THE CHINESE ROAD TO HIGH TECHNOLOGY

Also by Xiaobai Shen

CASEBOOK ON GENERAL MANAGEMENT IN ASIA PACIFIC
(*co-editor with Dominique Turpin*)

The Chinese Road to High Technology

A Study of Telecommunications Switching Technology in the Economic Transition

Xiaobai Shen

Foreword by Geoffrey Oldham

First published in Great Britain 1999 by
MACMILLAN PRESS LTD
Houndmills, Basingstoke, Hampshire RG21 6XS and London
Companies and representatives throughout the world

A catalogue record for this book is available from the British Library.

ISBN 0–333–74627–9

First published in the United States of America 1999 by
ST. MARTIN'S PRESS, INC.,
Scholarly and Reference Division,
175 Fifth Avenue, New York, N.Y. 10010

ISBN 0–312–22362–5

Library of Congress Cataloging-in-Publication Data
Shen, Xiaobai.
The Chinese road to high technology : a study of
telecommunications switching technology in the economic transition /
Xiaobai Shen.
p. cm.
Includes bibliographical references and index.
ISBN 0–312–22362–5 (cloth)
1. Telecommunication—China.   2. Telecommunication—China–
–Switching systems.   I. Title.
HE8424.S54   1999
384'.0951—dc21   99–18871
                                                                      CIP

This book is printed on paper suitable for recycling and made from fully managed and sustained forest sources.

10   9   8   7   6   5   4   3   2   1
08   07   06   05   04   03   02   01   00   99

Printed in Great Britain

To the memory of my father
Bai-Yu Shen

Contents

Foreword

During the late 1970s and early 1980s China experimented with novel ways of converting their previous command economy into what is called a 'socialist market economy'. But it was not until 1984 that a coherent set of science and technology policies were put in place to try to ensure that science and technology served the needs of a market economy. The reforms which were initiated meant dramatic changes to the system of innovation. Research institutes previously fully funded by the state now had to find clients who would pay for their work. New relationships with foreign companies were cultivated in an effort to acquire foreign technology, and the military was encouraged to develop its technology and to transfer it for civilian use.

The success with which these new policies were implemented varied considerably between provinces, research institutes and business enterprises. Where managers maintained the outlook of the command economy there were difficulties and failures. However, when the managers took a more entrepreneurial approach the new policies provided opportunities for innovation and often substantial economic gains.

Although the outlines of the new policies have been known to foreign scholars, and some aspects of their implementation have been studied, detailed case studies of successes and failures in policy implementation have been few and far between. Now, Xiaobai Shen has documented the development of Public Digital Switching Technology in China and presented the results in a way which illustrates the difficulties and successes in building local Chinese technical capabilities in this critical domain. By focusing on two different approaches to acquiring local technological capabilities Dr Shen has been able to demonstrate the impact of the economic and technology policy reforms in relation to the role of research institutes, joint ventures with foreign companies, the reform of state-owned enterprises and technology transfer from the West to China and from the military to civilian sectors.

This is an important book because it provides valuable insights into the actual workings of economic reform and technology policy implementation. It also shows that even in a market economy there is a need for clearly formulated technology policies. The book will be valuable to those interested in modern telecommunication systems in

China, but it will also be useful for policy-makers in other countries interested in the process of acquiring and assimilating advanced technology.

GEOFFREY OLDHAM
Former Director of Science Policy Research Unit
University of Sussex

Acknowledgements

This book is based on my PhD thesis which was completed in September 1997. I am indebted to my supervisors at the University of Edinburgh, Wendy Faulkner and Alfonso Molina, for their enormous help throughout my doctoral research – in developing, conducting and writing up this study. Special thanks to Wendy also for her help in getting financial support from various sources. I would like to acknowledge the contribution of Gregory Owcarz and Robin Williams, for their conscientious reading of draft chapters and for correcting my English. Particular thanks to Robin also for providing valuable comments on draft chapters at different stages and for his enormous help in editing this book, going through the whole manuscript almost word by word.

I would also like to thank my examiners – Geoffrey Oldham, former Director of SPRU, University of Sussex, and Martin Fransman, Director of JETS, University of Edinburgh – for their encouragement for turning the thesis into this book. Geoffrey Oldham also kindly provided the Foreword for the book.

Since the PhD thesis was completed, there have been rapid institutional and technical changes in Chinese telecommunications. For providing information during my recent visits to China regarding the subsequent development of HJD-04, I would like to thank, in particular, Professor Wu Jiang Xiang, Board Chairman of Great Dragon Telecommunications (Group) Co., Ltd (also Director of the Centre for Information Technology in the Zhengzhou Institute of Information Engineering of the People's Liberation Army) and Mr Zhang Feng Zhou, former Director of the Beijing Long-term Data Technology Corporation, part of the Posts and Telecommunications Industrial Corporation in the Ministry of Posts and Telecommunications, who let me interview them over the phone and supplied me with the then latest information. This allowed me to provide an ending to the HJD-04 case, whose future was uncertain when I ended the PhD fieldwork but which has been developing in a very promising way. This made the study more complete and underlined the general theses advanced about the range of strategies for technological development.

I would like to thank all the respondents who gave up their time and energy to talk to me and answer my questions in my fieldwork in China. Some also gave strong moral support and encouragement for this study, in particular, from MPT, Professor Liu Xi Ming, the No.1 Research Institute; Professor Qian Zong Jue, the Department of Science and Technology; Jiang Yong, Deputy Director of the Planning Division in the Science and Technology Department; Chen Yun Qian, Chief Consultant of the Research Centre for Economic and Technology Development; Li Zheng Fu, Director of the Science and Technology Information Centre. And from Shanghai Bell: Mr De Graeve (Belgian) Director and General Manager; Li Da Lai, Chinese General Manager; Rong Li Lai, Manager of the Localisation Department; and Xu Zhi Qun, Deputy Manager of the Engineering Department. I also want to thank Feng Ji Chun, Deputy Chief of the Department of Fundamental Research and High Technology, of the State Science and Technology Commission; Bou Fu Dong, Director and General Manager of the Luoyang Telephone Equipment Factory; Han Fu Er, Consultant for the Shanghai Municipal Science and Technology Committee, Shanghai Science and Technology Information Institute, amongst others. My friends, Feng Zhi Jun, Ma Bao Shen, Zhang Yong Qian, Gu Wen Xin, Fang Han Lun and Song Duo Jing were of great assistance in helping me gain access to the network of respondents. Without their support, it would have been impossible for me to carry out the case studies successfully.

My study was made possible by financial support from the UK Overseas Research Studentships Awards Scheme, the Henry Lester Trust, Edinburgh University's Vans Dunlop Scholarship Fund, and Cowan House Scholarship and the Great Britain–China Educational Trust. My deep thanks are due to them.

I would like to mention the staff and colleagues in the Research Centre for Social Sciences (including the former secretary) who were supportive and helpful in providing information for my study, as well as in helping me get to know Edinburgh and make my studying there much more enjoyable.

Finally I would like to thank my family, especially my mother and my sister whose immense love and care gave me the courage to take up and complete the study. In addition, my thanks are due to Klaus von Glahn whose trust in the British education system and his love of Scotland convinced me to choose Edinburgh University for my PhD study, and to Professor Fei Xiao Tong and Feng Zhi Jun in China who supported me in undertaking this study.

XIAOBAI SHEN

List of Abbreviations

BHCA	Busy hour call attempts (a measurement of call processing power)
BTM	Bell Telephone Manufacturing Company
CAE	Customer Application Engineering
CCG	Communal Co-ordination Group
CCITT	Comité Consultatif International Télégraphique et Téléphonique
CDE	Country Development Engineering
CIT	Centre for Information Technology in Zhengzhou Institute of Information Engineering of the People's Liberation Army
COCOM	Co-ordinating Committee for Multinational Export Control
DCs	Developing Countries
DGT	Directorate-General Telecommunications
IN	Intelligent Networks
ISDN	Integrated Services Digital Network
ISO	International Standard Organisation
ITC	Indigenous Technological Capability
ITT	International Telegram Corporation
LED	Light emitting diode
LSI	Large Scale Integrated (chips)
LTEF	Luoyang Telephone Equipment Factory of MPT
MMEI	Ministry of Machine Building and Electronics Industry
MPT	Ministry of Posts and Telecommunications
NICs	Newly Industrialised Countries
PABX	Private Automatic Branch Exchanges
PDSS	Public Digital Switching System
PTA	Posts and Telecommunications Administration
PTIC	Posts and Telecommunications Industrial Corporation
R&D	Research and Development
RASM	Remote Autonomous Switching Module
RMB	Renminbi (Chinese yuan)
SST	Social Shaping of Technology
S&T	Science and Technology

Part I
Introduction

1 The Scope and Context of the Study

1.1 FOCUS AND SCOPE OF THE STUDY

Developing countries (DCs) are keen to benefit from new advanced technology. However, its acquisition presents some potentially difficult dilemmas. Will the resort to exogenous technology leave them dependent upon the developed countries or multinational companies that supplied them? Will the inequality in capabilities force DCs to pay too high a price? Can DCs obtain the capabilities to *produce* high technology products for themselves? Can they even acquire the capabilities needed to *develop* new advanced technologies for themselves? Indeed, can developing countries catch up with the West?

Many have been pessimistic about the scope for DCs to acquire technological capabilities by transferring advanced technologies from industrialised countries. However, the recent successes of Newly Industrialised Countries (NICs) have forced a reassessment of such a blanket view (whether pessimistic or optimistic) and instead raised questions about the different strategies which might be available for developing countries and their effectiveness in particular circumstances. These concerns are at the heart of this investigation. They are explored in the specific case of attempts in the People's Republic of China to build up indigenous capabilities in public digital switching systems (PDSS) – the technology at the heart of modern telecommunications.

A detailed account is presented of the acquisition of PDSS technological capabilities, focusing on two contrasting cases: in the first, foreign technology is transferred into China as a complete system, through a joint venture project; the other is a locally developed system which utilises available foreign components and design tools. These cases point to the range of strategies available for utilising advanced foreign technologies, and provide important insights into the prospects for China's distinctive 'dual-track' technology policy of 'walking on two legs'.

The second concern of this study is with the problems experienced by a socialist state, particularly in relation to its lack of technological dynamism and innovation, and its attempts to overcome these by

3

restructuring its socio-economic system. It examines the process of economic transition in the People's Republic of China, which is attempting to transform its centrally-planned system to a market-oriented one. The study therefore bears upon the economic and techno-logical prospects of a country which is widely expected to become a leading player in the world economy in the twenty-first century.

There have been other studies of technological developments in China, including the development of telecommunications in China. However, these accounts have often been of a generalised nature, and mainly based on national statistics and published information on central policies. What is distinctive about this study is its highly detailed account of the development of public digital switching technology in China. The empirical analysis encompasses the roles of the key actors (individuals or organisations) or constituencies involved in technology development – for example, a military R&D institute, a state-owned firm, a joint production venture, and other relevant governmental orga-nisations. The cases document the changing behaviours of the actors involved in innovation and the relationships between them. It examines how these local processes were shaped by their historical settings and the particular influence of the broader social and economic context which was changing rapidly as a result of China's economic transition.

This introductory chapter sets the scene for the book. It briefly outlines the intellectual traditions and debates that informed this study, and provides an introduction to the structure and coverage of the book. It then introduces the social and technological context of this study, describing the former socialist economic and social system in China and its transition. Finally it addresses the importance of telecommunications *per se* and the historical background and char-acteristics of the Chinese telecommunications system.

Debates Underpinning this Study

This study addresses an extraordinarily broad range of issues. It sees technology transfer as not just a narrowly technical issue, but also as a profoundly social, economic and political one, linked not only to the domestic system, e.g. institutional structures and government policies, but also the world technology, economic and politics. To analyse these complex developments, the study applies perspectives and approaches from three disciplines: technology studies, development studies and the study of socialist economies (in particular the current transition of socialist states). In this way it aims at a better understanding of the problems (and opportunities) for developing countries – and, in particular, former socialist states – in technological development.

In the area of technology studies, there have been important developments in the understanding of the process of technological innovation. However, a rigorous and systematic analysis of the social determinants of technological change across different (economic, social and technological) contexts is still lacking. This is particularly the case in relation to the developing countries, given the focus of most technology studies on the advanced Western economies. The study explores whether and how insights from technology studies can be applied in developing countries and China in particular.

By applying a 'social shaping of technology' perspective, this study shifts from the generic accounts of underdevelopment (and, for example, technology transfer) that have prevailed in development studies, and instead opens up for detailed analysis both the processes of innovation and the content of technology. Drawing on social shaping insights, this study sees complex modern technologies not as stable and rigid technical systems but as a heterogeneous assemblage of diverse 'technological' and 'social' elements. Such configurational technologies may be relatively malleable or flexible and open to being reconfigured in their implementation and use. Applying these insights to the transfer of foreign advanced technology into developing countries suggests that technology transfer is a process of unpacking and local shaping of these technologies. There are therefore always choices, albeit within constraints, for developing countries to decide which technologies to adopt as finished solutions and which 'black boxes' need to be opened. This introduces a range of strategic options in utilising foreign advanced technologies: for example, between transferring developed technological systems and adapting them to local conditions, or buying in components and/or design-tools to develop systems locally and configuring them into complex systems matched to local requirements and conditions. The study then discusses the choices between different technology transfer strategies in relation to the existing indigenous technological competencies and/or the long-term plans for the accumulation of technological capability of a country.

This enables a focus on the strategies whereby developing countries might benefit from modern technologies developed elsewhere. Rather than linger on the often overly-generalised debates that have prevailed in development studies, this study seeks to develop a more detailed and dynamic account – and one which presents developing countries with a number of options in choosing how to deal with a changing world, and to handle the relationship between technology suppliers and recipients (at firm and at national levels). Developing countries might seek to strengthen their position and achieve a more balanced relationship with technology suppliers by building up their technological capabilities, while suppliers are seeking to further develop their capabilities, maximise and sustain their position in the global market. Rather than totally replicating supplier capabilities, and displace the supplier, it may be in the interests of developing countries to have a continuing engagement with the external developer to stay in touch with global developments. Indeed this is likely to become a more general feature. Given the powerful current trends towards globalisation, the goal of total self-sufficiency of a country in an area of advanced technologies is becoming less relevant – even developed countries may not find it feasible to maintain the full range of capabilities in a technology (as is already the case in relation to micro-electronics and computing, except for in a handful of the most developed countries). Developing countries and even small countries may, however, be able to acquire partial competencies in advanced technological fields, on the basis of which they may be able to achieve substantial economic and technological benefits.

The focus on strategies of developing countries to acquire technological capabilities raises questions about the influence of its broader economic and institutional context and appropriateness of policies in this setting. One concept that has recently been advanced to capture this is the idea of national systems for technological innovation. The concept revolves around an attempt to audit a nation's structural characteristics and policies and their effects on the rate and success of innovation, and implies a search for the optional conditions for a particular country. However, national systems are in a continuous process of flux – in the face of socio-economic and technological change – particularly in the developing economies and socialist economies in transition. For example, in China today, the social institutional structure and policies have been changing extremely rapidly as the country undergoes a profound transformation of its system from a centrally planned to a market-oriented one. There is thus little value in seeking to identify a particular 'best-practice' national system for China to emulate. This research will analyse the problems of the former central planning system and the changes taking place in the institutional structure and incentives during the economic transition. Attention will be paid to analysing the successive strategies and policies of the government and their implementation, and the steps and outcomes of reforming institutional structures, the general features of which can be seen to underpin effective innovation. In addition, broader considerations, such as domestic social tensions and international opportunities and pressures, are also taken into account. Economic reform and the transition of China's state planning system are thus of considerable importance.

China had adopted a socialist model of development for thirty years before its recent economic reforms, though this differed to some extent from the widely established Soviet model. Moreover, while many of the former socialist states have abandoned socialism altogether and moved rapidly towards a *laissez-faire* economic model, China is still hanging on to some elements of the socialist model in its economic transition. Therefore, issues related to the study of socialist economics and transitions are thrown up by this research. Drawing on the range of theoretical positions in the study of socialist economies, this research analyses the Chinese socialist tradition in relation to technological development and the transition to a more market-oriented economy. It examines their related institutions and government policies which have had a major impact on the technological dynamism of the country in the past and now. From the viewpoint of development strategies, whether China is or is not truly 'socialist' is not the main issue for this study. More important is the speed as well as the elements of continuity of China's development, not only in economic but also social and political terms. There are interesting comparisons with the former Soviet Union and other East European countries that appear to have abandoned their socialist tradition overnight and lost much of their state power.

Given its concerns with policy implications, the study assesses the major Chinese government policies which have had effects on technological activities particularly in relation to the case of public switching technologies. These include import substitution policies to protect domestic industry by providing subsidies to local firms, high tariff rates and regulations that served to restrict the import of foreign goods, and financial support for indigenous technological projects as well as the more open policies designed to attract foreign investment and technology inflow. In particular this study examines the twin-track technology policy, described as 'walking on two legs', which encouraged both the transfer of foreign technology into China and the development of indigenous technology. It discusses the conflict between these policies for long- or short-term development, the sequence and circumstances for their implementation and their consequences, including both their positive and negative outcomes and side-effects.

The Broader Relevance of this Study

As well as highlighting issues for China, this study intends to draw lessons and policy implications of general importance for other developing countries, especially those in transition. However, because of the uniqueness of China's size and its historical inheritance, there may be limits in the extent to which Chinese experiences can be extrapolated elsewhere. For example, the sheer size of the Chinese market gives it considerable bargaining power with foreign firms wanting to enter this market. In addition, given that this research is based on the particular empirical case of telecommunications switching technology, findings may not be directly applicable to other technologies – for example, automobiles, chemicals or textiles – which differ in their technical, social, economic and political features. In particular, the strategic importance of telecommunications and the fact that network integrity must be maintained nationally means that the state is a major player in regulating or actually running the telecommunications system. This may give greater opportunities for public policy and state intervention than might prevail in relation to other fields (such as computing, for example) where market forces may have greater hold, suggesting a different mix between public and private processes.

However, the focus on China is justified by the global importance of this country. China has one-fifth of the world's population, about 80 per cent of whom are peasants, with over 200 million living under the poverty line. Its success or failure will have a substantial impact on the political economy, as well as the environment, of the whole world. Although this research mainly focuses on public digital switching technology in the telecommunications sector, it at the same time provides a general picture of the Chinese economic and technological system, its tradition and current transformation. For developing countries, China's experiment will be an important experience and a source of lessons to draw upon for alternative paths of development. For those in the developed world, China might well present a growing commercial opportunity, as well as a threat. These are not fixed matters, but rather can be altered by the endeavours of the powerful developed world. As illustrated in this study, the key policy change on the public switching market was the response of the Chinese government to international pressures from Western suppliers to open up this market.

The Structure and Coverage of the Book

There are three parts to this book. Part I, the background to the study, has two chapters. Chapter 1 provides a general introduction, and Chapter 2 selectively reviews and discusses debates in three areas – development studies, the study of socialist economies and their transition and technology studies. It highlights the key issues and debates that have arisen and links these together to provide the theoretical framework and approach adopted in the study; and finally, the presumptions and research questions that underpin this study are presented, and the methodology is described.

Part II presents the empirical findings – its two chapters provide contrasting case studies of the development of two public digital switching technologies, one indigenous and the other foreign. Detailed accounts are presented of the innovation processes in each case. Chapter 3 explores the case of the transfer of a foreign PDSS, System-12, as a complete package. It examines the process of technological innovation (selection, adaptation and improvement) and changes in the social and economic arrangement (e.g. related government policies) over this period. The acquisition of technological capability is investigated in the joint production venture, Shanghai Bell and in components supply. Chapter 4 examines the case of the indigenous technology, detailing the process of building up the socio-technical constituency for the Chinese public digital switching system, HJD-04. This involved three players: a military research institute which initiated the project, a state-owned firm which produced the HJD-04 system, and a governmental organisation, the Posts and Telecommunications Industrial Corporation. Along with elucidating how social factors in the transition shaped technical features of this technology, and how technical and organisational elements were aligned together, it gives a close-up examination of the state-owned firm, how it acquired technological capabilities, the problems encountered and progress made.

Part III offers a detailed analysis comparing the indigenous and exogenous technology acquisition processes encountered in the case studies. It has three chapters. Chapter 5 identifies the range of strategies for acquiring technological capabilities revealed by these cases. It analyses these strategies in terms of the variety of options for purchasing technology, access to foreign technological competencies, and the scope for local shaping of imported technologies. It links them to existing indigenous competencies, technological learning and the ultimate goal – building up technological capabilities. Chapter 6 evaluates the influence of the broader social and economic context on PDSS technology development in China's economic transition. It examines the changes in government policies and the institutional structure and incentives for technological innovation. Finally, Chapter 7 reviews the main findings of this study. It presents the conclusions and explores the further implications of the study for other developing countries.

1.2   CONTEXT – CHINA'S TRANSITION

China has been seeking economic prosperity for generations, no matter whether the government was 'republican', 'nationalist' or 'socialist'. However, recent history has not favoured this ancient giant, the 'central kingdom'. While the West prospered, China, beset by the colonial powers, was subject to sustained political and economic turbulence and chaos (including civil strife and foreign invasions) until the 1949 success of the Chinese Communist Party. Since then, there have been several periods of rapid economic growth. Under the People's Republic, for the first time after a long period of impoverishment, the country was able to feed its population, which by then had reached one billion. The majority of the population came to believe in the leadership of the country, with the expectation that this government would deliver continued improvements in economic and social well-being.

However, like other socialist states, over time the initial impetus of the revolution gradually eroded, and people's confidence and inspiration faded away. Mao's political campaigns inside and outside the governing Communist Party did not save the socialist system from decline. From time to time, Mao's policy explicitly prioritised matters of ideology over economic pragmatism. Economic development became tangled up with political movements. Ever-changing policies resulted in fluctuations in economic development and reached its lowest point in the late stages of the Cultural Revolution (1966–76).

China has been reforming since 1978 when the Third Plenary Session of the Central Committee of the Communist Party of China was held in Beijing to inaugurate policies of economic reform and openness to other countries. In a relatively short period China has become one of the countries in the world with the fastest growing economy. Between 1978 and 1993, economic growth averaged 9 per cent a year. In 1992 and 1993, GDP increased by 12.8 per cent and 13.4 per cent respectively (Li Tieying, 1994, p. 3). China's share of world trade has doubled and 200 million people have been released from absolute poverty (Balls, 1993). 'The dynamism of the Chinese economy has been a major factor underlying the rapid growth of the region's trade and output which has contributed to maintaining stability in the world economy' (UNCTAD, 1994a, p. 7). Some consider that China will become the world's next economic super-power (Balls, 1993).

Unlike the former Soviet Union and other former socialist states, China is publicly seeking to combine socialism and market mechanisms. The motto of China's transition as defined by the Communist Party is to establish a 'socialist market mechanism in a planned economy' and to build up 'four modernisations' (upgrading industry, agriculture, national defence and science and technology) with 'Chinese characteristics'. The term 'socialism with "Chinese characteristics", reflects the challenge facing China's transition with no existing model to follow, as well as its pragmatism and the importance attached to social prosperity. This pragmatism is an essential element of Chinese culture, embodied also in the Chinese leadership, as captured by Deng Xiaoping's phrase 'whether a black cat or a white cat, the one who can catch rats is the best'. It is precisely this pragmatic attitude that Chinese reformers and ordinary individuals are displaying in pursuing the current process of socio-economic transformation. 'Chinese socialism' is the product of such a culture.

In China, not many people are seeking a clear definition of what the government means by a 'socialist market economy with Chinese characteristics'. Instead, since the market economy is new for China, people are learning about it while practising it. After thirty years under a state socialist system, and especially after the previous ten years of the Cultural Revolution, in which people have seen all too many of the errors and defects associated with socialism and a centrally planned system, people have high expectations for a market economy. Only recently have some of the problems endemic to market economies become apparent. These include the widening of economic inequality between individuals and between districts, high inflation, increasing unemployment and disruptive migration from the countryside to the cities and from poor districts to the richer coastal areas. People are now beginning to recall the merits of the previous socialist system.

China's reforms have taken place in three phases. The first phase, from December 1978 to September 1984, mainly concentrated on the agricultural sector. It sought to introduce a more market-oriented system and to give farmers greater scope for private initiatives. This ended successfully with a 'rapid increase in agricultural productivity, a dramatic reduction in the incidence of poverty' (Yenal, 1990, p. 707). From October 1984 to December 1991, the second phase of reform shifted the central focus to urban areas and was mainly directed to reorganise the industrial sector. Government policies sought to stimulate the dynamism of industrial sectors by introducing market forces to the entire system and giving much more autonomy to enterprises. In the third phase, since the beginning of 1992, the sphere of economic reform has broadened in many aspects and the process has been stepped up. The aim is to build up a new socio-economic mechanism for the country (Li Tieying, 1994, p. 7).

A major objective of economic reforms is to promote dynamism in the technological innovation system. Progress has been unprecedented as economic reform has stimulated the integration of economic development with technological innovation. However, in contrast with the other social, political and economic policies, the core of science and technology policies has shown key elements of continuity in the importance attached to both developing technology locally and introducing advanced technology from abroad.

As early as 1949, with the foundation of the People's Republic of China, one element of the technology policy was described colloquially as 'walking on two legs' – that is to say, to combine foreign and national aspects in technology development (Li Wan, 1991). Accordingly, the strategy for the development of science and technology aimed to establish a number of advanced industrial enterprises and to acquire large amounts of modern technology (Li Wan, 1991). There were many ups and downs in technology development before the 1979 economic reforms – largely due to political fluctuations as well as to fundamental problems of the socialist centrally planned system (in particular the poor linkages between R&D institutes and production organisations, and the lack of incentives for firms to adopt technological innovations).

In December 1980, the National Labour Conference on Science and Technology in Beijing had the explicit objectives of overcoming these problems. In particular it sought to integrate the S&T systems with economic development. The strategic motto was clearly presented,

> Economic construction should rely on scientific-technological progress and that science and technology has to serve economic construction. It was pointed out that the main task of scientists and technicians was the development of the national economy, and that the majority of the scientific-technological forces should be shifted to the main field of action – to serve the development of the national economy.   (Li Wan, 1991, p. 38)

This began the introduction of market mechanisms into the field of science and technology research and development. These new steps were explicitly aimed at catching up with the West and developing new technologies and high technology.

One of the important features of these new technological development strategies is the 'open door' policy, addressing 'rigorous promotion of technology transfer'. The purpose of opening China's economy up to other countries was in order to import funds and highly qualified personnel, and assimilate advanced science and technology and experience from abroad (Li Wan, 1991). Under this policy, in the late 1980s, the issue of the introduction of foreign technology came to be seen as all important. Newton's line – 'If I can see a little farther, then it is because I am standing on the shoulders of a giant' – was frequently quoted by those who believed that 'technology import is more efficient and uses less research personnel than research itself' (Li Wan, 1991, p. 44). It was believed that China should not only seize opportunities to import foreign technologies, but also make every effort to assimilate, remould and innovate the imported technology in a so-called a 'healthy cycle' (Li Wan, 1991). This is a concept that draws upon the experiences of Japan: the 'healthy cycle' is considered as a spiral series of developmental activities: import of advanced technology; assimilation; new creation; extension of exports and increased imports (Li Wan, 1991).

The Chinese government has stated that opening its economy to other countries and rigorous promotion of technology transfer represent a fundamental long-term state policy and a strategic measure to accelerate socialist modernisation. However, what really matters are the changes actually taking place in China's technological innovation systems and its benefits to the economic development (as well as any problems which may arise and lead to policy shifts).

Today China is undergoing a socio-institutional transition. The whole system is characterised by instability, as well as by an acute shortage of almost everything. Like other developing countries, China has been short of capital and natural resources in proportion to its population size (resulting from the rapid rate of population growth and the slow rate of capital accumulation) (Mu Gongqian, 1991). The behaviour of institutions like individual enterprises or firms, local government organisations, sectors, and even the state, is largely determined by the immediate external and internal opportunities and pressures bearing upon them. In these contexts, their scope for developing and implementing new policies is highly limited.

China is determined to catch up in technology and economic development. The Chinese government policies in technology development pursue dual development: on the one hand, of rigorously importing foreign advanced technologies, and, on the other, of encouraging assimilation and innovation of imported technologies. But, in reality, China is facing enormous constraints and problems along its road towards social prosperity. Old problems stemming from the socialist system are still there while new problems associated with the emerging market-oriented mechanism have surfaced.

1.3   TELECOMMUNICATIONS IN CHINA

My engineering background in telecommunications technology encouraged me to select public digital switching systems as the specific advanced technology for this study. The main justification for this choice however comes from the nature of PDSS technology *per se* – telecommunications technology is at the centre of the rapidly developing field of electronics and computing technologies, and the public switching system is right at the heart of public telecommunications service. It has great social, economic and political significance for both industrialised and developing countries alike. Accordingly, within China, the telecommunications sector had been under state monopoly control from the very outset, and had attracted considerable attention from the government since the economic reforms. As China reformed its economy, virtually all the large telecommunication equipment companies worldwide had lined up, with backing from their governments, to pursue the Chinese market (especially in the run-up to 31 December 1992, when the Chinese government announced a new policy which relaxed the previous strict controls over the import of digital switching systems).

Telecommunications services involve three operational areas – transmission, switching and terminals. The first two of these are complex, large-scale technologies. Network provision in particular is subject to marked economies of scale. It has been presumed that economies of scale and network 'externalities' (the growing benefits with larger numbers linked up to a system) would favour 'natural monopoly' of telecommunication provision, which would need to be run or tightly regulated by the state. The huge capital costs of telecommunications networks, especially the 'local loop' to individual domestic consumers, were presumed to prohibit competitive provision of fixed link phone services. Duplicate provision would be inefficient and too expensive. Public management, through nationalised service or state regulation, could further enable the network to be developed in line with broader social and economic policy objectives – for example, to allow equality of access. However, the traditional model, whereby the state was the guarantor or monopoly provider of telecommunications services, has recently come under sustained attack, with moves toward privatisation, opening up the sector for competition and so called deregulation (which often in fact involves re-regulation of the sector), spreading from the USA to the UK, the rest of the European Union, and the rest of the world.

In a context of rapid technological change and the growth and diversification of telecommunications service markets, it has been argued that state regulation or state monopoly provision have proved inefficient because of the lack of competition and have served as an obstacle for further technological innovation. However, some researchers such as Vickers and Yarrow (1986) and Ypsilanti (1988) suggest that privatisation and competitive provision may be not a better solution in the longer term, particularly in the provision of telecommunications network facilities.

Similar arguments have surrounded the supply of telecommunications equipment. Its enormous costs stimulate governments to seek domestic manufacture to improve balance of payments. Strategic considerations have motivated many countries to ensure national ownership or control of production facilities and innovation capabilities of the technologies involved. However, recent advances in switching technologies – the move to electronic switches, and in particular to programmed control and digitisation underpinning PDSS – have been associated with a dramatic escalation of research and development costs. This posed particular problems for poorer (for example, smaller and especially developing) countries which lacked the necessary financial and human resources. The scale of investments required is frequently beyond the capacity of individual domestic companies without assistance from the state or large foreign companies. PDSS posed a strategic challenge for developing countries. They offered greatly reduced costs and scope for rapid expansion and upgrading of telecommunications services. But they also posed a number of dilemmas. The first concerns whether to develop the technology locally or buy it in. In the latter case there were further dilemmas. Strategies of state control (or even nationalisation) of foreign firms, which might have been relatively successful in relation to earlier mature generations of electromechanical switching technology, might frighten away foreign companies, technologies and investment. Opening up the market for a single foreign supplier might make it more attractive for private firms to accept public requirements (for example, to keep costs low or allow for domestic production), but might lead to dependency. On the other hand allowing free entry and market competition could produce fragmentation of the telecommunications network and inefficiencies associated with duplication of technologies and incompatibilities between them.

In the past, China's telecommunications system was one of the poorest in the world. Before the beginning of economic reforms in 1978, China's telecommunications system had been under the control of the central government and served mainly the needs of a centrally planned economy, and the Party and government organisations. At the foundation of the People's Republic of China in 1949, the country had only about 300 000 local telephone lines (East Consulting Ltd, 1995). For the next 30 years, little changed. From 1949 to 1978, the central government was the sole investor in telecommunications networks and services; the total investment of the country in fixed assets in the telecommunications sector was only 5.2 million Chinese yuan (Zheng, 1992). In 1978, China had merely 3 972 000 telephone lines compared with a population of over 900 million, with about 4 phones per 1000 people (ITU, 1986). Telecommunications technologies in Chinese public network services lagged far behind the world level, and most telephone switching systems were manually operated.

It was the economic reform of the end of the 1970s that made apparent the serious constraints of the telecommunications infrastructure to economic expansion in China. As the country's door opened to the world, business communications within China, as well as with the world, increased rapidly. People's rising living standards also demanded telecommunications services. Telecommunications immediately became one of the most serious infrastructure bottlenecks for the economy. The low density of telephone lines and the consequent high rate of usage made the network badly congested. The call completion rate was so low that a popular saying stated that, 'for delivering a message, it would be faster to cycle than make a local call; it would be faster to go in person by train than to get through on a long distance call'.

The need to speed up the reconstruction of the telecommunications infrastructure, by expanding the telecommunications network and modernising its technologies and services, was acknowledged. Increasing attention was given to the area. Large sums of money were allocated to the telecommunications sector from home and abroad. During the 6th (1981–5) and 7th (1986–90) five-year plan, with government approval, a combined total of yuan (RMB) 26 billion ($3 billion) was invested in telecommunications (East Consulting Ltd, 1995). Since then annual investment has soared. In 1993 alone it totalled yuan (RMB) 40 billion ($4.9 billion) (East Consulting Ltd, 1995). As a result, since 1985, the growth of telecommunications has outpaced GNP growth. According to the Ministry of Posts and Telecommunications' figures, during the first half of the 1980s, telecommunications traffic in China grew by 17.5 per cent a year, increasing to 24.4 per cent annually during the second half of the decade (East Consulting Ltd, 1995). Since then these annual growth rates had jumped, rising from 40 per cent in 1991 to 58.9 per cent in 1993 (East Consulting Ltd, 1995).

In spite of this, the demand for telecommunications services continued to accelerate, as the economy continued to boom. In late 1992 (when my investigation in China began), it was a common sight to see people making a phone call while crossing the street in cities of the coastal area, even though the price of a mobile phone had reached 30 000 Chinese yuan (equivalent to £3000). 'Information', 'economic gain' and 'high-tech telecommunication equipment' began to be tightly interrelated in people's minds. As a result, the waiting lists of subscribers for telephone services jumped from 163 000 in 1980, to 1 670 000 at the end of 1992, even though the number of telephone lines installed had increased by 15 million lines between 1979 and 1992.[1] Installation fees for new subscribers rocketed steeply: in 1993, the top fees charged in Beijing could be as much as 5000 Chinese yuan (equivalent to £500) per line, and the waiting time was one year, or longer if no extra fees were paid (formally or informally).[2]

With a telephone penetration rate as low as 1.63 per 100 in 1992, China had a long way to go to reach European levels.[3] Still demand was expected to accelerate very rapidly. A Chinese scholar described this growth as involving several waves (Chen Yunqian, 1993). The first originated with business users, especially organisations involved in foreign trade in the south-east coastal area. Later on, it moved inland and to the north. The most recent wave (1993) involved domestic households. There was a 'bandwagon effect' associated with a compli-cated cultural process. When households with telecommunications equipment expanded from the emerging entrepreneur groups to include a number of 'open-minded' non-business residential families, people suddenly sensed a social trend. Traditionally, Chinese cul-ture stigmatised economic upstarts as arrogant money-worshippers, immoral opportunists, less educated or social climbers. However, apart from during the Cultural Revolution, wealth has never been rejected by Chinese society. More importantly, Chinese people do not like to be left behind any social trends. This is especially true in the case of telecommunications. When one's friends have got telephones at home, and one alone is outside the communication network, one feels excluded from the social circle. In these circumstances, some people were willing to pay 5000 yuan (in the order of ten months' basic salary) to have a telephone-set at home.

Economic and social demands had placed great pressure on the Chinese government. Tight budgets could not meet the needs of modernising the whole country's telecommunications infrastructure. Financial pressures led the central government to adopt a set of decentralisation policies intended to raise the necessary funds. First, local Posts and Telecommunications Administrations[4] were made responsible for the local infrastructure and allowed to raise funds from various local sources – for instance, from local government, business organisations, and individuals. Second, government control over telecommunications charges (which had remained unchanged for several decades) was liberalised, with the result that the Ministry of Posts and Telecommunications (MPT) adjusted charges in the 1980s, and local Posts and Telecommunications Administrations were given scope to make certain additional charges to meet their own circumstances. Given these policies, many local Posts and Telecom-munications Administrations set out to muster funds, including foreign soft loans. Many of these soft loans involved a stipulation (by the foreign government) to purchase foreign switching systems; this took purchasing decisions out of the control of MPT.

Central government issued new guiding principles to solve the fundamental problem of the lack of modern telecommunications technologies. This involved three steps: first, buying advanced technology products from overseas; second, transferring technologies by setting up joint production ventures; and third, developing Chinese technologies. This was in line with China's general strategy of dual technological development, which extended to PDSS technology.

The Chinese telecommunications sector was one of the most monopolistic industries. Since the founding of the Ministry of Posts and Telecommunications (see Figure 1.1) in November 1949, it had been a centrally controlled independent sector. It had its own financial, material and human resource systems. No local governments and no other organisations were allowed to take part in managing its business. It was regarded as quasi-militarised. Furthermore, during the cultural revolution, in 1969, the 'telecommunications' sector was separated from the 'posts' sector and its control resided in the People's Liberation Army. From 1973 when the MPT was re-established till to the 1979 economic reform, the MPT retained a very strong monopoly position in the country. During this period, it reinforced its own productive capacity, establishing 28 manufacturing firms in total. Economic reform has led many ministries gradually to decentralise control over their companies. However, the MPT, instead, reshuffled its organisations and rearranged these 28 manufacturing firms under the leadership of the Posts and Telecommunications Industrial Corporation (PTIC) which was founded in 1980 (Gu Ming, 1992, pp. 16–21). So, although MPT appeared to loosen its control over these firms, it still retained considerable influence through the PTIC. For these firms, this was only a change from one headquarters to another. Therefore, for quite a while after the onset of economic reforms, all switch-producers under the MPT retained their traditional status: they were still state-owned; their material suppliers, annual production volume and technology development projects were all decided by MPT; and end products were provided to users through the same system. In the early 1980s, they were still producing electro-mechanical cross-bar switches.

On the other hand, soon after the inauguration of economic reforms, China begun to explore opportunities to transfer more advanced switching technologies from abroad and seek partners to set up joint production ventures. However, instead of setting up manufacturing bases in China, most foreign companies preferred to sell their finished products directly into the Chinese market. From

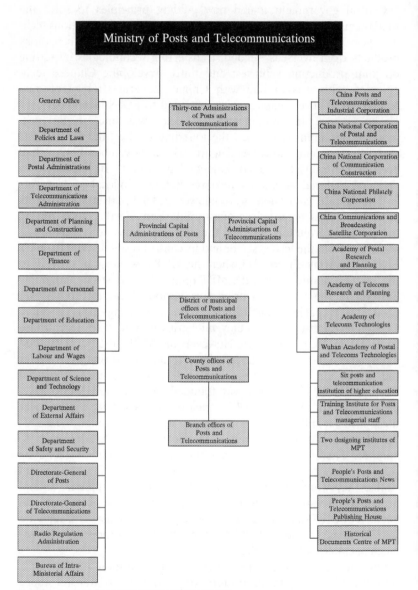

Source: The Economist Intelligence Unit, 9.1995 (East Consulting Ltd, 1995).

Figure 1.1   *Ministry of Posts and Telecommunications*

1980 onwards, when the first PDSS (F-150, a Japanese system) was installed in the southern province of Fujian, about ten different systems from eight countries had gradually entered the Chinese market, including System-12, EWSD, Neax-61, F-150, E-10b, System-X, AXE10, etc. China's PDSS market came to be dominated by foreign systems.

Some multinational telecommunications equipment companies recognised the importance of Chinese markets in the long term. They responded quickly to China's call for technology transfer and were also willing to bring in capital to set up joint production ventures. By 1991, three joint production ventures had been set up. Then a request was issued to restrict the number of foreign systems operating in the public network. It was based on the argument that the number of different types of foreign PDSSs had already brought about the need for complex interfaces in network, difficulties in maintenance, spare-parts supply, and mastery of software techniques. However, the debate about whether or not it was necessary to tighten controls over the range of foreign system types ended in controversy over costs and political risks. Some studies were conducted in order to find a better solution, but *de facto* the opening up of the market weakened MPT's monopoly control. The Chinese government came under enormous pressure from the demands of the domestic market and state financial shortages, as well as from foreign governments. Finally, under increasing pressure from the government of the United States of America, the Chinese government had to make a concession – not only to keep the market open but also to open it still wider. Since 1 January 1993, in response to conditions imposed for China to rejoin the General Agreement on Tariffs and Trade, the tariff for direct imports of PDSSs has been reduced, and two further PDSS technology transfer projects, from AT&T and Northern Telecom, have been approved by the government.[5]

Following the government policy of decentralisation, customers (that is, the local Posts and Telecommunications Administrations) preferred foreign advanced systems, even at much higher prices, to low-price Chinese cross-bar technology. Indeed, the 1980s was a decade of 'foreign technology fever' in telecommunications. Orders for cross-bar products decreased sharply, and many cross-bar switch producers were running at a loss. There were two alternatives for the Chinese switch industry: either develop new technology indigenously, or bring in foreign technology and capital by setting up joint ventures. In the event, foreign technology was so much in demand that government policy gave privileges to joint ventures: these included low tariffs, autonomy in personnel recruitment, and fewer restrictions on management than in a state-owned company. In some instances, locally produced foreign systems were treated as Chinese systems – for example, MPT provided subsidies for local Posts and Telecommunications Administrations to buy locally produced System-12, when Shanghai Bell was running at a loss.

While joint ventures were booming, local state-owned companies were suffering. The transition from a centrally planned system to a market system had been uneven across enterprises. Joint ventures and new private companies were not subject to the traditional constraints on state-owned companies, whereas state-owned firms had inherited heavy social and economic burdens which were difficult to change.

In the socialist tradition, state-owned firms made up the industrial foundation of socialist China. They functioned not only as a manufacturing body but also as a staff community undertaking extensive social services for its members. State-owned firms had unduly large workforces and people's jobs were permanent. Once one entered the factory, one became a member of the community; even one's dependants were included in the welfare schemes. Under this system, the resources of materials and manpower (including all staff from managers to labourers) were allocated by the state; financing was controlled by the state; the volume of production was decided by the state, and even its products were assigned under ration to users, all in accordance with the state's plans. Incentives were provided by the inspiration and commitment of the people, encouraged by mass education in socialist and communist thought. Workers were supposed to be masters of the firm and, in turn, the firm took care of their well-being.

By the mid-1980s, there had already been a profound change: state protection gradually decreased as state-owned companies were pushed into the market place. Existing institutional arrangements – once well suited for the central planning system – did not fit the new circumstances. In particular, having a substantial workforce, previously regarded as an advantage, became a heavy burden, and incentives which worked in the past were no longer effective. This rigid system of jobs for life and wages dissociated from individuals' performances was popularly known as a 'big rice bowl'. The most notable feature of the state-owned company was its low productivity and its inefficiency. During China's transition a much higher percentage of state-owned companies than other enterprises were running at a loss (Sun, 1992).

State-owned companies all over the country had been facing increasing challenges in the changing economic and social environment.

This was also true of state-owned companies producing telephone-switching systems. Unlike the joint ventures, they were struggling to become profitable, and many were on the edge of bankruptcy. They faced two challenges: first, they needed to develop workable new technologies to replace the dated technology of cross-bar exchanges; second, they needed to restructure their operation. Moreover, state-owned firms were competing with joint ventures from an unequal position. This was due largely to the uneven pace of reform with respect to different parts of the state machine – that is to say, government policy, the legal system, tariffs, and so on.

The introduction of foreign switching technologies created new problems. Foreign systems, although advanced and sophisticated, were not suitable for the poor conditions of the Chinese network. All these systems, to varying degrees, encountered severe problems. Lacking PDSS technology of their own, the Chinese were dependent on foreign suppliers who controlled not only technologies but also the market prices.

As a part of the government guidelines for three-step technological development strategy noted earlier, in 1983 China established an R&D project to develop its own PDSS technology under a state scheme to promote technological innovation.[6] The earliest switching system, DS-2000, was based on the knowledge of Japanese system F-150. The project was successfully completed in 1986. Subsequently, a more advanced version, DS-30, was developed.[7] During the same period, another system (HJD-04) was being developed as a joint project involving a military R&D institute – the Centre for Information Technology in the Zhengzhou Institute of Information Engineering of the People's Liberation Army, a state-owned manufacturing company and the industrial procurement unit of the MPT. It is this development of HJD-04 that forms the central focus in my second case, as a contrast to the case study of System-12 produced by a joint venture – Shanghai Bell.

2 Frameworks for Understanding

2.1 INTRODUCTION

This chapter describes the intellectual context of this study – encompassing the academic debates which informed the study and the methodology adopted. The complex technical and socio-economic issues raised in this research span at least three disciplinary areas: development studies, writings on socialist economics and technology studies. As the fields reviewed are each extensive, it has been necessary to be selective in this account of the literature and main debates. The sources used, and the framework presented here, reflect the particular concerns and values which have underpinned this study.

Section 2.2 reviews development studies, and in particular the issues relating to technological development and its relationship with economic development in developing countries. From the vast range of theoretical writings on socialism, section 2.3 addresses problems of the socialist centrally planned economy, especially in terms of its institutional structure and incentives relating to technological dynamism, and focuses upon debates about the role of markets and state within socialist economies. Section 2.4 examines the range of relevant approaches within technology studies and their relevance to this study.

Section 2.5 draws out from this literature review the research questions, which will be explained in the case studies that underpin the rest of this book, and then provides an account of the methodology adopted.

2.2 PERSPECTIVES ON TECHNOLOGY FROM DEVELOPMENT STUDIES

Today, it has been by and large acknowledged that development is not purely an economic phenomenon, but is rather a multidimensional process involving the reorganisation and reorientation of entire social as well as economic systems. In particular, technological development has come to play an increasingly important role in the economic and social life of developed and developing countries.

The Challenge of the Newly Industrialised Countries (NICs)

A key feature of the global economy in the last decades has been the dramatic processes of economic and technological development in a number of peripheral economies – the so-called newly industrialised countries, notably Hong Kong, Singapore, South Korea and Taiwan. These experiences present a sharp challenge to existing theories and models of development studies. The high growth rates experienced by East Asian NICs obviously contradict the pessimistic conclusion assumed by advocates of dependency. On the other hand, it is fairly clear that the model of development under way in the NICs is far removed from the traditional concepts of modernisation theorists, of creating developing countries (DCs) in the image of the social order now present in the developed countries (or the concept that DCs had to replicate their particular development paths and methods, e.g. *laissez-faire* system and industrialisation). The NICs' success has attracted the attention of scholars from a variety of tendencies – whether modernisationists, dependency advocates, neo-Marxians, structuralists or neoclassical economists (Dutt, Kim and Singh, 1994). It has stimulated detailed investigation of the NICs' practices across a broad range of dimensions (e.g. institutional structure, government policies).

The interpretations drawn from the NICs' experiences are often highly controversial. The theoretical approaches of individual scholars tend to lead them to reach different conclusions. For instance, neoclassical economists see their *laissez-faire* model in the successes of Taiwan, South Korea, Hong Kong and Singapore (Wolf, 1990); others attribute this to the role of government intervention (Amsden, 1989; Wade, 1990; Singh, 1992). Nevertheless, these studies have promoted a resurgence of research interest by development studies on the role of modern technologies in the economic and social development of a nation; and moreover the role of government and social institutional frameworks in technology development and acquisition of technological capabilities. Two questions therefore arise: first, whether the tradition of development studies is applicable to the experiences of NICs; and second, whether NICs' experience are transferable to other developing countries, for instance, China.

Modernisation, Dependency and Intermediate Technology

There are many theoretical approaches within the post-war literature on development studies. A variety of retrospective schema have been proposed to categorise these diverse approaches. These include, for example, the mainstream modernisation theorists, structuralist approaches and dependency theories. Various writers reviewing this field have sought to synthesise and categorise this diverse literature (Clark, 1985; Colman and Nixson, 1994; Chenery and Srinivasan, 1988; Dutt and Jameson, 1992; Hirschman, 1981; Taylor, 1992; Todaro, 1994; Smith, 1995). However, scholars from different academic, social and political backgrounds have treated theoretical concepts differently, or given different emphasis to particular elements, and have thus arrived at different classifications of the main theoretical trends and the relationships between them (Smith, 1995). For example, in many accounts the 'structuralists' are attached to the dependency school; however, in some other schema, structural-change theories are associated with those, such as Lewis, Chenery and some post-Keynesians (Todaro, 1994), who are broadly associated with the stage-model that derives from modernisationist accounts. These differences are not 'just academic' but reflect sharp political differences within the field of development studies. Thus there have been controversies about the contribution of various traditions. For example, modernisation theory has been strongly criticised on the grounds of its implicit ideological support for neo-colonialism or imperialism (Barratt Brown, 1974; Leys, 1975, 1977; Smith, 1995; Warren, 1980; Cardoso and Faletto, 1979). However, others have seen modernisationists as making an important contribution to the theoretical development of development studies, linking them to those of developmentalists who were ambitiously seeking a unified model of development (Smith, 1995).

Despite these differences of view, modernisation theories and dependency theories are more or less consistently recognised by most scholars as representing two contrasting views in development studies. Whilst the former was articulated largely by scholars from the industrialised countries, the latter emerged from DCs (notably based on experiences in Latin America). It would probably be too simplistic to say that these two theories have been the mainstream in development studies. However, they do often represent contrasting points in a spectrum, which provide a useful opening into the area of development studies, its ideological, theoretical, and empirical diversity, and the controversies that have arisen. It is also worth reviewing these because the substance of these two perspectives still influences development studies today (although not many still acknowledge this contribution). Moreover, some of the issues raised in these two perspectives are still relevant to today's practice in DCs.

The most outspoken and influential theory in the Modernisation tradition can be traced to Rostow's stages of economic growth (Todaro, 1994). According to Rostovians or modernisationists, all countries pass through the same set of historical stages in the same sequence, and if there are slight variations in terms of timing, duration and other factors, these do not detract from the main process. Less-developed countries are backward in terms of their cultures, political systems, social institutions and economic resources. As a result, modernisationists believed that, as an extension of the already developed part of the world, what less-developed countries must do is 'to compress an essentially linear process into the shortest possible time-scale' (Clark, 1985, p. 165). 'The way to become "less backward" ' is to borrow, buy or copy those corresponding features of the rich countries felt to be instrumental in bringing about economic growth' (Clark, 1985, p. 167).

Modernisation theories came under attack from many scholars not only for their economic implications but also on empirical, ideological and methodological grounds. The most eminent critique came from a range of writers from Latin America who developed theories of 'structural underdevelopment', which have also been described as 'dependency theories'. From this perspective, the conditions in the less developed countries were examined as part of a broader international picture. 'Underdevelopment is seen as being caused by the dominant influence exercised by developed capitalist countries as a result of certain political and economic institutions which lock poor LDCs [less developed countries] into a dependent relationship' (Colman and Nixson, 1994, p. 29).

Perhaps the heaviest criticism was derived from empirical studies in the Third World which showed that the Western model of develop-ment had brought negative consequences including unemployment, dependency and disequilibrium. Latin American and African coun-tries are seen as typical victims of this development approach. And the Western model of development was condemned as 'maldevelopment' or 'distorted development' (Goulet, 1983). It was believed that, even where high economic growth had been achieved, mass misery still continued. There, a small portion of people gained wealth through economic growth. However, the majority was by-passed, and these benefits did not trickle down to the poor masses.

Dependency theories have a very pessimistic view of the prospects for technology transfer, let alone the acquisition of technological capabilities by developing countries. With regard to technology transfer, it is believed that the ownership or control over advanced technologies is not transferred, and there is merely a geographical movement of technology from one set of geographical boundaries to another, but still within the control of the metropolitan economy. Developing countries do not have effective access to the whole range of existing technologies, and the price structure is always based on the seller's market. Apart from these, Western technology is regarded as a two-edged sword, simultaneously creating and destroying different kinds of values – destroying old values and uprooting people in alienating fashion, and threatening indigenous values, local economies or local institutions in developing countries (Goulet, 1983). Indigenous technological competencies are even less possible to achieve, as developing countries are considered to be poor and lacking technological resources, not only equipment but also know-how and manpower. Therefore, the more a developing country relies on advanced Western technologies, the more it will reinforce its dependency on industrialised countries.

Some of the most radical critiques have led to extremely pessimistic views, based on notions of 'a series of interlocking vicious circles of poverty and stagnation', 'backwash effects', 'low-level equilibrium traps', 'backward-sloping supply curves of effort' and the like, which assert the impossibility of economic development in less developed countries (Clark, 1985). Some even concluded that 'stopping economic growth would be the solution' (Riedijk, 1982, p. 2). However, these dependency theories have been subject to increasingly severe criticism (Leys, 1977; Palma, 1978; Warren, 1980).

For the purpose of this study, it is not necessary to review all the writings within these two perspectives. Instead, I will draw out those aspects which are most relevant to the theoretical framework of my research. As we have seen, the core theory of modernisationist perspective, the linear-stage model of development, has hardly any credibility in development studies today. However, its implicit presumptions have become deeply rooted in much contemporary thinking about development. Let us leave aside for the moment two long-standing criticisms of modernisation theories – first, that politically and ideologically they reflect colonialist and imperialist views, and, second, that their schematic form does not provide a useful framework for critical analysis or for policy prescription. However, we can still acknowledge the usefulness of a range of detailed empirical studies conducted within this framework. For example, modernisation theories generalised the features of experiences of economic and technology development in the West, in particular the powerful integration of technology and market economy. This point is closely related to the interests of this research, and I will explore it in detail below.

The 'dependency' or 'structural underdevelopment' theories opened new perspectives for developing countries in understanding their situation within the worldwide economy and the sphere of international politics. This structural perspective is obviously useful for comprehensive analysis of the technological, social and economical development in developing countries. However, from the early 1970s onwards, dependency theories came under increasing criticism on both theoretical and practical grounds. The latter, in particular, was in response to the success of NICs in which sustained and rapid economic growth has taken place with the state playing a strategic role. Dependency theories could not provide adequate explanation of this. (I will return to this in the following section.)

Despite this, it is undoubtedly the case that dependency theory has provided many important insights into the characteristics of developing countries and the interaction between them and developed capitalist economies. For example, one of the important contributions of dependency theory is to show that the problems of development are not only a question of economic growth, but that the broader social dimensions must be addressed. It highlights a range of social issues in developing countries, including social security systems, unemployment, income distribution, poverty. Technological change, and especially the negative consequences of technology transfer from industrialised countries, are given particular attention. On top of these difficulties are added also the effects of the discriminatory trade barriers imposed by industrialised countries. 'Textiles are the most obvious, though not the only, example' (South Commission, 1990, p. 29). The DCs have been playing a role in providing low-price food and raw materials to industrialised economies, in order to buy highly value-added industrial goods as well as technologies.

The critique advanced by dependency theory has been one factor stimulating the emergence of an important concept about technological development in developing countries. This is 'intermediate technology' (or appropriate technology), which points to an alternative development approach that seeks to encourage self-sustained growth through the design and development of technologies that build upon locally available skills and resources, and appropriate to the local, social and cultural circumstances. A leading role in espousing this concept has been played by Schumacher's publication, *Small is Beautiful* (Schumacher, 1973). Various bodies, such as the Intermediate Technology Development Group, which was established in London in the late 1960s, have sought to put these ideas into practical application.

Like dependency writers, Schumacher and his supporters attributed many disastrous manifestations in the world to modern technologies. They concluded that:

(1) many Western technologies are inappropriate to local conditions in developing countries;
(2) there is a huge imbalance in technology trade between richer and poorer countries;
(3) technology transfer has reinforced dependencies of all kinds; and
(4) the values of less developed countries are being manipulated and people are being mobilised to support goals reimposed from the external-metropolitan economies of industrialised countries (Schumacher, 1973).

To counter these tendencies, they therefore called for alternative development approaches. Intermediate technology is supposed to be appropriate for local conditions in less developed countries and regions, and to meet certain criteria, e.g. being easy to access, easy to learn, and being suitable for small-scale regional or district production with local resource supplies (Schumacher, 1973).

The intermediate technology approach appears to provide a very promising model of technological development in developing countries, by encouraging indigenous technological capabilities. However it has obvious weaknesses. First of all, the ideas about which technologies might be appropriate have been confined to a very limited category of artefacts and technologies – which effectively rules out a wide range of existing technologies, particularly advanced technologies. Second, the practical achievements of appropriate technology have been very limited. These points, in turn, draw attention to weaknesses in the theoretical framework of this approach – and in particular its treatment of technology. Schumacher and his supporters recognised the fact that technology embodies social factors of the country which developed the technology, but they did not pay enough attention to the possibility that exogenous technologies could be sufficiently flexible to be useful in a wider range of circumstances or could be adapted to the particular local context of developing countries. Further, they have largely confined their search for technologies appropriate to developing countries to a series of relatively inefficient traditional technologies, to the exclusion of modern technologies which are often extremely resource efficient (Beckerman, 1995).

One of the reasons for these theoretical and practical shortcomings can be linked to shortcomings in Schumacher's conceptualisation of technology. Schumacher saw socio-economic values as becoming embodied in technological artefacts – that were conceived as stabilised 'black boxes'. Their implementation and use would therefore impose certain socio-economic arrangements and outcomes. In this respect, Schumacher's perspective on technology can be seen to have incorporated some features of the 'technological determinist' approaches (Williams and Edge, 1996) which were extremely prevalent when he was writing. From this perspective, therefore, technology transfer tends to be virtually treated as the synonym of technology transport from one place to another.

The three intellectual traditions of development discussed above – modernisation theory, dependency theory and the intermediate technology approach – each have their strengths and weaknesses. Together they bring a wide range of perspectives for this research into the scope for development in less developed countries. Modernisation theory is very much confined to the model of Western industrialisation, but it produced a range of detailed empirical studies. These empirical studies were valuable particularly in integrating technology and the market economy, although largely based on the experiences of economic and technology development in the West. The dependency school of thought draws attention to the obstacles to economic and technological development in DCs. Together with associated structural approaches to understanding development, it addresses not only the economic dimension, but also other social and environmental issues and explores how the roots of underdevelopment lay far beyond the domain of less developed countries and arise from their position in the world political economy. However, its general view is so pessimistic as to provide little hope for developing countries wishing to industrialise and to acquire advanced technologies. It does not suggest effective strategies for DCs and it fails to explain the relative success of some NICs. The intermediate technology approach gives a close-up view of the problems and especially the negative social consequences of technology transfer from industrialised to developing countries, and emphasises the scope for developing indigenous technologies.

However, it confines itself to a very limited choice of technologies, which particularly excludes advanced technologies.

The need for modern technological development is now widely recognised as crucial to economic development in developing countries. There are still doubts as to whether it is feasible for developing countries to catch up and overcome the existing gap between developed and less developed countries, and debates about how DCs might achieve this and thus escape economic and technological dependency. The economic success of Asian NICs has raised the hopes of developing countries. Studies of these experiences draw attention to some of the strategies which may achieve technological dynamism. However, there have been controversies about the assessment of their technological capabilities and the validity of their experiences for other countries (particularly since the recent financial crises and economic setbacks in some Southeast Asian countries).

We also note the increasing attention paid in contemporary development studies to the role of the state, and the social and economic structure of a country, in technology development. Developing countries' technology development cannot be treated as a subject which has a universally applicable recipe. Each country has its own peculiarities arising from its social and economic development history and position in the world economy and politics. Thus, development, including technological development, would better be seen as a strategic issue, and to some extent a race between developing countries, and a race with a powerful developed world. Decision-makers seeking to develop successful technology strategies need to understand the strengths and weaknesses of a particular country and the scope for resorting to external opportunities in the world.

This brings us on to the need to examine the social and economic system in China, and in particular the problems associated with its socialist system from 1949.

2.3 PROBLEMS OF THE SOCIALIST CENTRALLY PLANNED ECONOMIES

The collapse of the political and economic systems in the Soviet Union and the Warsaw Pact countries, and the challenge of resurgent new liberal policies to Western forms of social democracy, have thrown traditional concepts of socialism into a deep crisis. Many writers on the left have been forced to reassess their approaches. Some of the fiercest controversies have arisen between writers within the Marxist tradition, involving sharp polemics about the nature and definition of socialism. Instead of digging to find out authentic socialist theory, this review focuses on the practical issues which socialist states like China are facing and particularly those arising with their transition.

The Central Planning System

Contrary to the expectations of nineteenth-century Marxists, twentieth-century socialist revolutions had taken place in largely pre-industrial or industrialising countries. It is generally acknowledged that the early socialist regimes in Russia and China alike achieved great advances in industrialisation.

However, the initial dynamism which followed the transformation of these semi-feudal and chaotic societies was not sustained. The central state planning system, which seemed so effective in developing large-scale basic industries and providing the essential social needs of food, clean water and housing, seemed less well suited for producing non-essential consumer products that populations sought as their living standards rose. Leftwich (1992) comments that socialist states have been facing systematic constraints associated with the centralised planning system. They need to achieve international competitiveness, develop alternative planning and management systems capable of dealing with the complex flows of resources which characterise more developed economies, and meet popular demands associated with non-essential consumption – for consumer durables, improved housing, better quality and variety of food, etc.

White (1988) has examined these problems in the case of China. Within this system of planned state industry, relations between state economic organs and industrial enterprises, and among enterprises themselves, are not based on commodity exchange regulated by the 'law of value' through the markets, but are subject to unified co-ordination and control at various levels of the state planning network. The pattern of industrial output is predominantly determined by state officials not market demand; production functions are set by the plan according to relatively unchanging, standardised technical coefficients; most prices are regulated administratively and are only marginally subject to pressures of supply and demand; money plays a passive, accounting role, monitored closely by a centralised banking system with cash playing only a marginal role; industrial manpower is administratively allocated by state labour bureaux; inter-sectoral product flows are determined by a balancing process based on physical input–output ratios; supplies of raw material to industrial enterprises and purchase of their products are both handled administratively by specialised state agencies. Under such a system, although firms are formally independent accounting units responsible for calculating their own profits and losses, in reality they are administratively subordinate, responsible for carrying out the planned targets issued by superior state organs. White concludes that, 'Just as capitalist enterprises in competitive conditions are theoretically "price-takers" so socialist enterprises in such centralised conditions are theoretically "plan-takers"' (White, 1988, p. 155).

These criticisms of the problems of socialist planned economies have now been well rehearsed with a substantial recent contribution by writers from the former socialist states (e.g. Brus and Laski, 1989; Kornai, 1986; Zhou, 1982 and other Chinese economists).

Studies of socialist countries show that the information on which central planning is based is always inadequate and that the state machine is too large and rigid to react to a situation that is continually changing at various levels, including consumers' demand, requirements of firms and institutions in the supply chain, and a changing external context (e.g. of global technologies and world trade) (Brus and Laski, 1989). As described by Brus and Laski (1989), the 'inconsistent plans cannot be fulfilled in their totality by definition', let alone the 'unforeseeable reactions of the economic actors to unexpected events which must be included' (p. 42). The informational weaknesses of the system interact with weakness of incentives: the lack of competitive incentives and the fragility of those linked to consumers' choice (Brus and Laski, 1989, p. 44).

The lack of incentives for change within an essentially static system is the other fatal problem. The socialist incentive system relies on people's inspiration, government mandate and officially organised competitions (Zaleski and Wienert, 1980), which are in reality often unreliable. Because people had life-long tenure of employment within organisations, their sense of motivation, based upon general inspiration for socialist construction, gradually became eroded. The incentives for hard work and better performance gradually declined and could only be sustained at a low level. Moreover, labour allocation was conducted by the state, and human mobility was limited. Government agents at various levels of the state planning network became bureaucratic organisations and were not able to play an active role in monitoring and promoting technological development.

Institutional Structure

The lack of technological dynamism has come to be seen as an increasingly critical problem of state socialism. It stems from the lack of integration between the research system (specialised R&D institutes) and industrial organisations, and the weak links between technology designers and producers and technology users. R&D institutions were by and large separated from industries, and manufacturing firms were separated from product users. In the main, government agencies were not able to play an active role. Information exchange between players was inadequate, apart from the rather crude requirements of central planning. Therefore, the bigger the system, the more rigid the system was for technological changes.

R&D institutions themselves have little interest in understanding what industries need, since their finances are provided by the state, and R&D projects are not selected according to the demand from industry (Balàzs, Faulkner and Schimank, 1995a). Similarly, industrial enterprises have no need to co-operate with R&D institutions, partly because most technologies are freely provided by the state. Firms find their output targets set on a continuing 'ratchet principle' that impels them to seek increased output without concern for cost, quality or customer satisfaction. So, although they are the 'carriers of innovation' they have little space to improve their performance. In turn, customers only had limited scope to impose their requirements because of the supply-driven system. They found that they had little option except to accept what was produced.

All these factors resulted in low productivity, and a waste of techno-logical resources. Worse, firms – the supposed carriers of technological change – and other relevant institutions lack motivation to improve this situation. Although the socialist system is supposed in theory to promote technological development by controlling science and tech-nology to ensure free education of people and technology exchange by any enterprises (Bhalla, 1992), in practice it failed to deliver the expected results. Apparently, central planning without market forces is not able to provide necessary and adequate incentives for techno-logical development.

Transition

Since the economic and political collapse of the Soviet Union and the Warsaw Pact Allies, there has been a sharp turn from central planning towards capitalism in most of the former socialist states in the Soviet Union and Eastern Europe. Other less developed socialist states, like China and Vietnam, with economic systems that differ from the Soviet model, have shifted to a more pragmatic stance and committed themselves to economic reforms while ideologically still hanging on to the socialism. Whatever the different reactions which might be derived from diverse theoretical approaches and presumptions of the various school of thought, they are embarking on the process of transition.

Clapham (1992) regards these transition processes as part of a global phenomenon that is not restricted to the former socialist states. He refers to the demise of the 'statist orthodoxy' whether in its socialist or capitalist/Keynesian variants, and the concomitant ascendance of 'a newly dominant orthodoxy [which] emphasises the need for market incentives, and sees incorporation into the capitalist world economy as the essential motor for growth'. He believes that this restructuring affects not only socialist states, but also 'actually existing capitalism' (Clapham, 1992, p. 9).

Others have seen the problems of planned economies in terms of the interaction between the socialist and capitalist worlds, and view the successes or crises of socialism as a product of the economy and politics of the world. As Qadir and Gills (1992) indicate, the crisis of penury in the Third World is an integral element of a much broader and deeper economic crisis in the global political economy and a process of restructuring that affects all states, developed and less developed, 'capitalist' as well as 'socialist' (p. 9). Colburn and Rahmato (1992) argue that no (developing) country succeeded entirely in breaking out of the capitalist dominated world economic order and constructing an 'independent economy'. For all, there is no escaping the dependence on generating export earnings, i.e. participating in world trade in order to earn foreign exchange (p. 10).

State Interventions versus Markets

There is an acute debate about the feasibility of socialism. Some scholars from a socialist perspective have turned to the solution of the market, while others have argued that markets are incompatible with socialism. At the more pragmatic end of this spectrum there has been a debate about the respective roles of states and markets.

Authors like Alec Nove, Geoff Hodgson, Wlodzimierz Brus and Kazimierz Laski attempt to reconcile socialism with the market (McNally, 1993). The influential text by Alec Nove, *The Economics of*

Feasible Socialism (1983), illustrates a model that combines these two. Investment and the infrastructure, in general, would be planned by the state. Health and education would continue to be non-market parts of the economy. So-called natural monopolies, such as utilities, would remain with the state. The rest would operate within a market. For instance, services and consumer goods would be in a market situation. Accordingly, they would set their own prices and conclude their own contracts, which would be based on profit and loss. Meanwhile, the centre (the state) would have a number of vital functions, such as major investment, monitoring decentralised investment directly or through the banking system, playing a major role in administering 'naturally' centrally planned productive activities, while setting the ground-rules for the autonomous and free sectors, with reserve powers of intervention when necessary, and operating the functions connected with foreign trade (Nove and Thatcher, 1994). Brus and Laski (1989), on the basis of their past experiences in Poland, are more aware of the problems that may arise in the process of realising such 'market socialism'.

Authors like Ticktin, Bettelheim, Sweezy, McNally and Elson, and many from a Trotskyite or Maoist persuasion, all argue that markets and socialism are incompatible. Bettelheim and Sweezy insist that there is a viable socialist economic model without involving the market (Bettelheim, 1970; Sweezy, 1978). However, McNally admits that the market cannot be eliminated overnight and would have to play some roles for a considerable period of time in the transition to socialism (McNally, 1993).

Leland Stauber (1987) looks at this issue from the features of Western capitalism, and explores the implications and problems of a broader form of socialism drawn upon the practical experiences of socialism within Western capitalist economies. Based on the analysis of modern capitalist economies in the United States and Western Europe, he sees the problem of the 'simple dichotomy' in which 'on one side of the fence lies the combination of private ownership of business corporations with an emphasis on the market and decentralisation to the level of firm', and 'on the other side of the fence lies the combination of the principle of public ownership with a large amount of government economic planning and hence a large amount of government control required to implement such planning' (Stauber, 1987, p. 321).

Stauber further points out that contemporary Western Europe displays practices that do not readily fit the ideologies either of capitalism or traditional socialism, but which exhibit many significant elements of market socialism (Stauber, 1987). In his view, the term 'market socialism' can be used to denote any of a wide range of institutions and policies that emphasise simultaneously the market within the decision-making process and public or social ownership within the property system along with tax policies designed to eliminate and prevent large private fortunes. A range of types of market socialism can be conceived, extending from only modest departures from the most centralised of central planning systems, at one end, all the way to a situation in which corporate business firms are publicly owned but where their control is structured so that their management operate with a degree of freedom and autonomy no different whatever from that typical of privately owned corporations in contemporary capitalist systems.

Such concepts of market socialism bear obvious similarities to Western social democracies, particularly the more egalitarian participatory system such as in Scandinavia. These observations undermine the traditional dichotomy that has been drawn between socialism and capitalism.

Even Ticktin (1992) has noticed that modern capitalism is no longer the classical capitalist system based on the free market. He points out that in modern capitalist countries, governments are playing a substantial role in the economy, intervening via interest rates, subsidies, taxation, etc., and controlling prices and production by large firms. In reality, 'the law of value, or the market, is greatly limited in operation' (Ticktin, 1992).

From a historical perspective, after the Second World War, a large number of developing countries turned to socialism. In the developed capitalist world, collectivist policies such as state intervention to create a substantial public sector, policies and regulations to reduce unemployment and to redistribute private wealth, as well as the development of a social welfare system, have been extensively adopted in many Western European countries. For example, the Swedish model of 'welfare capitalism', before its crisis of 1991, was admired by people in China and regarded as 'more socialist' than that of socialist countries. However, we can also see that in newly industrialised countries like Japan, Singapore and South Korea, the state has made a critical contribution to their successful industrialisation processes, as discussed in the previous section.

This suggests the conclusion that the current crisis of socialism in both the socialist and industrialised capitalist world does not necessarily point to the demise of socialism or the role of the state. On the contrary, the transition of socialist states and reformation of socialist theories may prove to have been a step in the evolution of our understanding of socialism or in particular advanced socialism. At the same time, the modern capitalist system is far removed from its early beginnings, and capitalism which retains 'an extensive repertoire of socialist rhetoric' can be regarded as 'advanced capitalism' (Clapham, 1992). State control and central planning do not deserve to be discarded; rather they should be thoroughly assessed. If we break out of the 'dichotomies' between state and markets, between socialism and capitalism (see Stauber above), there is no need for socialist states to forgo any effective means such as market mechanisms in pursuing social and economic development. For the same reason, state control does not need to be confined to merely central planning, and central provision of public goods. Practices in Western capitalist countries have shown that governments have many instruments of influence over firms, even those which are privately owned. These instruments include both regulatory controls and positive financial inducements, e.g. subsidising, indicative planning with its co-ordination of investment decisions, promoting consultation, etc. (Stauber, 1987).

Socialist developing countries might need to continuously use the state and central planning as an instrument to use limited resources effectively, secure social stability and support the attempts of embryonic industries and less experienced firms to participate in the world market. At the same time, the state will perhaps inevitably have a role in combating problems that have emerged alongside economic development – for example, mass unemployment, large-scale bankruptcies, polarisation of the wealth of people, social instability, etc.

Governments have played an important role in the success of the NICs. Many argued that the modern notion of development rests on a concept of the state as the main generator of socio-economic progress (Hodder, 1992). In particular, for technology development, competition generated by market forces could induce individual enterprise towards technology protection. In such a case, government intervention is able to facilitate co-operation at the national level. So although the socialist system has shown a number of weaknesses and problems, particularly in the institutional structure for technology development of a country, the positive features of the industrial planning system should not be downplayed. As Riskin (1981) pointed out, in some accounts the negative stereotype of this system is a mirror image of that idealisation of the market to which some reformers are prone.

2.4 NEW APPROACHES FROM TECHNOLOGY STUDIES

Technology studies in many ways provide the integrating perspective for this study, not only because of its central focus on technological innovation, but also because the field has been developing extremely rapidly over the last two decades and has generated a wealth of concepts and frameworks for analysing detailed processes of technical and social change, and explicating the role of the broader socio-economic context. What has emerged across a number of related branches of enquiry is a much more sophisticated and complex account of the nature of technology and the relationship between technology and society which has 'opened the black box' of technology; unpicking for detailed analysis its composition and the processes by which it is developed and applied. In contrast to traditional accounts, which saw technology in a reified way, as largely exogenous to society, these emerging views point to the close interaction between social and technical elements (often captured by the concept of the 'socio-technical'), and for example draw attention to technologies as embodiments of knowledge and social practices, emerging within particular socio-technical constituencies and broader institutional settings. These emerging frameworks call into question the way in which technology has been conceived and used as an explanatory factor in other areas of study (particularly in development studies). Three aspects are pulled out for detailed examination. First is an approach to technology transfer as a process not just of acquiring particular bits of equipment but of gaining *technological capabilities*. Second are the ongoing attempts, under the rubric of 'systems of innovation', to characterise the contribution of particular *institutional and policy settings* to successful innovation. Third, and most fundamental, is the development of a model of the *social shaping of technology* (where I examine how this can be applied to understanding the social shaping of technology in developing countries).

Technology Transfer and Indigenous Technological Capabilities

Technology transfer and indigenous technology development, and the presumed dichotomy between them, have traditionally been at the centre of discussions of technology development in developing countries. More recently, with the shift to a more sophisticated processual analysis of technology, we have seen an evolution in this discussion which now addresses how 'indigenous technological capabilities' are attained. It is necessary to start by clarifying these concepts and their relevance to this study.

Earlier studies concerned with technology transfer from richer to poorer countries focused largely on the enormous problems which most developing countries suffered. These problems related mainly to the cost, suitability (or 'appropriateness') and effectiveness of the technology transferred (Fransman, 1984). Since the late 1970s, with the recognition of the success of certain NICs in acquiring and developing advanced technological capabilities, the assumption about the extremely weak position of less developed countries in technology transfer began to be challenged. Since then, there has been a fundamental shift in focus in the study of technology in developing countries (Fransman, 1984 and Colman and Nixson, 1994).

Intellectually, this shift paralleled a turn in technology studies to address the detailed processes involved in technological change in developing countries (Fransman, 1984) and in general (MacKenzie and Wajcman, 1990). Increasingly researchers became interested in what happened to technology as it was imported and assimilated by DCs. Accordingly, greater attention began to be given to the processes involved in unpacking, mastering and adapting imported technologies.

In contrast to the modernist presumption that technology transfer was an unproblematic means of acquiring technological capabilities, studies showed that technology was not fully transparent, but involved important tacit elements, and that its transfer accordingly involved a significant degree of uncertainty. The process of unpacking, mastering and assimilating imported technologies thus required firms to solve numerous problems, the answers to which were not always provided by the supplier of the technology. The assimilation and reproduction of technology therefore itself involved a process of technological innovation, to a greater or lesser degree (Fransman, 1984). The process of technology transfer cannot be reduced to a simple model of 'transport' by which artefacts and knowledge are 'poured in' to the recipient by the donor, but is closely related to the technological capabilities of the recipient. The effectiveness of technology transfer – including the selection of both technology and supplier, and the maximisation of the recipient's bargaining position – requires indigenous technological capabilities. For example, in the first place, strategic planning demands a certain level of technological knowledge and understanding of current technological developments. A long-standing debate here has focused on the relative merits of acquiring large-scale, sophisticated technologies versus small-scale, intermediate technologies. In the recent past increasing attention has been given to the importance of acquiring advanced technologies. Experience shows that both have a role to play in different contexts. What is essential is that developing countries need properly qualified manpower to assess competing technologies on their own merits and to select those that are found to be most suitable under the circumstance (Huq, 1991). Moreover, the recipient's knowledge about the technology concerned will be an important factor influencing its bargaining strength, e.g. the information it has about alternative sources of supply, the resources it is prepared to expend on getting such information, and, paradoxically, how much it knows about the knowledge it is buying (Balasubramanyam, 1973).

The longer-term significance of technology transfer is the possibility of replicating knowledge and applying it more broadly, beyond the boundaries of the firm originally involved, for recipients to assimilate, adapt and improve upon the original technology transferred from abroad. Rosenberg points out that the geographic transfer of very productive forms of physical capital may be of little use, unless the appropriate human resources are simultaneously available *in situ* to provide for the operation, maintenance, repair, and upgrading of the facilities, as well as to interface with and learn from foreign engineers and specialists (Rosenberg and Fischtak, 1985, p. viii).

Therefore, issues regarding the technological capabilities of the recipient come to the fore in relation to technology transfer. For developing countries in particular, possession of the requisite indigenous technological capabilities for effective technology transfer becomes critical. In turn, it offers the possibility of further building up indigenous technological capabilities by strategically and effectively acquiring exogenous technological capabilities through technology transfer.

There have been many definitions of indigenous technological capabilities, and definitions are often closely related to the perspectives and purposes of the person using the concept. Many popular definitions identify different components of technological capabilities in relation to the process of technology transfer and put them in a hierarchical order. For example, Dahlman and Cortez identified five types ordered as follows:

(1) Capturing technology which includes searching for available technologies, selecting those appropriate to specific local needs and conditions, and negotiating favourable terms.

(2) Translating product and process knowledge into products and productive facilities.
(3) Operating those plants, processes and equipment.
(4) Improving plants, products, processes, inputs and equipment.
(5) Creating new technological knowledge, in order to satisfy specific needs and local conditions. (Dahlman and Cortez, 1984, in Molina, 1987)

Lall (1992), perhaps from an economic point of view, stresses 'investment capabilities', 'production capabilities' and 'linkage capabilities', and describes these technological capabilities as a sequence involving mastery of technology proceeding from simpler to more difficult activities (though he indicates that different firms and dierent technologies may adopt different sequences).

In spite of this diversity of interpretations, there is consensus that capability in innovating technology and creating technological knowledge is crucial for DCs to 'catch up' through technology transfer.

There are also different accounts of the accumulation of technological capabilities. Many stress that technological capabilities are firm-oriented. It is argued on theoretical grounds that 'technology is conceived as firm-specific information concerning the characteristics and performance properties of production processes and product designs, and to the extent that it is tacit and cumulative in nature' (Rosenberg and Frischtak, 1985, p. viii). Empirical studies have suggested that 'most technological learning is localised in firms', and 'even in the industrially advanced countries, measured R&D activities are only the tip of the iceberg' (Bell and Pavitt, 1992, p. 25). Thus, firms are regarded as of central importance in the accumulation of technological capabilities, and, at the same time, technological learning, the mechanism transforming the activity of technology transfer into the accumulation of indigenous technological capabilities.

Notwithstanding technological learning at the firm level, some writers address also the importance of technological capabilities at the national level, which require not only a clear vision of how to utilise exogenous advanced technological capabilities strategically, but also a supportive environment for technological learning and innovation. Researchers such as Lall (1992) distinguish technological capabilities at two levels: firm and national levels. He points out that the nation's technological capabilities are not simply the sum of individual firm-level capabilities. There may be a synergy between individual firms, and more important is a common element of response of firms to the policy, market and institutional framework (Lall, 1992). Bell and Pavitt define the country's technological capabilities as being incorporated with the resources needed to generate and manage technical change, which include not only skills, knowledge and experience, but also institutional structures and linkages (in firms, between firms and outside firms) (Bell and Pavitt, 1992). The OECD (1987) refers primarily to a country's technological capabilities as the supplies of human capital, savings and the existing capital stock, as well as the technical and organisational skills required for the use. It notes the interactions between incentives and capabilities, and institutional framework: 'Both incentives and capabilities operate within an institutional framework; institutions set rules of the game, as well as directly intervening in the play; they act to alter capabilities and change incentives; and they can modify behaviour by changing attitudes and expectations' (OECD, 1987, p. 18).

In order to identify the linkage between indigenous technological capabilities and the effectiveness of technology transfer from abroad, this study distinguishes these commonly recognised technological capabilities into two levels: at the basic level is the capability of production, operation, maintenance, resource allocation, management, marketing, etc.; at the advanced level is the capability for innovating technologies and creating new technological knowledge. Once an assessment has been made of the level of technological capabilities required – largely determined, according to this dichotomy, by whether these are geared to meet domestic demands or to compete in the world market – it is clear that the level of existing technological capabilities will have important consequences for the objectives of technology transfer and for the selection of the package of technology to be transferred.

It is likely that the lower the level of technological capabilities the recipient possesses, the more extensive must be the package transferred. In situations of limited indigenous capability it seems likely that the capacity to operate, produce and maintain imported technology and any upgrading will rely heavily on the technology supplier, which is liable to induce financial and technological dependencies. It has been widely presumed that developing countries transferring technology on this basis can at best hope to become a follower of their technology supplier. In contrast, possessing advanced technological capabilities was seen as crucial to the prospects of DCs to pursue more ambitious objectives for technological development.

This study is concerned to explicate the processes of selecting, unpacking, adapting and utilising foreign technologies and through them ultimately acquiring technological capabilities rather than the form of the commercial relationship between suppliers and recipients. The main focus is therefore on the interplay between technology transfer and indigenous technological capabilities. It gives credence to the view that the process of technology transfer, of selecting, unpacking, adapting and innovating imported technologies, demands indigenous technological capabilities, while, in turn, the accumulation of indigenous technological capabilities requires strategic and effective technology transfer.

Closely related to these processes is technological learning – defined as the means by which exogenous technological competencies are transformed into indigenous technological capabilities. However, technological learning is by no means guaranteed by the existence of technology transfer initiatives. It may be passive, inefficient and incomplete, because of the lack of incentives, resources and supportive mechanisms to encourage such technological learning to take place. An important question concerns whether technological learning is localised, and newly acquired technological capabilities do not spread beyond the recipient organisation, or whether more widespread learning allows this knowledge to become more widely diffused across the society. The character of such technological learning does not depend solely on the behaviour of those immediately involved but is greatly influenced by the broader social and economic context. This context, encompassing the institutional framework and incentives stemming from both state intervention and market forces, which has important consequences for whether the necessary resources and incentives are in place.

To summarise, this study sees the extent of existing indigenous capabilities as a key consideration for strategies for technology transfer. They shape choices about which exogenous technological capabilities need to be acquired, and influence the prospects for absorbing and utilising those capabilities effectively through technological learning. The study distinguishes technological capabilities at two different levels: distinguishing the basic level of production, operation, maintenance, resource allocation, management, marketing, etc. from the advanced level of innovative and creative technological capabilities. The starting point of this enquiry was the assumption that although the technological capabilities at the basic level are essential, the advanced-level technological capabilities in innovating imported technologies and creating new technological knowledge are crucial in enabling developing countries to catch up with the developed world. Further, the study distinguishes a nation's technological capabilities from firm-level technological capabilities. Whilst accepting that most technological learning is localised in firms it argues that the nation's capabilities are not just the sum of the many individual firm-level technological capabilities. Particularly in developing countries, many local firms are so weak in terms of their existing technological capabilities that assistance from other technologically advanced firms and institutions, such as R&D and financial institutions, becomes crucial. Wider technological learning thus becomes essential in allowing DCs to fully exploit the transfer of exogenous capabilities, to absorb and enhance them and build up indigenous capabilities.

The broader institutional context provides the foundation for any consideration of strategies for technology transfer, particularly regarding the state of indigenous technological capabilities at the national level – regarding materials, financial and human resources and the capacity to generate and manage technological innovations. It shapes the scope for technological learning to build up indigenous technological capabilities (at the level of the firm and nation). Careful deployment of these resources is particularly important for developing countries, in particular those seeking to develop longer-term innovative and creative technological capabilities. It is to these structural questions that we now turn.

Institutions and Incentives for Technological Development

Scholars such as Nelson (1992), Fransman (1991), Lundvall (1992) and Bell and Pavitt (1992) have been focusing on the national system for technological innovation in developed and developing countries. They seek to identify the essential characteristics of 'best practice' of a country's national system – comprising institutions and policies and the key features which are associated with successful technological development.

Bell and Pavitt (1992) sought to distinguish the characteristics of the countries which have been successful in generating and managing technical change from those which have not. They address these at 'micro' 'meso' and 'macro' levels in terms of the features of particular firms which have different sources of, and opportunities for, technical change and technological accumulation; local incentive mechanisms, and inter-sectoral linkages; and policies and institutions that support the development of indigenous capabilities. They then seek to link this to the related performance of the country and its technological accumulation. Key features are identified as being associated with successful technological accumulation: a substantial inward flow of foreign technology, closely coupled with the rapid development of indigenous capabilities in firms; heavy investment in education, training and skills; incentives for innovation and imitation; favourable product market conditions; and institutions and policies to encourage learning.

Bell and Pavitt (1992) have systematically compared institutions and policies in developed, developing countries and centrally planned systems. They argue that the accumulation of technological capabilities must become a policy objective of a country in its own right, rather than being treated as a by-product. They emphasise the indispensable importance of the state role in encouraging technological accumulation (learning) within firms, given the risks of 'market failure' in this respect.

Similarly, Lundvall (1993) criticises the presumption of many economists of the rational behaviour of economic agents and the existence of pure markets. His work also explores the relevance of the concept of national systems of innovation, highlighting the ways in which real world economic systems may be organised differently and wherein the behaviour of agents, rooted in different systems, may be governed by different rules and norms.

A series of studies has been undertaken in recent years of many different countries. Some features are commonly recognised as important across different national systems. These include user–producer relationships and intra- and/or inter-sectoral collaboration.

This shift of concern from addressing the generic features of successful national innovation systems towards investigating particular aspect and processes which may be associated with technological dynamism is also accompanied by a concern to examine how these may vary with different forms of technological innovation and across different technological fields. Thus Freeman and Perez (1988) and Lundvall (1993) distinguish stationary technology, incremental innovation, radical innovation and technological revolution. For example, Perez (1985) suggests that the current period which is dominated by information and communication technologies and micro-electronics, heralds the onset of a new techno-economic paradigm, requiring a radically different set of social and institutional arrangements. This includes, for example, a high level of industrial collaboration and government intervention. Perez further suggests that the new paradigm will offer DCs important opportunities to catch up with the West.

However, most of these studies are concerned to identify particular 'best practice' with a national system. Apart from being essentially regarded as static, this is not practical on two accounts. First, factors deemed to be successful in inducing innovation in one country may turn out to be less significant in a different national context. Second, national systems are not static (especially a country like China which is in transition). A national system in the real world is changing and, moreover, must change in response to the evolving world system and technology paradigms. The current transition in socialist countries is perhaps the most dramatic illustration of this. The pace and scope of social and institutional change poses particular difficulties in characterising the national system at any one moment, let alone in defining the circumstances that would best promote innovation in that system. For example, it requires not just the selection of appropriate policies but perhaps also their rapid adjustment. With this regard, it is important to address not only the form of the institutional system and the content of policy, but also the process, timing and circumstances.

The Social Shaping of Technology in Developing Countries

In its understanding of the character of technology and the relationship between 'technology' and 'society' this research is based on the view of technology as socially shaped. Thus, the characteristics and implications of technology may be influenced by a broad range of social and economic factors, as well as narrowly 'technical' considerations. From this perspective, technology transfer, in theory, can never be a pure process of geographic movement, rather technology will necessarily be transformed to adapt to the different social and economic context. One implication is that it may be possible for developing countries to adopt advanced technologies from abroad and make them suitable for the local environment. No doubt, to achieve this purpose, indigenous technological capabilities in the recipient country are required.

According to the theory of social shaping of technology (SST), technology does not develop according to an inner technical logic or any other single rationality, such as an economic imperative. Instead, every stage in the generation and implementation of new technologies involves a set of choices between different technical options. Alongside narrowly 'technical' considerations, a range of 'social' factors affects which options are selected – thus influencing the content of technologies and their social implications (MacKenzie and Wajcman, 1990).

SST highlights the 'choices' inherent in both the design of individual artefacts and systems, and in the direction or trajectory of innovative programmes; and it stresses the social influences upon, and negotiability of, technology. This contrasts with traditional 'linear' models of innovation which conceptualise innovation as divided into separate phases, with a one-way flow of information, ideas and solutions from basic science, through R&D, to the diffusion of stable artefacts through the market to consumers. In this way SST criticised 'technological determinist' views, that sought to exclude technological development from social analysis and explanation, and which saw technologies as requiring particular social outcomes or 'impacts' (Williams and Edge, 1996).

SST research investigates the ways in which social institutional, economic and cultural factors have shaped:

- the direction as well as the rate of innovation
- the form of technology: the content of technological artefacts and practices
- the outcomes of technological change for different groups in society.

It intends to 'identify opportunities to influence technological change and its social consequences'; to 'broaden the policy agenda'; to offer 'the prospect of moving beyond defensive and reactive responses to technology, towards a more pro-active role' (Williams and Edge, 1996).

In respect of technology development in developing countries, the SST perspective has some similarities with classical intermediate technology theory, in so far as it points to the way that technologies embody social and economic elements from the context in which they originated. However, these two theories point to different conclusions about the scope for developing countries to transfer advanced technologies from industrialised countries and apply them to their own ends. Classical intermediate technology theories see advanced technology transfer as inextricably linked to dependency and therefore confine what they see as appropriate technology to a very limited category.

SST research emphasises the instability and negotiability of technologies. So although values may get built into artefacts they are not automatically reproduced when they are used; instead the possibility remains for their transformation to meet specific local circumstances. Indeed SST empirical research shows how flexibility in use is a deliberate feature of many advanced technologies such as microelectronics: technologies which were purposely designed to meet the needs of a wide range of customers, often around public or industry standards, as part of a strategy to build and exploit mass markets (Williams, 1997). The implication is that such technologies as the telephone and computer can be used not only in industrialised countries but also in developing countries. Underpinning these contrasting interpretations are very different views of technology, and their social bases.

Whereas classical intermediate/appropriate technology theories tend to see technologies as internally monolithic, and embodying particular priorities and presumptions (about social goals, about the skills and resources available in the society) which will be reproduced when those technologies are used, SST sees complex modern technologies as heterogeneous assemblages (of diverse technologies and social elements) and therefore capable in principle of being reconfigured in their implementation and use. Indeed an important feature of modern, complex technologies, such as information technologies, is their configurational nature, as combinations of standard components and customised elements, configured to meet particular exigencies of use (Fleck, 1988a, 1988b). In the dynamics of development of information technology, many elements have become available as standardised, 'black-boxed' commodities, including, for example, hardware (e.g. microprocessors, personal computers) and software (e.g. operating systems, and generic utilities such as databases, network management functions, etc.) designed around their potential utility in a wide range of technical and social settings (Brady, Tierney and Williams, 1992).

In a broad sense, the local shaping of technology in a developing country can be seen as the adaptation and further elaboration of technology development on the basis of technologies transferred from abroad. From the viewpoint of SST theory, we can clearly see the possibilities for developing countries to acquire technological capability by transferring foreign technologies and through it to locally shape these technologies. Some accounts from development studies suggest that there are many disadvantages and problems for developing countries to transfer foreign advanced technologies, e.g. the incompleteness of their knowledge of the transferred technology; the

Western social and technical rationality and presumptions which may be embedded in transferred technologies which may not be appropriate for the developing countries; and trade barriers favouring industrialised countries. This research argues that the potential flexibility in use and negotiability of technologies, emphasised by SST research (particularly in relation to modern Information and Communications Technologies), invite developing countries to look into technology strategies and government policies relevant to the local appropriation and further development of technology. For example, where technology transfer only resulted in incomplete knowledge transfer, developing countries need to consider only acquiring the knowledge which is acquirable and needed at the moment. Other kinds of technological knowledge – for example, that needed to build 'black-boxed' technological artefacts – may remain within the 'black box'. With regard to embedded Western rationality, developing countries have to reduce negative effects through either selectively purchasing or locally shaping imported technologies to meet the local needs.

In these respects, of course, it becomes important to understand the scope for the flexibility and negotiability of a particular technology in its design, production and use.

From the viewpoint of a developing country, the scope for local shaping of foreign technology is concerned with the characteristics of the technology transferred and the nature of transaction agreed between suppliers and recipients. It might be useful to identify some characteristics of technology employed typically in today's advanced technology transfer from industrialised countries to developing countries.

There is a spectrum of types of technology transfer ranging from the purchase simply of physical assets to the complete transfer of technological competencies including also foreign know-how, management skills, etc. Although, both entail technology transfer in the form of physical assets, the latter is more complex and extends into more explicit 'social' issues. In terms of 'know-how', the latter involves more comprehensive transfer of knowledge not only of using the technology but also production, possibly re-engineering, operation, installation and maintenance, etc.

In considering the scope for local shaping it may be useful to differentiate technologies in terms of their form, scale and complexity. Here we can draw upon the distinction between discrete technologies, systems technologies and configurational technologies. In so far as discrete technologies are stand-alone technologies designed to carry out particular functions, it may be possible to apply them widely, including in developing countries. Examples include word-processors, and computer-controlled machine tools – which relate to activities that are widely encountered (Fleck *et al.*, 1990). Fleck (1988a) con-~Although both entail technology transfer in the form of physical assèts.trasted these with system technologies which typically encompass a greater range of activities than discrete ones and thus may be more tightly linked to particular applications settings. System technologies developed for use in developed countries may need to be adapted to fit them to the rather different requirements and circumstances of developing countries. However, system technologies tend to be rather rigid in their construction and may be difficult or costly to adapt. An example is provided by the System-12 public digital switching system covered in this study.

Configurational technologies match the application complexity of systems technologies, but are designed to allow great flexibility in development and application. Development costs are reduced by drawing upon existing components technologies – which can be selected to match the particular applications requirements. This makes it more flexible for developing countries to reconfigure such solutions to their local needs and exigencies.

Information and communications technologies in particular are increasingly taking the form of configurational technologies (Williams, 1997). Modular design and the use of open standards facilitates the substitution of internal components. The selection of components and design for flexibility in application can make it easier to adapt them to meet the specific needs of a wide range of users. In such a case, foreign technologies can be locally configured in the developing country to meet local criteria, such as being suitable for local production and local markets, using local resource, etc. Configurational technology extends the scope for recipient-side innovation.

To some extent every technology needs to be re-configured when being transferred from one society to another. In fact, their degree of configurability varies greatly depending on the nature of the technology design and the nature of component technologies. Obviously, the more configurable the technology, the more the technology can be locally shaped.

One important advantage of the more open architecture of configurational technology solutions is the scope for applying standardised component technologies which may be available on the

ıs cheap commodities (thereby offering lower prices for
s and bigger markets and bigger profits for suppliers).

ьy contrast, system technologies would seem to be generally more
difficult to master than configurational technologies. Their more or
less unique proprietary architecture and elements mean that they
embody a wide range of (perhaps proprietary or locally specialised)
technological knowledge which must be acquired if a developing
country is to learn how to design, make and apply the system
themselves. On the other hand, the possibility of building configurational solutions from component technologies gives a firm or a nation
more choices about which areas of competence they need to acquire
themselves, and which areas can be 'bought in' as black-boxed technological solutions. For developing countries, there are always 'black
boxes' when transferring foreign advanced technology, since mastering
technology or adapting technology is a gradual process. In addition,
some black boxes are more difficult or costly to open than others, and
the extent to which they can be opened depends on local technological
capabilities, market price and decision of suppliers. In this respect,
developing countries have to concentrate on the most appropriate
choice regarding which technology black-boxes to open and when.

2.5 RESEARCH QUESTIONS AND METHODOLOGY

By applying the above discussed theoretical framework, this study
aims to examine the empirical case of PDSS development as examples
of the different strategies for technology transfer and the acquisition of technological capabilities, as well as analysing the influence of
the broader social and economic context of the transition in China.
The research also sought to draw implications for developing countries
in general.

The Main Research Questions

- What has China achieved in the development of public digital
  switching systems to fulfil its domestic demands for modernising its
  telecommunications infrastructure, as well as to build up technological capabilities?
- What strategies has China adopted in selectively utilising advanced
  foreign technological competencies? What implications can we
  draw for other developing countries?

- What can we learn from the Chinese PDSS cases about the relationship between technology transfer, indigenous technological capabilities and technological learning, and moreover the broader social and economic context in which the activity of PDSS technology development is taking place?

Methodology

Given the complexity of the issues addressed in this study, I have adopted a double methodological approach. On the one hand, I seek the detailed account of technological development processes made possible by actor-centred approaches, such as actor-network theory (Latour, 1988), socio-technical systems (Hughes, 1983) and, in particular, socio-technical constituencies (Molina, 1990). On the other hand, the research design addresses the influence of broader structural and historical factors (Hughes, 1983, and others like Edquist, 1985).

The first approach helps to identify possible constituencies which are potentially influential to technological development. In particular, it highlights the interaction between 'technical' and 'social' elements – the way 'the technical' is both shaped by and shapes 'the social'. According to Molina (1990, 1995), technological development processes involve the emergence and development of technical and social elements – machines, instruments, institutions, interest groups – that interact and shape each other in the course of the creation, production, and diffusion of specific technologies. These two groups of elements evolve and change their mix in ways which result in technology growth or decline.

The second approach seeks to understand the context within which technological processes take place, and particularly to analyse institutional structures of the national system for technological dynamism and the role of government policies, and how they affect the behaviour and success of local actors. However, this study is also centrally concerned to understand the character and significance of China's economic transition. The contextual part of the study, therefore, explores the modification and transformation of institutional structures over time in response to changing government policies and other changes in the domestic and international environment.

My selection of the cases was extremely constrained by the limited number of technology transfer initiatives in the field at the time of my investigation. Although there were many foreign PDSS technologies being used in China, only three joint production ventures had been set up to manufacture public digital switching systems (PDSS):

- *Shanghai Bell*: this is a joint venture between the Posts and Telecommunications Industrial Corporation (on behalf of MPT), the Alcatel Bell Telephone and the Belgian government, producing System-12;
- *The Beijing International Switching System Corporation*: this involves Siemens AG and the Ministry of Machine Building and Electronics Industry (now Ministry of Electronics Industry), manufacturing the EWSD system;
- A Sino-Japanese joint venture producing system Neax-61.

Shanghai Bell was the earliest established joint venture and its first contract for a technology transfer programme had been officially completed. Its product – System-12 – had widely been used in the Chinese public telecommunications network. The Beijing International Switching System Corporation joint venture had emerged more recently, and its EWSD system was still at its early stage of development. The Sino-Japanese joint venture project was progressing even more slowly. In such circumstances, the choice of Shanghai Bell and its System-12 was obvious.

A more difficult task was to select a Chinese PDSS system, and moreover to gain access to the state-owned company which manufactures the product. Getting to interview high-ranking officials in the Ministry of Posts and Telecommunications and other relevant departments in the central government also proved difficult. I needed not only to find the right person who would be able to provide the information that I required, but also to get permission to interview them. The problem was that these people were typical officials (or bureaucrats) working at the highest level of organisations, which had a tradition of collective decision-making and secrecy.

I travelled to China in October 1992 to begin fieldwork. My first move was to get more detailed information about possible cases, especially about the Chinese PDSS systems. I had several formal and informal discussions with two of the country's leading switching specialists and other senior telecommunications engineers. These discussions confirmed that two locally developed large-scale public digital switching systems had been technically approved by the authorities, the DS-series and HJD-04, though further technical improvements were still required for a full licence before they could enter the public telecommunications network.

The DS-series project began almost immediately after the introduction of the first foreign public digital switching system into China in the early 1980s. This was an MPT-funded project and designed in the MPT's R&D institutes. The DS development project had been carefully planned, representing the attempts by the Chinese government to develop such a technology on their own, and gathering the best and available technological resources within the sector. Accordingly, the process of R&D followed more or less the existing (traditional) pattern of R&D in China. I could foresee that this would be a good case to reveal the problems of institutional structures typical of the old centrally planned system in China and incentives in relation to technology development.

By contrast, HJD-04 was not an officially planned product, and its development process did not fit in any traditional pattern. The project had been initiated by a military research institute. The technical, financial and organisational elements required to complete the project were only built up later. Among many institutions involved in this process, there were three main players:

- the key figure who initiated this project, Professor Wu, and his Research Centre for Information Technology at a military research institute, Zhengzhou Institute of Information Engineering of the People's Liberation Army;
- a state-owned manufacturing firm under the MPT, the Luoyang Telephone Equipment Factory (LTEF);
- a *de facto* procurement unit of MPT, the Posts and Telecommunications Industrial Corporation (PTIC).

It proved a great effort for HJD-04 PDSS technology to gain official approval. In other words, this system is a product of the new social and economic phenomenon, reflecting the country's current social and economic transformation. Moreover, from the technological point of view, HJD-04 adopts a very different technical strategy from the early developed switching systems, and one which I considered to be very interesting in relation to the acquisition of technological capabilities by developing countries.

Although the scope of the study had been established, the research design still needed to be modified or changed in the course of data collection. A study like this, that relies on detailed case-studies as the main method of research, may well encounter unforeseeable outcomes in the course of the investigation. New areas of interest are identified as well as uncertainties and difficulties in the research. The way in which these issues are handled in the course of fieldwork is critical to the quality of the entire investigation. Because research design, data collection and data analysis are often inseparable in practice, many decisions could not be made until particular data had been collected and preliminary analysis done.

In Shanghai Bell, I carried out twenty-eight interviews, ranging over workers, engineers and managers of most departments and both Belgian and Chinese general managers. During my investigation into System-12, on the basis of new information arising from the interviews, I also interviewed people not with Shanghai Bell:

- one of the System-12 users, Shanghai Telecommunications Administration;
- the former Chinese general manager of Shanghai Bell who took part in negotiating the technology transfer process;
- the System-12 Project Leading Group Office for Shanghai Municipal Government which jointly involved Shanghai Bell and Shanghai Municipal Government for the purpose of System-12 'technology localisation' (the actual meaning is: local production of components).

In the case of HJD-04, I had from the outset encountered resistance to my gaining access to the manufacturing firm, LTEF. LTEF, like other state-owned companies which were traditionally 'plan-takers', had no reason to expose itself to any unofficial investigations. My approach was through the help of a personal contact in the Municipal Science and Technology Committee of the regional government which had some modest influence over LTEF (which was more directly under the leadership of PTIC, the MPT's procurement arm) to make my investigation semi-official.

I carried out eighteen interviews in the Luoyang Telephone Equipment Factory (LTEF) of MPT in a similar range to those in Shanghai Bell and two interviews in the Posts and Telecommunications Industrial Corporation of MPT. I also spent a very informative half-day with Professor Wu and his research team in Zhengzhou Institute of Information Engineering of the People's Liberation Army. The three key actors in this same technology project presented sometimes quite different accounts about its development.

To understand the broader context for PDSS and telecommunications technology development and the background of the state policy formulation and implementation, I carried out fifteen interviews with researchers and officials in a number of R&D institutes and central governmental organisations, including:

- the Economic and Technology Development Research Centre of MPT;
- the Science and Technology Information Centre of MPT;
- the State Science and Technology Commission;
- the State Planning Commission;
- the Ministry of Posts and Telecommunications;
- the Ministry of Machinery and Electronics Industries (now the Ministry of Electronics Industries).

Part II
The Case Studies

3 System-12: Wholesale Technology Transfer

3.1 THE INITIATION OF SYSTEM-12 TECHNOLOGY TRANSFER

This case involves the comprehensive technology transfer of a foreign developed PDSS, System-12, through the establishment of a Belgian–Chinese joint production venture – Shanghai Bell.

The System-12 technology transfer was set up immediately after the inauguration of economic reforms in China. This demonstrated the Chinese government's early determination to modernise its telecommunications systems and build up indigenous technological capabilities by acquiring advanced foreign technologies. The central government played an important role in searching for collaborators and setting up this project. This section details the objectives of the Chinese government; its initiatives and the international environment for such an advanced telecommunications technology; and describes the scope of this technology transfer.

First Move – Searching, Mutual Selecting, Negotiating

As mentioned in Chapter 1, the Chinese government decided from the outset that direct import of finished foreign PDSS could only be a short-term solution for China. As the most populous country in the world with a huge potential market, transferring technologies by setting up joint ventures was considered necessary for China to increase local added value, maintain local employment and speed up the process of industrialisation; and more important, through technological learning, to build up indigenous technological capabilities. Facing pressing demands for an adequate telecommunications infrastructure, the Ministry of Posts and Telecommunications (MPT) approached almost all the prestigious telecommunications companies across the world, to explore opportunities for technology transfer through joint venture projects. At that time, several state councillors and premiers, during official visits to industrialised countries, explored the possibility of transferring foreign switching technologies.[8]

However, at that time, most telecommunications companies in the world were only interested in exporting their finished products into China. Bell Telephone Manufacturing Company (BTM) was one of the few who were willing to exploit the potentially huge market through wholesale technology transfer of manufacturing components through a comprehensive 'turnkey' project.

'In 1980, BTM was convinced that its technology could be successfully transferred to the People's Republic of China', given China's 'skilled personnel, sound Chinese financial policies, and a suitable partner, PTIC' (Zhou[9] and Kerkhofs,[10] 1987, p. 186). Obviously, the attractions of a potentially large market and the opportunity for long-term technological and commercial partnership with a successful local manufacturer were key elements for BTM in their decision to draw up a contract for the technology transfer project. The first preliminary agreement between BTM and the Posts and Telecommunications Industrial Corporation (PTIC) was therefore signed in Luoyang,[11] in November 1980. PTIC initially proposed that this joint production venture would be situated at the Luoyang Telephone Equipment Factory (LTEF). BTM preferred an alternative location. The final agreement was to set the joint venture at the factory of another MPT telephone exchange producer in Shanghai.

The Chinese side was convinced that System-12 was, at that time, the most advanced technology as well as the technology the most appropriate for the Chinese telecommunications network. For example, System-12 was the only switching equipment available at that time with fully distributed control. It was designed to avoid the weakness of central control systems, so to be relatively fail-safe. It was able to handle the complex user-interface and large call-processing densities which were essential for operating in China. ITT's (International Telephone and Telegram Corporation) reputation was an additional attraction, as, at that time, BTM was a daughter company of ITT. In addition to these considerations, the Belgian government had agreed to issue a long-term loan at a 'country to country' level, which guaranteed the Chinese continued financial support. The most important factor was that BTM agreed to transfer technologies for component production, including the production technology of its custom LSI (large scale integrated circuit) chip. This was remarkable. At that time no other supplier was prepared or able to offer the transfer of such advanced technology.[12]

The initiation of the System-12 technology transfer project involved the Belgian and Chinese governments, MPT, BTM, ITT and PTIC.

Since this was by far the largest high-technology transaction in the history of China's foreign trade (Zhou and Kerkhofs, 1987), the Chinese side set up a strong negotiating team. Within this team, the Chief Representative was a deputy minister of MPT (also a senior specialist in telecommunications technology). Many senior experts in both technologies and foreign trade from various state institutions also took part. The negotiation was an arduous marathon lasting 33 months. As far as the Chinese side was concerned, the major technological issue was whether the System-12 technology suited the conditions of the Chinese telecommunications network. For this, the features of System-12 were checked one after the other. Trade negotiation was also time-consuming. The whole process was a challenge for the Chinese team. As noted above, the most thorny issue was the transfer of the production technology for the custom LSI chip, as it was a high technology within the category of COCOM's (Co-ordinating Committee for Multilateral Export Control) restrictions.[13] The Chinese side insisted that all the technologies of component production had to be included in the transaction, lest component provision be stopped in future as a result of a change in political relations between the two countries. On this issue alone, both sides took a year to reach an agreement.

BTM undertook to lobby COCOM to ease the control.[14] The Belgian government, from time to time, took up the matter as its involvement became necessary. In 1983, the Belgian Minister of Foreign Affairs sought to convince the US government to lift the restrictions against China. In June 1985, even the Belgian Prime Minister intervened. The Belgian Embassy in Washington acted on behalf of the Belgian government in obtaining the US government approval for LSI technology transfer. In this period, BTM delegations had travelled frequently to Washington and Paris to pursue this goal. Even ITT was involved in these efforts. In March 1987, approval for the transfer of the (LSI) chip production technology to Shanghai Bell was at last obtained from the USA and other relevant governments.

Scope of the Technology Transfer

The contract for the rest of the technology had been agreed and signed on 30 July 1983, nearly four years before the final agreement on technology transfer of the LSI chip! BTM's equity share amounted to

32 per cent of the total, the Belgian government contributed 8 per cent and the PTIC of MPT held the remaining 60 per cent.

According to the contract, PTIC was primarily responsible for providing land, buildings and necessary facilities for the plant and for exploiting the domestic market for locally produced System-12 exchanges; BTM provided the technology together with various services; and the Belgian government contributed capital. The joint production venture, Shanghai Bell Telephone Equipment Manufacturing Company (Shanghai Bell), was registered with capital of 27 000 000 US dollars and designed to produce 300 000 lines per year of System-12 switches (Alcatel Bell Telephone, 1992a).

The technology to be transferred between BTM and Shanghai Bell included manufacturing and installation technology, as well as engineering technology. This was to be carried out during the contractual period of 15 years with an extension option for a period of 5 years. It concerned the transfer of hardware and software technologies. The hardware technologies included: custom LSI chip production of 3-micron CMOS (Complementary Metal Oxide Semiconductor) and 8-micron Bi-MOS; thick film hybrids, double-sided and multi-layer printed circuit boards, and assembly line technology; computerised test facilities; and numerically controlled equipment for piece-part manufacturing. The software included full Country Development Engineering (CDE) and Customer Application Engineering (CAE) capabilities and computer systems.

BTM was committed to transfer all the technologies that the Chinese requested. However, the Chinese did not order all the technologies, but only those which were considered necessary. For example, the Chinese did not use the fully automated production assembly that BTM used in its own factories, in order to save on capital costs. The Chinese decided to conduct manually many jobs which could be carried out by hand without having an impact on production quality.[15] In other words, where possible, the Chinese preferred to use labour rather than expensive automatic machines. Some equipment which they judged they could make in China was also not ordered. One example is the automatic operator-position, which was later developed jointly by Shanghai Bell and a local university.[16]

The earliest System-12 technology transferred was the 'release-5.0' based on the evolution line circuit technology,[17] which at that time was the latest version. Subsequently, Shanghai Bell selectively transferred the later innovations of System-12. In 1989, Shanghai

Bell obtained the last development of the version 5 – release-5.2. In 1992, a new contract between BTM and Shanghai Bell was signed, deciding that the project of technology transfer would extend for another twenty years from 1994 to 2014.[18] The new version of System-12 to be transferred was release-7. With the hardware, the size of the exchange would be smaller than the existing one – release-5. With the requisite software, release-7 was able to provide ISDN (integrated services digital network), IN (intelligent network) and so on, as well as to meet the new requirements of the international standards body CCITT (Comité Consultatif International Télégraphique et Téléphonique). The new contract also included an updated technology for manufacturing LSI with 1.2μ. The registered capital of the company increased to 40 000 000 US dollars and the planned annual production volume from 1995 would be 4 000 000 lines.

3.2 ADOPTING THE FOREIGN TECHNOLOGY

From the outset, the Chinese decided to adopt foreign technological capacity as a whole, not only technologies for production, engineering and services, but also institutional organisation and management. The Chinese side believed that only after adopting all these would it be able to judge whether they are appropriate for the Chinese environment. To this end, considerable effort was made by the Chinese. The Belgian company's experience in technology transfer was also crucial. In spite of this, Shanghai Bell encountered a range of acute problems. These resulted variously from the technical imperfections of System-12 *per se*; and the inappropriateness of this technology to the Chinese environment; common problems of using foreign equipment and services, e.g. maintenance and spare parts supply; as well as the weakness of indigenous technological capabilities, particularly in relation to production quality.

Chinese government policy and its direct support for Shanghai Bell helped the company out of the crisis which arose at the beginning of production, and provided the joint venture with privileges – e.g. low tax, autonomy in management, human and material resource supply, etc. – which allowed Shanghai Bell to conduct its business free from many of the constraints from which local firms were still suffering.

Implementation

The product and manufacturing technology transfer had three phases. The first comprised the assembly of components or parts as well as testing, including incoming inspection, the assembly and test of cables, back-panels, printed boards and racks. The entire process undertaken was to BTM standards: it used the most modern production and test facilities; all components or parts and other materials were directly imported from BTM or from the companies which BTM specified; every single incoming item and each sub-assembly was inspected. This detailed quality control continued until the final system tests which were followed by a performance trial (Zhou and Kerkhofs, 1987).

The second phase involved the establishment of a workshop for the production of printed circuit boards and metal and plastic piece-parts. Again, these were all a copy of the BTM's, ranging from workshop equipment, and functional tests over all sub-assemblies, to waste water treatment, etc, The installation of the equipment was completed by the end of 1986, and the production line was brought into operation in the first quarter of 1987 (Zhou and Kerkhofs, 1987).

The final phase was the manufacture of the LSI chips. In order to save capital investment, instead of following the original plan to establish a completely new production facility in Shanghai Bell, a new arrangement was agreed between the Chinese and Belgian sides to set up a joint venture, between Shanghai Bell and an existing chip producer, the No. 14 Shanghai Radio Factory, to manufacture the chip. Under the new arrangement, the No. 14 Shanghai Radio Factory contributed 60 per cent of the equity and Shanghai Bell 40 per cent. This new contract was signed in September 1988, and the joint venture was named as Shanghai Belling. Product and manufacturing know-how were transferred from BTM via Shanghai Bell to Shanghai Belling for System-12 custom LSI chips. In the middle of 1991, Shanghai Belling began to provide System-12 custom LSI chips for Shanghai Bell (Alcatel Bell Telephone, 1992a).

As well as hardware, transfer of engineering know-how was essential to foster a batch of Chinese engineers able to operate independently. There were two major areas, CAE (Customer Application Engineering) and CDE (Country Development Engineering), which were needed to allow the Chinese to adapt the system and build operational software packages to meet specific custom applications. CAE is the know-how by which the system is made according to individual customer requirements, as each exchange office has its specific physical layout, and each exchange involves a different number of subscribers and trunk lines with different conditions. The hardware know-how involved mastering the techniques for enabling specifications to be prepared for manufacturing; software expertise was required to understand and operate programmes, in order to produce the system load tapes for each exchange.

The CDE was necessary for the system to be customised to meet the specifications of the Chinese network. For example, in China the telecommunications network embraced exchanges of different generations, which were using different signalling systems, and System-12 therefore needed specially designed software to identify these signals. Furthermore, as the specifications for the network had been updated over time by MPT, CDE know-how could enable the system to follow the changes.

Hardware and software installation and testing in the field of each exchange office were critical undertakings. The first locally produced System-12 was installed in 1985 but was not 'cut over' (brought into operation in place of the existing exchange) until a year later in December 1986. This was the most problematic and critical time in the early stage for Shanghai Bell.

The technology was transferred by means of technical assistance, management participation, training and documentation. During the 'pre-operation' period and the early years of operation, technical assistance by BTM reached the highest level. Later on, the number of Belgian engineers gradually dropped. Since 1987, after the inauguration of the first exchange, the Chinese had taken over all positions, and were able to operate the whole process on their own. In December 1992 (the time of my visit), there were merely three Belgian technical assistants left in Shanghai Bell, compared with over 12, on average, during the first three years of operation.

Management participation began with attempting to copy BTM's style, encouraged by the Chinese government's desire to introduce modern management methods into national enterprises. The posts of Director of Shanghai Bell, and of managers of engineering and quality control departments, were held by BTM experts. In the first six years, all Belgian managers sent to Shanghai Bell had strong engineering backgrounds. With the increasing technological capability of the Chinese engineers and rapid expansion of production, managerial problems came to the fore. In 1991, BTM, for the first time, appointed a managerial specialist to be the Belgian general manager of Shanghai Bell in order to enhance management capabilities.

Since 1989, Shanghai Bell's production capacity had been increasing rapidly. Compared to its designed annual capacity of 300 000 lines, its actual output was 336 000 lines in 1989, 455 000 lines in 1990, 736 000 lines in 1991 and 1 380 000 lines in 1992. 'The Chinese have produced four times what was foreseen in the beginning. This is a great growth, unpredictable!', as the Belgian general manager of Shanghai Bell concluded.[19] Furthermore, the production volume continued to increase to 2 700 000 lines in 1993. The expansion rate was not 10 per cent as at most other companies, but about 100 per cent per year. According to the plan, by the end of 1994, after the completion of new workshops, the annual production volume would be 4 000 000 lines.[20] Shanghai Bell expected to be one of the largest exchange producers in the world by that time.

Privileges and Troubles

Quality control in the process of production was the main issue in Shanghai Bell, while production capacity was rapidly expanding. In 1989, the first year of full-scale production, the Department of Productivity and Quality Management was established in Shanghai Bell, with a Belgian quality control specialist in charge.[21] He set up routines in the production process in line with world class standards including motivation, examination in each section, regular reporting, record-analysis and internal and external auditing. As with BTM, the target of production quality control in Shanghai Bell was to reach the level of ISO (International Standard Organisation) 9001.[22] A year later, a young Chinese engineer took over the position. However, the level of quality control was not attainable in the short term, since it is closely related to people's understanding which is associated with their broader social situation and general culture. Because of the old tradition, for many, the 'quality' of production was merely a question of the reject rate. A Belgian manager had a vivid explanation:

> You should not expect there will be an overnight change. Quality is, first of all, the people's perception. Look! [standing by his office's window, he pointed through the window, to the area – one of the poorest housing areas in Shanghai – where Shanghai Bell's workshops are located]. People are living in environments like these. How could you expect them to have a good sense of quality?!
>
> (Director of the Engineering Department, 2 February 1993)

The young director of the Department of Productivity and Quality Management described the current situation:

> Workers are still not aware enough about the importance of quality. There are two major problems: first, quality of production is often ignored when quantity of production becomes urgent; second, understanding of the importance of quality has not penetrated much beyond management circles. Quality incidence changes in cycles. After managers stress the importance of quality, then workers begin to pay more attention and quality becomes good. However, it usually declines bit by bit over time, until, when it reaches 'red line', the managers have to 'sound the alarm' again.
>
> (Director of the Department of Productivity and
> Quality Management, 9 November 1992)

System-12 was developed in industrialised countries. No matter how experienced the developers were, some problems were inevitable in applying the technology in China. On top of that, when the technology was first introduced into China in the early 1980s, System-12 technology *per se* was still immature.[23]

Some problems were obvious. For example, System-12 uses English as a communicating language between human and machine, and all the technical documents and the kernel and common application software were written in English. In the documentation transfer alone, 'several hundred thousand documents' had to be translated into Chinese (Zhou and Kerkhofs, 1987, p. 191). Moreover, many posts using the computer required operators who could understand English. For candidates applying for a job in Shanghai Bell, in most cases, one special requirement was English language comprehension. Further there was a compulsory requirement for new recruits to undertake certain English courses to reach the level specified by the firm.

Another related problem was technical training for customers. As a normal requirement, to operate System-12 needs special technical training for customers. In the case of Shanghai Bell, it had to add teaching the technical terminology in English to training programmes. In the early stage, Shanghai Bell's technical training courses used BTM's textbook which had been translated into Chinese. Because it was a (poor) translation, the book was so difficult to read, that, as the manager of the Training Centre described:

Those who could easily understand the technology avoided reading this book, whereas those who would read this book in order to understand the technology did not get any help from this reading.
(Manager of the Training Centre, 29 January 1993)

When System-12 was installed in large or middle-sized cities, it was not difficult to get reasonably educated people who had learned English. These people, after taking technical training courses in Shanghai Bell, could undertake the operation posts. However, as System-12's market share was expanding and some exchanges came to be installed in small towns or villages, it became very difficult to find suitable candidates for even the technical training course who could, at least, understand English.[24]

Irritations also came from using imported equipment and machines. All machinery and equipment used for exchange production in Shanghai Bell were specified by BTM, including the brand and/or producer. Problems arose with their maintenance and spare parts supply, because most of them were imported from abroad – apart from a few produced in joint ventures in China. For example, the surface mounting technology was a fairly advanced technology for the production of printed circuits. Shanghai Bell bought this British-made machine at a cost of $200 000.[25] However, since its installation, the machine broke down often, and Shanghai Bell could not get it repaired in time. Chinese engineers tried to make the broken parts themselves. However, because they lacked the proper material, locally made parts wore out easily, making the machine break down more often. The inserting machine provided by Universal, which was supposed to work continuously, broke down approximately every twenty four hours. Since Universal had already set up a joint venture manufacturing the same machine in China, spare part supply was much easier.[26]

In the early stages, one of the biggest problems for System-12 technology was the condition of the Chinese telecommunications network, which was poor in general and uneven over the country, in terms of facilities and equipment. For instance, transmission lines varied from bare open wire in remote districts to fibre optic cable. As a result, signalling conditions differed from place to place and changed from time to time depending on weather. Different generations of exchange technology were operating in the same network, ranging from manual exchanges, early step-by-step, Strowger, and cross-bar electro-mechanical exchanges to advanced digital switching systems. Moreover, when the first Shanghai Bell system was installed in the Chinese network, even the signalling systems used in the network differed between exchanges. System-12 was a sophisticated technology, designed with a presumption of high transmission quality. In the very different rough conditions of the Chinese network, System-12 often failed to identify correctly the different kinds of signal.

During the first few years of operation, Shanghai Bell encountered acute problems, both technical and financial. Serious technical problems occurred on installation because the technology itself was immature and because BTM experts were not familiar with the Chinese telecommunications environment. Interrelated with this, there was a financial crisis. During the early stage of technology transfer, Shanghai Bell was only assembling piece-parts imported from BTM. However, the price of these piece-parts was high, with the result that the total cost of assembled exchanges was higher than directly importing finished exchanges. To make matters worse, Japanese companies were offering their exchanges at a cut price. At that time, Shanghai Bell's System-12 cost $250 per line, compared with $150 per line on average for the Japanese systems.[27] Shanghai Bell barely got any orders from the domestic market.

During this period of time, the production volume was very low: 66 000 lines in 1986, which fell further to 15 000 in 1987 (Alcatel Bell Telephone, 1992a). The company was running at a loss. Between the 1984 inauguration of production and 1987, Shanghai Bell had run up a total debt of $15 000 000.[28] Shanghai Bell was not able to pay fees for technology transfer, and even felt hard-pushed to pay the Belgian engineers' salaries. At the same time, BTM was unhappy and threatened to stop the transfer.

In this situation, MPT adopted strong measures to attract customers. Users buying Shanghai Bell's System-12 could receive an MPT subsidy of $30 per line. In total, MPT provided 60 000 000 yuan RMB (equivalent to around $17 000 000) in subsidy.[29] With this support, Shanghai Bell regained its momentum. In 1988, it recovered and produced 189 000 lines. That year was the first year of profit for Shanghai Bell. After the 1989 Tiananmen debacle, foreign government soft loans were greatly reduced, and the domestic political situation drove the market towards locally produced systems. Ever since, Shanghai Bell's production has been rapidly increasing, and its position in China was privileged in many respects.

As a joint production venture, Shanghai Bell was allowed to pay much less tax than domestic companies.[30] Shanghai Bell was free of tax for the first couple of years, and tax charges were reduced by 50 per cent in the following few years. After this, as it was classified as a high-tech company, tax reductions were still applied.[31] In addition, the state granted a licence for Shanghai Bell to import components at a low tariff rate. It was given the right to purchase components directly from overseas and, moreover, allowed to collect a certain portion of its payments from Chinese customers in foreign currencies.[32] A joint venture like Shanghai Bell was also given management autonomy to decide the internal organisational structures and material rewards.

MPT gave considerable attention to Shanghai Bell's creation, resource allocation and the market for System-12. From the outset, it set up a dedicated bureau in Shanghai to co-ordinate with local government on the building of Shanghai Bell's factory. To ensure its domestic market, MPT decreed in an internal circular[33] that System-12 was one of the principal switching systems for use in the Chinese telecommunications networks. MPT also endeavoured to obtain funds and loans required by Shanghai Bell from relevant government departments.

In terms of human resources, at the end of 1983, MPT brought together a group of highly skilled staff from MPT's R&D institutes, universities and factories across the country to Shanghai Bell to set up the plant. Among them were many experienced senior engineers, and knowledgeable professors in the telecommunications field. They played a crucial role in building up the company in the early stages. Thereafter, most of them returned to their institutes, and some subsequently used the knowledge they had obtained of System-12 to carry out various R&D projects for Shanghai Bell. In October 1985, when the first production assembly was to be put into operation in Shanghai Bell, MPT again took on the role of recruiting capable graduates and experienced young engineers all over the country to join the workforce. Many of them, later on, became departmental directors, and section managers, and formed the technical nucleus of the company.[34]

As a joint venture located in Shanghai, Shanghai Bell had received substantial support from the Shanghai Municipal Government. In particular in the early stage of constructing the joint venture, the Shanghai Municipal Government helped the company to obtain the resources it required within its territory, from electric power supply to new workforce recruitment. As Shanghai Bell was regarded as a source of advanced technologies for the region, it was treated even better than its state-owned counterparts by the government. In May 1991, with the Shanghai government nomination, Shanghai Bell was conferred the title as one of the Top Ten Joint Venture Companies in China. In June of the same year, the Shanghai Municipal Government awarded the Shanghai Bell's Belgian director the 'Magnolia Medal' – a high honour paid by the city.

As mentioned in Chapter 1, following the Cultural Revolution, China was short of almost everything. Shanghai, one of the biggest industrial bases and the commercial centre of country, suffered from shortages of electricity power supply, water, housing, etc. For many local manufacturing companies, power cuts occurred for several hours almost every day, especially in summer at 'peak-hours'. However, because of the particular concerns of the local government, Shanghai Bell was able to avoid this problem from which other companies suffered badly. The harsh conditions facing other companies was expressed by a non-Shanghai Bell engineer:

> The power supply in our factory has been often cut off. Sometimes we were notified beforehand, sometimes not even this. Frequent cut-offs in power supply causes unstable temperature of the soldering torch and therefore often causes quality problems, as well as low productivity. In summer, when the power supply gets worse, even air-conditioning in the workshops was restricted to only several hours a day. You can imagine how awful it is to stay in a workshop with natural temperature at 35–38 centigrade for eight hours, not to mention working with soldering.
>
> (A non-Shanghai Bell engineer in the workshop, 2 February 1993)

As noted in Chapter 1, under central planning, human resources were arranged by the government. This was based on the regulation requiring registration of residence. In other words, people were not mobile unless there was government approval, e.g. because of their particular level of education and/or occupation. Because Shanghai was already an overcrowded city, Shanghai enterprises could only employ Shanghai residents. Any other new recruitment had first to be approved by the municipal government. During the first ten years of economic reform, these regulations were still effective. In the case of Shanghai Bell, which had recruited manpower from all over the country, the Shanghai government always gave a green light to this.

3.3 ASSIMILATION OF THE FOREIGN TECHNOLOGY

After the first stage of technology transfer when Shanghai Bell tried hard to master the technology as a whole, Shanghai Bell realised that it could not simply copy these technologies but that it had to adapt them to the Chinese environment. This section tells how Shanghai Bell, in the face of difficulties, gradually mastered more and more of the technology and were able to work better on not only System-12 *per se* but also on production process technologies. In particular, as a joint venture having a special position in China during the transition period, Shanghai Bell had learned to take advantage of its connections with its locality and the Chinese government as well as overseas to strengthen its capabilities in marketing, sourcing and management. At the same time, while enjoying support and protection from the government, it made efforts not to fall into the rut that state-owned companies found themselves.

Adapting System-12 to the Chinese Environment

System-12 software consists of several layers. The generic system kernel is the basic layer which is common to all System-12 applications in all countries, providing the operating system, database, input/output and system maintenance functions. In addition, there are the application layers. Some application software was specially designed for the system to meet country-specific requirements (e.g. CDE), some is needed to fit the switching requirements of particular customers (e.g. CAE). If System-12 is applied in a country where telecommunications technology is largely internationally standardised, then its application-related software has a higher degree of commonality. As already described in section 3.2, China had very complex conditions, and its technologies in public network were far from the international standards. Therefore, to ensure the success of System-12, a proper adaptation of this system to the Chinese telecommunications environment was essential.

However, this adaptation took time. It did not happen in Shanghai Bell straight away. Rather it arose through a gradual learning process, which included growing demand from the market. As the Chinese general manager described:

> In the first instance, we had technical problems. However, we did not quite understand the system and were not able to change the slightest detail of the products. That time we had to rely on the Belgian engineers. Now, we understand more and more about the technology and begin to do a few changes here and there with help from experts. We do this and are allowed to do this, because of

our customers' needs. However we cannot do much as we are still learning; besides, these changes need BTM's approval.

(Chinese General Manager of Shanghai Bell, 1 February 1993)

As mentioned above, the transmission conditions in the Chinese networks made it difficult for the exchange to identify signals. For this, Shanghai Bell developed supplementary instruments to monitor and identify the condition of the transmission lines. This was done with the help of local universities and R&D institutes.

With the continual development of the country's telecommunications infrastructure, the regulations and specifications for the networks and services had also been modified. To integrate System-12 with the country's specifications, Shanghai Bell, from the outset, set up a task force to update CDE. According to the previous agreement between BTM and PTIC, CDE projects would mainly be performed by BTM engineers, and only a few Chinese engineers in Shanghai Bell would be selected to participate, as this task requires deep understanding of the system. However, as it turned out the Chinese team undertook 80 per cent of the CDE software development work compared with 20 per cent by BTM – the latter mainly in the form of supervision and consultancy.

At the same time, MPT and Shanghai Bell established a working group, named the Communal Co-ordination Group (CCG). Its major task was jointly to set targets for System-12 technology innovation in line with the development of the telecommunications network. In particular, this sought agreement on CDE innovation between MPT (which was both user and administration) and Shanghai Bell (supplier). CCG organised working seminars involving a deputy minister of MPT as the chair, and many senior engineers and senior research fellows from various MPT R&D institutes, and key officials from relevant MPT's administrative organisations to discuss the issues. A successful result was the CDE software package-5X, which involved more than 30 person-years by the time of its completion. At the end of 1992, the first toll exchange equipped with the package-5X was put into operation in Shanghai. With the CDE package-5X, which integrated the MPT's specifications that were compatible with new CCITT regulations, the exchange was able to provide many new features for advanced services. In February 1993, the fourth CCG meeting was held in Shanghai, with up to 80 participants, to discuss further targets for the new version of System-12 NGLT (new generation line circuit) – release-7. The new CDE project was to be completed by the end of 1994 in time for the expansion of Shanghai Bell's production in the second half of 1995.[35]

To meet a wider range of customers' demand, Shanghai Bell developed a remote autonomous switching module (RASM) with a capacity of about 1000 lines, which was suitable for rural areas where population densities are low, and also for engineering teams working in areas without existing telecommunications networks. The technology was designed by several Chinese engineers and was patented in August 1990. It proved to be welcomed by users, since China has a large rural area where people could not afford the expense of System-12 to this date.[36]

However, there were differences of opinion within Shanghai Bell about whether it was necessary for Shanghai Bell to master every single technology of System-12. Almost all the young Chinese managers believed that the most important issue was the profitability of the company: they thus saw the need for technological capabilities solely in terms of the ability to adapt System-12 to satisfying user requirements, and strengthen Shanghai Bell's position in the market. They argued:

> Just as China is a 'tree' in 'the world national forest', so Shanghai Bell can play a part amongst all System-12 producers in the world. The relationship we prefer is technological complementarity between one another, each with its own particular strengths. Now we, Shanghai Bell, can produce the best software and tapes for the Chinese market, and one day we will achieve more.
>
> (Deputy Director of the Engineering Department, 10 November 1992)

In contrast, many older engineers had different views. They hoped that Shanghai Bell would build up its own strong R&D base, and could undertake the development work independently, anticipating the eventuality that the supply from overseas might be cut off.

Adapting the Production Process

As mentioned in section 3.1, in manufacturing System-12, Shanghai Bell introduced the latest production facilities and production processes. Over time, these production technologies were updated in line with BTM's technological innovation. Although these technologies were at the world level (e.g. in 1992 the surface mounting technology was the most advanced technology in circuit production in the world), they were still foreign technologies which Shanghai Bell depended on. In other words, Shanghai Bell always had to follow BTM and transfer the technologies which are adopted by BTM in order to upgrade its technology. The deputy manager of the Operation Department (production) described the situation:

We are still at the level of 'copying' in terms of production technology, including the production process, production organisation and techniques. When BTM has any technological change, we copy it. The equipment we are using, its types, producers, and variables, are decided by BTM. That was the agreement between BTM and us. Even if we want to use a more advanced machine, we have to get BTM's approval.

(Deputy Manager of the Operations Department, 6 November 1992)

Nevertheless, there were some technical achievements that Shanghai Bell was proud of. As mentioned in section 3.1, for economic reasons Shanghai Bell did not transfer some technologies that were not considered to be the core of the production process. In the early production stage, their functions were undertaken by manual labour. With the growth in production, Shanghai Bell developed some of this ancillary production equipment in co-operation with local universities and R&D institutes. One example was the automatic test apparatus for checking the DC–AC converting board.

The development that Shanghai Bell was most proud of was a new set of CAE. This set of software tools was used for running an automatic production process transferring the specifications of each application on to programmed data tapes which were then loaded into the production system to produce individual exchanges. In the beginning, Shanghai Bell used the CAE which had been developed by BTM, which did not work very well in practice. Chinese engineers in Shanghai Bell therefore gradually modified the software package: they began by adding a patch to the package, and then another one. Over time, their understanding of the software package also developed. When the number of the patches grew substantially, over 300, they rewrote the whole package. It proved to be simple to use and very effective and involving fewer problems.

Although this set of software tools was aimed to improve production by Shanghai Bell itself, it came to attract the attention of other System-12 producers. The first buyer to come to the door was Alcatel-SESA (the System-12 producer in Spain). They were turned down by

Shanghai Bell. SESA turned to its sister company BTM for help. BTM did send engineers to Spain to help improve its existing CAE software, but the result turned out to be not as good as Shanghai Bell's. At the end of 1992, SESA came back to Shanghai Bell, and eventually made a deal that Shanghai Bell would sell the software package to SESA and in return SESA would provide Shanghai Bell with $1.8 million of business per year over five years.[37] Shanghai Bell was very proud of this success. Both the Chinese general manager and the Belgian general manager declared that Shanghai Bell was able to provide the best application software for the Chinese market.[38]

For BTM, Shanghai Bell had gradually become a technically reliable partner. When BTM's customers in China needed technical assistance, it often asked Shanghai Bell to send engineers to solve problems. Once, its international exchange (trunk)[39] in Beijing needed a capacity extension, and some new functions to be added. As BTM was short-staffed, it turned again to Shanghai Bell for help. Despite the fact that the Chinese engineers had never done any international exchange work, the mission was successful.[40]

Accumulating Marketing Capabilities

In the Chinese PDSS market, demand was huge and always exceeded supply. By the end of 1992, orders taken by Shanghai Bell were already queued up to 1994 and their share in the Chinese PDSS market exceeded 50 per cent. Its products had covered almost all the provinces of the country. Despite this, Shanghai Bell sought to ensure its future market. While increasing the scale of production, it gradually brought down the price. Compared to $250 per line in 1984, the price of the exchange was reduced by 50–60 per cent in 1992.[41] In addition, Shanghai Bell's marketing strategy was to cover as many districts of the country as rapidly as possible with its products. This was because they knew that once they had installed the first exchange in a region it would often lead to further purchases later on, for reasons either of technical continuity or of economics. For example, noting that the Tibet area did not have any System-12 exchanges, Shanghai Bell offered them one for free.

Over time, Shanghai Bell's installation team became more and more experienced, and its workforce was meanwhile expanding. Compared to the first installation of Shanghai Bell's System-12 which took about a year, the current set-up time for an exchange, from hardware and software installation to system debugging and to final cutting-over, needed only about a month. The quality of installation also improved. As the production capacity of Shanghai Bell expanded rapidly, the activities of the installation team increased dramatically. In 1992, it installed around 318 exchanges – nearly one exchange per day.[42] To meet the demands, Shanghai Bell used fully its connections in the sector. It hired several MPT engineering teams to carry out installation works in neighbouring areas which they were familiar with. It also used engineers who had been technically trained in Shanghai Bell (for more details see section 3.4) to carry out a relatively difficult job in installation – software testing. This measure proved to be economical for Shanghai Bell, as well as effective.

To provide adequate after-sales-services, Shanghai Bell had built up a number of maintenance centres, in Beijing, Shanghai, Hefei, Guangdong and Shandong (by the time of my visit), and was planning to set up more in all 30 provinces and autonomous administrative districts and municipalities of the country. Apart from that, Shanghai Bell's computer centre had been providing 24-hour services for users. It also established a Customer Association with members across the country. Every six months, it invited users to a meeting to give feedback on using Shanghai Bell's products. The meeting in April 1992, for instance, gathered over four hundred users. Shanghai Bell also arranged a 'System-12 Column' with two pages in a telecommunications journal – *Telecommunications Technology* – whereby Shanghai Bell regularly introduced the system to users and discussed troubleshooting experiences. In addition, Shanghai Bell circulated widely an occasional publication named *Bell Dispatches*, the first edition of which was published in 1992. Alongside this, in its user's computer network, it ran an 'information' system which included many items on the utilisation of System-12. Some essays were instructions written by specialists and others were engineers' experiences; all were carefully classified to allow users to search easily on-line. Taking advantage of MPT's traditional arrangement, involving the development of a couple of highly experienced engineers in each district, Shanghai Bell co-operated with them to solve technical problems on-the-spot.

In line with general Chinese government policy, Shanghai Bell was encouraged to export its products. However, because of the pressing demand for PDSS in the domestic market, Shanghai Bell's exports were very limited. A few System-12 exchanges were exported to Russia, Vietnam and Cuba. More widespread export of System-12 by Shanghai Bell would have been against Alcatel's interests, as the Belgian general manager noted:

It is common knowledge that, through technology transfer, the technology supplier wants to create markets rather than create competitors. I think, if Shanghai Bell attempts export, the process of technology transfer will be slowed down by the Alcatel side. Obviously, Alcatel doesn't want to have a rival who is as strong as itself in technology.

(Belgian General Manager of Shanghai Bell, 10 February 1993)

On the other hand, Shanghai Bell had achieved high value-added exports of system-load-tapes and their CAE software tool package which were attractive to other System-12 producers which had sold or were going to sell System-12 in the Chinese market. These producers included SESA (Spain), BTM (Belgian) and SEL (Germany). Other System-12 producers from Norway, Italy and Australia were still in the process of negotiation with Shanghai Bell at the time of the fieldwork.

Accumulating Sourcing Capabilities

With the expansion in production capacity by Shanghai Bell, more human resources were required. Learning lessons from state-owned companies, Shanghai Bell sought to recruit young graduates. Every year, it enrolled selectively a certain number of graduates from universities and colleges. Moreover, in the recruitment of manual workers, Shanghai Bell took a very cautious stance to avoid creating a possible labour surplus in the future. Instead of recruiting permanent staff, it 'borrowed' a large number of labourers from other companies which were economically stagnant and suffered a burden of labour surplus. In this way, Shanghai Bell had, on the one hand, avoided an excessive increase in its labour force, which might become burdensome to it, for example by requiring provision of long-term welfare facilities, while on the other hand, solving the current problem for both Shanghai Bell itself and the companies which had a labour surplus.

By the end of 1992, the number of enlisted employees in Shanghai Bell was 1313, and their average age was 28.6-years-old. There were also over 300 labourers who had been temporarily transferred from the other factories and institutes.[43] Most of them were low-skilled workers. They received the basic salary from their original companies, which was a relatively small portion of their income compared with the bonus that Shanghai Bell gave them. Although their average income was less than that of Shanghai Bell's employees, it was still much more than what they previously received.

Shanghai Bell also managed to get many highly skilled external staff working for the company. They were all engineers sent by customers to Shanghai Bell. By agreement between Shanghai Bell and its customers, after their 6-month training course, these engineers would continue their further practice in Shanghai Bell for 1.5 to 2 years. As a result, given their previous experiences in the field and their newly acquired knowledge about System-12, they were very capable indeed. They played an important role in helping Shanghai Bell to install and maintain System-12 in the field, as already mentioned. The benefits of this arrangement were mutual. Most of these engineers were happy to work for Shanghai Bell at that time. With their salary from their own company plus the portion Shanghai Bell provided on top, their income became much higher than usual, and also, working with Shanghai Bell, they could acquire new expertise.

Shanghai Bell's policy was to use external human resources as fully as possible in order to keep the company's complement of staff at a low level. In terms of R&D, Shanghai Bell co-operated with local universities and research institutes. In installation and maintenance, it sought help from MPT engineering teams and experienced engineers in local PTAs. It hired local professionals for other logistic services, such as providing food and medical service to its staff rather than establish its own hospitals and canteens. Through this policy, Shanghai Bell's employment only increased by 54 per cent from 855 in 1989 to 1313 in 1992, compared with a 317 per cent increase in its production capacity during the same time.

The Chinese general manager's joke told the truth – that Shanghai Bell had been a 'big school', fostering a great number of qualified engineers for the country. Every year, around 3 to 4 per cent of the engineers left the company to work elsewhere, whilst more new ones joined. Among those who left Shanghai Bell were many good engineers. As the deputy manager of the Engineering Department (himself 28 years old) said, 'they are good enough to find good jobs elsewhere easily'.[44] For example, when Motorola established a new joint venture in Shanghai, it recruited three senior engineers, two of whom were from Shanghai Bell. Some went even further, to join a local PTT in Australia. Although, for Shanghai Bell, this was still far from a threat to the company, as it could always find proper candidates to fill the vacancy, top managers were convinced that there were things the company should do to keep these capable engineers.

Apart from providing material incentives, such as high salaries and relatively luxurious housing conditions, top managers gradually realised that material incentives were not everything, but that job satisfaction was also important. At that time, some newly established joint ventures and private companies were offering much higher salaries to get the manpower they needed. However, Shanghai Bell, for reasons we discuss below, was not able to respond in this way. The problem was that there were too many capable young engineers in Shanghai Bell, but there were not enough interesting jobs for them. For these capable young engineers, routine work in the production field was too repetitive, and most posts required little creative instinct. To use these young people's talents fully, as well as to keep them there and not join Shanghai Bell's rival companies, the Chinese general manager was planning to set up some R&D projects allowing them to devote their energy to projects which would also be useful for System-12 production, installation and services.[45]

A joint venture like Shanghai Bell attracted considerable government attention. Its managers, and in particular Chinese managers, who understood the importance of this connection, had learned how to utilise the government's concern. While the Belgian managers found the government intervention irritating, Chinese managers seemed to be more relaxed about it. For example, Shanghai Bell's annual production volume was usually decided jointly by BTM and the Chinese government through their representatives on Shanghai Bell's Board of Directors. In 1992 when it was time for both sides to work out the production volume for 1993, and soon after the Board of Directors had decided that the year's production volume was to be 1 500 000 lines, a new message came through from the Chinese government indicating that the production volume should increase greatly. The State Planning Committee proposed a number as high as 2 200 000 lines, and MPT pushed this even further and made the figure 2 700 000 lines. The Belgian side was irritated, and also thought this proposal was unfeasible. However, Shanghai Bell's Chinese top managers reacted differently. They investigated the reasons for this recommendation and decided that fulfilling it would be also good for Shanghai Bell. First, from the Chinese government's point of view, at that time, it had already become inevitable to open the domestic PDSS market for the USA. To ensure Shanghai Bell's position in the market, the government wanted Shanghai Bell to expand its market share as far and as quickly as possible. This coincided with Shanghai Bell's interests for long-term development. Second, now that the State Planning Committee had given this quota, it gave Shanghai Bell the possibility of low import tariffs for the components needed to produce

2 200 000 lines. Shanghai Bell therefore accepte
moreover, reached this level of production in 199
Apart from taking advantage of the Chinese gov
Shanghai Bell was also able to use fully its t
overseas. By 1993, many System-12 components c
locally. Nevertheless, Shanghai Bell still continued t
of these components, even though this irritated th
Shanghai Bell had a particular purpose for this – to keep open its links
to technological changes in the world. As the deputy manager of the
Department of Engineering explained:

> I have to say that, in terms of technology, the core technology of
> System-12 is still not in our hands. The future of System-12 depends
> more or less on technological development in the industrialised
> world. We do not want to drive foreign suppliers away. Rather we
> want to be kept informed by their product changes. Although we
> have to pay more, compared to purchase local products, we would
> like to keep the pace with the world.

(Deputy Manager of the Engineering Department, 30 February 1993)

Mixed Style of Management

At the outset, the management in Shanghai Bell was to copy BTM.
Later Shanghai Bell gradually developed its own style which was
considered to be a hybrid between Chinese and Western methods. In
the very beginning, the Chinese decided to adopt Western management approaches, in particular those of BTM, in terms of its
institutional settings and managerial methods. For this purpose,
some young Chinese managers were sent to BTM and to management
schools in China and abroad to learn advanced modern management
theories and methods. However, very soon, practice proved that it was
impossible to apply many Western methods to the Chinese environment. Inevitably, the outcome of adapting Western management
method to the Chinese environment was a mixture of both. Western
methods were used to deal with questions of productivity and efficiency whereas the Chinese way was used to deal with staff incentives.
First of all, the objectives of the company was market growth and
achieving profits. Shanghai Bell's management had been concentrating
on this target, with the result that it had achieved a high level of
productivity. In 1992, the production output was 1 380 000 lines, with

800 workers. Accordingly when production volumes reached 000 000 lines after the completion of a new workshop in the end 1994, Shanghai Bell planned to keep the number of workers as low as 1400, compared with the BTM's estimate of at least 1650.[46] Although there were political organisations in the company, such as the Communist Party, trade unions, the Youth League and Women's Association, their importance had already given way to productivity: their organisational activities only took place after work; and they took up only the smallest fraction of the company's agenda, compared with state-owned companies, where the Party's activities were always given high priority.

Material incentives were explicitly adopted, as already noted. In comparison with state-owned companies, Shanghai Bell offered much higher salaries, although the salary level was still far from the highest in the Shanghai area. As an early established joint venture, Shanghai Bell was allowed to raise the salary level for its employees only by up to 30 per cent above the average of state-owned companies. This was set by the government in order not to provoke workers in state-owned companies, especially in MPT's companies. Over time, as more and more joint ventures and private companies had been set up and started to compete with each other in offering higher salaries, the average salary had increased rapidly. Shanghai Bell, as a large company was simply not able to follow the pace. In 1992 it raised its general salary levels, but very soon the other companies caught up and overtook it.

To compensate for this, Shanghai Bell provided employees with housing.[47] It spent 50 per cent of the company's total welfare expenditure on housing for staff. By the end of 1992, about 10 per cent of its employees lived in company flats. The flats which were provided for key persons, such as department managers and senior engineers, were fully furnished, and some were even equipped with all household electrical appliances. For ordinary Shanghai residents, it was just paradise and could not be better. One department manager, a flat-holder said:

> I won't expect any better than this, and I think that our company's offer is the best in the whole Shanghai area, although our salary is a bit low.
> (Deputy Director of the Engineering Department, 30 February 1993)

A condition attached to this offer was that if one left Shanghai Bell then one should leave the flat too.[48]

Chinese management traditions tended to treat the company as a family. Its administration system was fairly hierarchical, but the relationship between the upper and the lower levels was not necessarily very formal. The authority of a director of the company could be very much parent-like. Even a manual labourer at the lowest level was encouraged to approach directors or higher-level managers of the company for help with personal problems, even bypassing intermediate management. In this respect, Shanghai Bell still kept the old tradition. A department manager explained:

> People still turn to us for help when problems occur with their family, such as when a child is ill or couples have a row, etc., although these are now not considered to be our responsibility according to the job specification. However, we have got used to it. The company takes care of them, and they take care of the company.
> (Deputy Director of the Engineering Department, 30 January 1993)

The Chinese general manager of Shanghai Bell believed the combination of Chinese and Western management method was necessary, and said:

> Working for foreign companies will make you feel that you are only working for a company which belongs to strangers. But in our company you still feel you are working with people who belong to your 'family', feeling part of it, and sharing. When a member of staff has got a problem, he or she can approach me directly, either with or without an appointment, in working or non-working time, as long as I have got time. This is Chinese culture. Although Western management provides us with efficiency in production organisation, we still need staff who are devoted to hard working. The fact that we, Shanghai Bell, could achieve such a production expansion, has to be attributed to the combination of Chinese and Western management.
> (Chinese General Manager of Shanghai Bell, 1 February 1993)

Belgian managers were very sympathetic to their Chinese counterparts, believing that they must be exhausted dealing endlessly with problems, such as wages, housing and so on, which they themselves could not have stood. They were happy with the division of management responsibilities, whether explicit or implicit; the Belgian managers would concentrate on production and leave personnel issues altogether to Chinese managers.

3.4 TECHNOLOGICAL LEARNING

Technological learning in Shanghai Bell had taken place throughout the whole process of System-12 technology transfer. This section in particular looks at the learning activities planned and organised by Shanghai Bell, as well as the Chinese government and Shanghai municipal government. The major foci are: technical training courses which were run by Shanghai Bell to educate its own staff and its customers; and the project of local production of System-12 components which was linked to Chinese government policies for technological development and was mainly organised by the Shanghai government to promote technology renewal in local industries. This section examines the successes and difficulties that arose with domestication of imported components, which related to the attitudes of local companies including Shanghai Bell, which had been changing during the period of China's social and economic transition.

Training[49]

Since the establishment of the joint venture, there had been a variety of training programmes in Shanghai Bell. In the beginning, engineering training programmes combined BTM's classroom training and participation in BTM operational departments, as well as training at the premises of the other technology suppliers in the USA and Hong Kong. The engineers who were trained abroad, in turn, came back to initiate training courses in Shanghai Bell, transferring their acquired skills and knowledge to the others. Ever since, training whether technical or managerial had become an important part of the operating agenda of Shanghai Bell. As a result, according to a comparative survey in 1987, the performance abilities of the Chinese engineers in Shanghai Bell ranged from 70 per cent up to as high as 100 per cent of the performance abilities of BTM engineers in similar functions (Zhou and Kerkhofs, 1987).

From 1987, Shanghai Bell began to run a series of training programmes for both staff and customers. In 1991, it set up a training centre, which expanded rapidly because of demand.

Shanghai Bell introduced a new measure in staff training, that all new recruits had to be trained before taking any job post. The compulsory training for potential engineers was for six months, and three to four months for new shop-floor workers. In addition, every employee was encouraged to take after-work courses run by external training or educational organisations. For this, the company provided 70 per cent of tuition fees, on condition that staff obtained 'diplomas or certificates' at the end of their courses. With these diplomas or certificates, they could apply for a more suitable post in Shanghai Bell. Apart from that, because of the complexity of System-12 technology, people involved in one part of the work were not necessarily familiar with other parts. In these circumstances, staff were encouraged to take training courses in order to get more knowledge about the context and how their jobs fitted in the whole system. As a result, the number of staff receiving training increased over time. By 1993, staff training provision had increased to 160 person-years, compared with only 43 in 1989.

Shanghai Bell's philosophy on customer training was that if more people know about the system, the market will be larger, more maintenance work can be carried out by users, and less work will be left for Shanghai Bell itself. It therefore encouraged customers and potential customers to take training courses to learn System-12 technology. Shanghai Bell set up its customer training programme with three levels: 'A' level training was for system engineers within 6 months including classroom and practical training; 'B' level was for technicians, lasting three or four months; and 'C' level was for operators, lasting only two to three months. The users were trained to carry out various jobs including test, installation, operation and maintenance. Those engineers taking 'A' level training, in particular, would stay to get further work experience in Shanghai Bell. As noted above, after this period of time working in Shanghai Bell, they would usually be able to deal with various problems independently. Some of them, later on, were even hired by SESA (the Spanish System-12 producer who paid them a salary so high that it did indeed make Shanghai Bell's engineers jealous).

In 1987, Shanghai Bell could only carry out 'C' level training, until 1990 when the three levels of training courses (A, B and C) were all set up. Since 1989, orders for System-12 had increased dramatically. Simultaneously, the number of customers receiving training increased too. By 1990, the number had reached 297, including 44 'A' level students, 42 'B' level and 211 'C' level, compared with only 102 students in 1987. Shanghai Bell therefore began to anticipate problems that might arise with the increasingly large scale of training in the foreseeable future. Usually, one exchange needs two operators working on each shift. Accordingly, for round-the-clock operation, there are at least six people who need to be trained. On average, one exchange has

Shanghai Bell's annual production volume was 1 380 000 ... '92, the numbers needing training would be more than .., ьhanghai Bell could not deal with such a large training ...crtaking. As early as 1989, the company began to seek help from MPT's universities and technical high schools to run its customer training courses in their premises, using their teachers and facilities.

Apart from this, Shanghai Bell had set up a mobile training team which was equipped with a System-12 exchange in a container lorry. The team ran a range of intensive training courses for officials in local telecommunication administrations, and local sales-agents. The training courses lasted from 4 days to a month. By February 1993, 1216 people had been trained in this way.

As noted earlier, the BTM's teaching materials used by Shanghai Bell in the beginning proved to have many disadvantages. In addition, because the division of labour in Shanghai Bell changed over time, it had different job classifications from the original ones that BTM used (BTM's job division was finer and more specialised than that of Shanghai Bell). It therefore became more problematic to use BTM's teaching textbook. To overcome the problems, Shanghai Bell called several senior engineers together to edit a new set of textbooks for training courses. By the end of 1992, three of the four textbooks had been completed.

Domestication of Imported Components – Reacting to Government Intervention

As part of its technological development strategy, to ultimately achieve indigenous technological development of the country, in the 1980s, while more and more advanced technology transfer from industrialised countries took place, the Chinese government pursued vigorously its policy of import substitution. A range of related regulations and practical measures sought to compel companies to replace imported components with locally produced ones. For example, first of all, the government applied a high tariff to direct import of components. Second, to ensure that this policy would not drive away advanced foreign technology transfer to China, the Chinese government granted exemption or a low import tariff to individual projects which were considered to be in the national interest. Third, to promote spin-off of advanced foreign technologies, the government urged the companies which were using imported components to gradually reduce imports and replace them by locally produced ones. To help realise import substitution, government financial support was available for promising projects. The Ministry of Machine Building and Electronics Industry (MMEI) and the State Foreign Trade and Economic Co-operation Committee were jointly in charge of controlling import licences, granting low import tariffs, setting up targets for import substitution and examining their implementation by companies.

The MMEI and the State Foreign Trade and Economic Co-operation granted licences for Shanghai Bell to import components at a low tariff. At the same time, they put pressure on Shanghai Bell to take action about the local production of components. They set up targets for import substitution for Shanghai Bell. The target for the first few years was 20 per cent of total components, and gradually increasing to 70 per cent by 1993. Shanghai Bell's performance in this matter was regularly examined and linked to the renewal of their licences to import components.

Since achieving import substitution relied on not only Shanghai Bell, but also local industries and resources, government financial support, etc., the issue was always negotiable. The government knew that there was no point in trying to force Shanghai Bell to buy local products which nobody in China could produce or which could not meet the quality criteria. Besides, there was even a specified method for measuring companies' achievement in import substitution, which was internally issued at the end of 1987 by the State Planning Committee. According to this formula,

$$\frac{Total\ cost\ of\ all\ components - Total\ cost\ of\ imported\ components}{Total\ cost\ of\ all\ components} \times 100\%$$

individual items add different weight to the level of import substitution. The bigger the differential is between total costs at local price and the imported price of this item, the higher its contribution will be to the import substitution. Hence, the companies' choice of components for local production could lead to different results. However, variables in this formula can be interpreted differently. For instance, an 'individual component' can be an assemblage of components. To count it as an item or break it down to details may have different results, because of price differences. A computer can be either counted as one item or many items; the price of a whole computer and the sum of the prices of its individual components are different.

It was the Shanghai municipal government that actively pursued local production of System-12 components, as it considered Shanghai Bell to be a source of advanced technology to bring the local industries to a new level. In 1988, it adopted the Shanghai Bell's System-12 project as one of the fourteen 'Major Projects for District Development'. The new Shanghai Mayor[50] even came to visit Shanghai Bell on the second day of his arrival in his new post. The local government meantime established an office, named as the Shanghai Bell System-12 Project Conducting Group. This organisation was jointly run by Shanghai Bell, the Municipal Electronic Equipment Bureau, the Municipal Economic Committee and the Municipal Planning Committee. The local production of components for Shanghai Bell's System-12 comprised 38 sub-projects. The major role of the Shanghai Bell System-12 Project Conducting Group was to examine the feasibility of individual sub-projects, to raise funds for them and co-ordinate between Shanghai Bell and local companies which were considered as potential components producers. Financial support for this project from the State Planning Committee and the local government comprised grants of 10 000 000 yuan RMB (equivalent to about $2 860 000) as well as access to foreign currency loans (for which the Municipal governments could draw on a 150 000 000 US dollar reserve held by the Chinese government).[51] Shanghai Bell received a portion of this amount, 3 000 000 yuan (RMB), for R&D.

Shanghai Bell followed the government's instructions and set up the Domestication Division in the company to deal with local production of System-12 components. In the early stage of production, due to various technical and financial difficulties, Shanghai Bell had very limited interest in this undertaking. However, subsequent developments made it give greater attention to conformity to government requirements. Under this pressure, Shanghai Bell co-operated with the local government and actively engaged in the project of import substitution. To achieve the target of local production of components set by the Chinese government was not an easy task. In the late 1980s, China already possessed more than 100 electronic component assembly lines, but none of these could meet Shanghai Bell's standards. For exchange uses, components have to be functionally very stable and durable. To meet this criteria required not only technology and finance, but also technological support from BTM and increased technological capabilities of local producers (which was, after all, the government's motive in building up these capabilities).

BTM did not oppose the project of producing System-12's components locally. It was instead supportive, as it assumed this project would lead to cheaper component supplies for itself. BTM prepared all the documents required with technical details (Shanghai Bell had to pay for these) and sent specialists and engineers to inspect local companies' production facilities and to help them master the production technology,[52] as well as to help Shanghai Bell set up a test system for examining locally produced components.

More sceptical attitudes towards this project came from local firms, state-owned companies, who had relatively better production facilities and human resources, who would be System-12's potential component producers. During that period, the financial position of most state-owned companies in Shanghai was rather secure – the economic reforms did not yet provide them a strong incentive to seek new markets and technological opportunities. At the same time, they were still constrained by traditional approaches, relying on the state. As a result, they were happy to get involved in a project arranged by the local government and it allowed them to get extra money from the government for renewing facilities and technologies. However, they lacked a sense that they should take full responsibility for making products of sufficient quality for the customer.

Therefore, while things did not work out exactly as the central government had requested, an important role emerged for the Domestication Division of Shanghai Bell to deal with the government officials in charge. First of all, it drew up a tactical plan corresponding to the targets scheduled by the government in that period and also sought to find the best methods of calculating to show a higher import substitution rate! Its other functions were to write convincing reports for the government and often to negotiate with officials in charge in relevant government organisations, in particular those in the Customs Office. For example, in February 1993 (the time of my fieldwork), Shanghai Bell had 200 lots of imported goods, including over 700 different kinds of components, held by the Customs Office at Shanghai airport, while the workshops in Shanghai Bell were waiting for the new supplies to come in. There was a dispute between the Customs Office and Shanghai Bell which was, as usual, over the import duty, and in particular about which import rate Shanghai Bell should pay according to its record of import substitution.

Things like this happened often, and the shortage of imported materials and components became one of Shanghai Bell's head-aches. This above all irritated the Belgian managers, especially after

1 January 1993 when the Chinese PDSS market was opened up under strong pressure from the US government. The tariff for importing finished systems was merely 9 per cent whereas for the components which Shanghai Bell needed it remained about 30 per cent.[53] The Belgian general manager could not find any justification for this:

> We are manufacturing System-12 locally. Why do we have to pay higher duty for importing portions of the components required for local production? Shanghai Bell is a business organisation which has to compete with others in the market in terms of price and quality. We of course would like to buy locally produced components, which would involve less trouble. However, we cannot find proper products. One cannot expect us to produce good quality and cheap products, while, at the same time, buying the components which are expensive and worse quality. It's just impossible!
>
> (Belgian General Manager of Shanghai Bell, 10 February 1993)

Most of the young Chinese managers in Shanghai Bell did not believe that the import substitution policy – and in particular the high pressure put on Shanghai Bell by the government – was necessary. They argued in favour of the market mechanism. 'If buying them in would be cheaper and better quality, why should we insist on producing them locally?' a department manager said straightforwardly. 'We should buy better quality and cheaper products from the market regardless of whether they are Chinese or overseas'. Others agreed in principle that the import substitution policy was good for the country as well as for Shanghai Bell in the long run, as local production would make component supply much more convenient. However, they felt that the government's intervention against them was too onerous, and it would not help very much to achieve the target.

The government requirement of local production of components was not insignificant. As a manager in the Operation Department described, 'The cost of importing 1 500 000-line components is about 120 000 000 RMB. If the tariff could be reduced to 10 per cent, it is a big deal for Shanghai Bell'. The Chinese general manager of Shanghai Bell expressed the extremely pragmatic stance of the company:

> The government has its view for the entire country, similarly we have ours. We are seeking profit for the company. However the government policy changes, we will pursue our own goals. When government is pushing us to adopt import substitution, well, we will

do it, as long as the interests of the company would not be compromised. We have our own programme. When the time comes, we are going to vigorously pursue local production of components, to establish a large local supplier network to strengthen our position.
(Chinese General Manager of Shanghai Bell, 1 February 1999)

The head of the Domestication Division hated the situation of having to play calculating games with the government officials. 'That is a waste of time and does nobody any good,' she said. However, she valued the policy of local production of components in general:

To get a local company to make quality products is hard work. It needs so much effort, and sometime we had to give up. Our local industries need to learn new technologies and most of all new concepts of production. They do need help. Without government policy, this process might take much longer. Nevertheless, when it succeeds, we all feel happy. Shanghai Bell can also benefit from that. Supply from abroad has many disadvantages – for example, transport. Once, we were waiting for a lot of chemical material, but it did not arrive till the workshop had run out of the material. Later on we were informed that the cargo ship with Shanghai Bell's articles on had sunk. Import substitution, as I believe, needs the initiatives from three sides: the government, local industries and us – Shanghai Bell. It is very difficult without one of them
(Head of the Domestication Division, 28 February 1993)

Difficulties and Successes[54]

At the beginning, government intervention to achieve local production of System-12 components did not obtain strong support from local firms, so the outcome of the project was far less successful than expected. Some sub-projects were ultimately abandoned for various reasons. And some completed ones proved to be not very successful because of either the high cost of production or unsatisfactory quality.

System-12 had about 4000 individual components in total, which could be classified into four groups: racks and sub-racks and printed circuit boards; nine types of large scale integrated circuits (LSI); circuit boards and tapes; and components such as hybrid circuits, relays and others. By February 1993 at the time of my visit, there were 794 items, which were able to be locally produced. However, most of them were low-technology components.

Several major factors had influenced the accomplishment of local production of components. First was the financial issue, relating to the dilemma of whether to select low- or high-technology projects. In most cases, local production of components with low technology involves low costs, whereas to produce high-technology components locally was unlikely to be attainable by local companies given existing local technological capabilities and low levels of investment. Some projects require a large amount of capital investment, in order to introduce new assembly machinery and/or to even transfer new technologies from abroad. For instance, the project for the relay production alone absorbed around $8 000 000. If selected projects all required expensive high technologies, only a very limited number of projects could be undertaken within the limit of available finance.

Apart from that, the uncertainties surrounding technological development, future markets, etc. made many projects less attractive to local producers and made people wary of making too large investments. According to the head of the Domestication Division in Shanghai Bell, in some cases local producers were not taking up the opportunities at all: some spent the project money but did not produce reasonable results; some even used the project money for other purposes, since they were doubtful that the final outcome of the projects would bring them a profit. To them, the future market was unpredictable, and, at that moment, demand for components from Shanghai Bell was not that large, and there were, as yet, no other customers for such products. Some projects had been abandoned before completion, as System-12 technology had been changing. It was difficult to anticipate whether one day some components would be no longer needed because of new technology. The project to produce a specific resistor by Shanghai Radio Factory No. 1 provides an instructive example. This had already completed the R&D and sample production stages, but was terminated because of the lack of further financial investment for mass production. According to the government's original plan, a state bank would issue a loan to support the development of production. However, when the bank learned that Shanghai Bell might not need this resistor in future because of technical innovation, it withdrew its commitment to this project, determined that such a large sum of money would not be another untraceable loan lost in the state sector.

Second, problems often resulted from the weakness of the entire industry in production-related technologies across the country. For example, the Ministry of Machine Building and Electronics Industry

(MMEI) had a state-owned company, manufacturing electronic components for national defence products. Since the demand from the national defence sector had been shrinking, the company was running at a loss. MMEI was very keen to get the company out of its financial problem, and determined that Shanghai Bell could be a suitable customer for its two products: transistor and TTL (transistor transistor logic) circuits. It therefore did not grant Shanghai Bell a low tariff for importing these two components, and indicated that there was a local company which was able to produce them. However, MMEI overlooked the fact that in China most defence companies which were considered to have the capability to make high-technology products were only able to produce small batches of samples to satisfy a limited number of customers. These technological capabilities were not geared for commercial production. In particular, when this company was manufacturing products for the defence sector, it did not need to consider the cost very much. In addition, most products required were made in small quantities which did not require mass production technologies. Obviously, if the company attempted to make products in high volumes in the same manner as with small batches, the production costs would be very high – so much so, that the price of these components would be higher than the imported ones. Shanghai Bell therefore refused to buy these transistors and TTL circuits. This became a longlasting negotiating battlefield between Shanghai Bell and MMEI.

Last, but not least, were quality problems closely related to the weak production technology. It was a common phenomenon in the country, that sample products were usually fine, but the quality of mass-produced products often was much lower. The head of the Domestication Division described the confrontation between Shanghai Bell and local producers, saying:

> No matter whether high-tech or low-tech products, we have often had battles with local producers about quality, which often ended up with unpleasant feelings on both sides. They thought we were unreasonable and hypocritical, and went to the municipal office to complain that we did not like to use local products. Quality problems can be traced back to our socialist tradition: no market, no competition; users could only buy whatever producers made, and producers took this for granted. We understood the problems of local producers. However, we could not accept their products.

We have our standards, which we have learned from BTM. Local producers have to face the challenge too.
(Head of the Domestication Division, 28 February 1993, Shanghai)

As a very typical example, on one occasion Shanghai Bell needed to buy some screws – a commonly used product. It sent an order to a local screw producer and attached to the order the technical specifications of the screw. However, when the screws were delivered to Shanghai Bell, many unexpected problems were found. For example, the thread of the screw was not deep enough; the surface finish was not smooth enough, etc. Shanghai Bell insisted on returning them, since these defects would reduce the screw's endurance and, further, influence the telephone-exchange's quality. The manager of the local producer was astonished and did not understand this, since, for his company, this product met all their standards, and they had certificates of inspection. Besides, the company had been producing screws for ages, and they had never ever come across such a complaint.

Another example was that Shanghai Bell was considering a local producer for a component – an LED (light emitting diode). After having checked all the technical features, the engineer from Shanghai Bell found that the angle of the light beam was not wide enough and asked the local producer to modify this from 75 degrees to 120 degrees. He explained that as the LED was used on the front panel of the exchange, a wider angle could make it more visible for operators. Although the engineers at the local company still believed that Shanghai Bell was pernickety, and the change was unnecessary, they eventually agreed to make the change. However, that was not the end of the story. After the angle was modified, another problem was found: the brightness of the LEDs differed from one to the next, which meant that when they were fitted on the same panel some would look brighter and some dimmer. This again caused friction between two sides. The producer argued that this was too tiny an imperfection to be a problem, whereas Shanghai Bell side persisted with its standard.

Despite such problems, over time, local production of System-12 components has gradually been realised. This was not because government stepped up its intervention. Rather Shanghai Bell and local companies had become active players.

Since 1989, the production capacity of Shanghai Bell had been rapidly expanding and its demand for components was growing. Even existing local production of components, such as the production of racks and sub-racks and printed circuit boards in Shanghai Bell and the production of LSI chips in Shanghai Belling, could not keep up with demand. To have increased component imports would have increased problems of supply, which had led to inconvenience and sometimes had affected their ability to meet orders in time. Local component supply proved more reliable because transport problems were reduced and it also avoided the need to deal with government officials to get import licences. Cost reduction was another important factor, since local production was usually cheaper than imported products, because of lower labour costs and international transport costs. For example, in the case of cable import, the cost of air transport was higher than the cable itself. More importantly, the foreseeable future market of System-12 was clearly seen to be promising. For all these reasons, Shanghai Bell determined that it was the time to reallocate its component supply nearby.

During the same period of time, the macro-economic environment pushed local manufacturing companies towards the market place. The state no longer took responsibility for selling whatever a state-owned company produced. Companies had to survive in the market-oriented economy by themselves. They had to find new products and new markets, and to produce the products which could meet market requirements. In these circumstances, most local companies wanted to be a component supplier for Shanghai Bell. Even providing packing boxes for Shanghai Bell had made a box producer into a booming concern.

As both Shanghai Bell and local companies were all keen to produce components locally, things became much easier. Lacking finance, they went together to lobby the government, as well as mustering funds from their own channels. Even for quality problems their attitudes were no longer mutually hostile. Shanghai Bell provided local producers with as much help as they needed, such as approved technical documents with detailed specifications for each component, and helped solve technical problems in local production. At the same time, to let component producers understand the importance of product quality, Shanghai Bell invited local producers to visit the their production workshops, to see how their components were fitted into the system through the assembly line and were functioning in the switching system. To ensure the local production quality in the longer term, Shanghai Bell established a programme with each local component producer for periodically inspecting the production process and examining products, as well as random checks. This programme sought to track down the source of quality problems and finally helped local producers to solve them. To take the example of a local producer providing Shanghai Bell resistors: every technical feature of the resistor was tested and matched the required specifications except for the hardness of the material for its two pins, which was slightly too soft. For the local producer, it seemed merely a tiny technical differentiation. However, after visiting the production line in Shanghai Bell and seeing that while going through an automatic inserter many pins of the resistors were bent before being properly inserted into the printed circuit board, they realised that they were wrong.

By the time of my fieldwork in February 1993, government direct intervention for import substitution had gradually reduced, although its control on import licences and tariffs was still there. However, Shanghai Bell had established a supply network, which had been expanded to about 50 local companies. All locally produced components had obtained BTM's approval. Each component had more than one supplier (e.g. the hybrid circuit had three suppliers). Because of competition between them, the price was also kept down.

During the course of domesticating production of System-12 components, local companies' awareness of product quality had gradually developed, and production capabilities had been strengthened, although quality problems were still occurring from time to time, as these could not just disappear overnight. Even the most successful import substitution project, the Shanghai Belling joint venture project, to manufacture large-scale integrated chips (LSI) for System-12, still had a reject rate of end products of 60 per cent, lagging behind the producers in industrialised countries. But compared to the reject rate at as high as 98 per cent at the early production stage, it still represented substantial progress.

3.5 SUMMARY AND CONCLUSIONS

In the initiation of System-12 technology transfer, the Chinese government played the sole role in searching for available technologies across the world, selecting the appropriate switching system, and negotiating the transaction. The government was determined to bring China's telecommunications to the world level and, eventually, to build up indigenous technological capabilities based on its three-step strategy of technology development. This was clearly reflected by its persistence in transferring all aspects of PDSS technology including the LSI chip production technology, which would not only suit China's telecommunications network, but would also bring the opportunity for China to gain access to the most advanced technology and ensure that China was able to produce the entire technology system independently in the near future. As a result of its efforts, the technology transfer agreement more or less laid the foundation for the co-operation between the Chinese and Belgian sides and so ensured the future success of the project.

All these government actions were crucial during the early stage of economic reforms for several reasons. First, after having been isolated from the world businesses for so many years, individual Chinese companies lacked experience to deal with international trade. Because the significant differences in political, social and economic systems between China and Belgium were very likely to pose considerable obstacles for companies on both sides, Chinese government involvement meant that the PDSS collaboration was a matter to be dealt with at the country-to-country level. Second, since a large-scale technology transfer project like the public digital switching system required a large investment, there were very few companies in the world that could handle the finance without any state help. Third, the collaboration engaged the Belgian government in the successful lobbying of COCOM to lift the ban on transferring LSI production technology to China.

Again it was direct and indirect government support that overcame acute problems arising in the course of implementing System-12 technology transfer. First of all, since in China the social and economic transition had only just started and this was still a centrally controlled system, government direct involvement was needed to handle the new establishment of a joint production venture like Shanghai Bell, which had to go through bureaucratic procedures at various layers in order to get official approval and to deal with difficulties – from land, human and material resources to utility supply – that were still allocated on a planned rather than market basis. Government approval was needed in particular at that time for Shanghai Bell to be allowed to adopt Western methods of management and to free it from the normal economic and political obligations (e.g. about taking on staff, involving political organisations in the management). MPT's support in gathering capable human resources across the country, and Shanghai local government's approval for this, greatly assisted

Shanghai Bell in quickly mastering a wide range of technologies (needed for example to overcome technical problems occurring in the first installation of System-12 in the Chinese environment). The large MPT subsidy ensured the market for Shanghai Bell and extracted it from the crisis that arose at a critical early stage of development.

Having such a favourable environment, Shanghai Bell was gradually able to adapt System-12 to the poor conditions of the Chinese tele-communications network, and to modify some parts of the production process. Most important was high productivity which Shanghai Bell achieved through its efforts in building up technological capabilities in management, marketing, and resource allocation. In China's changing environment from a centrally planned system to a more market oriented one, Shanghai Bell learned to take advantage of its position as a newly established joint venture. It developed pragmatic policies and measures, and articulated its domestic and overseas strengths, drawing upon its natural connection with both.

Despite the significant success of Shanghai Bell in developing production capacity and in application software technologies, its tech-nological capabilities in the innovation of System-12 and core production technologies, especially hardware technologies, were still very limited for several reasons. First of all, as a consequence of this model of technology transfer, the technology of designing and updating the core technology of System-12 was difficult for Shanghai Bell as a manufacturing company to master, especially as only limited technological support was available from within the country. Shanghai Bell has also limited opportunities for exporting System-12 exchanges, as this would offend BTM. However, it may be debatable whether it is necessary for Shanghai Bell to be able to independently innovate the core technology of System-12.

Apart from this, many hardware technologies, for example pro-duction technologies, in China were very poor (a general feature of the old socialist system), and would take quite a while to improve from scratch in terms of design of production processes and production quality control in particular. The best example was the produc-tion quality control. Its improvement had to start by changing people's perception of what quality means. Some problems, e.g. the incon-venience of using English as a human and machine interface language, were not economical to solve.

In terms of the production domestication of System-12 components, we can see that government intervention was not that successful until the domestication of supply became in the interest of Shanghai Bell and local industries, as a result of changes in the macro-environment in China's transition. This issue showed clearly the different interests between the state and individual companies in building up technological capabilities. It also demonstrated the important role of both state intervention and market forces in providing incentives for technological development.

4 HJD-04: The Chinese-Developed System

4.1 THE PROCESS OF DEVELOPING THE CHINESE HJD-04 SYSTEM

The Chinese HJD-04 system was born out of the socio-economic transition taking place in China. Its development process reveals interesting elements of technological development that are very different from the System-12 case. This section starts by describing the three major actors involved in the development process, and then illustrates the entire process of the Chinese PDSS technology development, divided into two phases: first the initiation phase – how a military research team became the initiator of this project and how other social and technical elements necessary for creating this technology were built up, through the development of collaboration also involving a switch manufacturer and telecommunications procurement organisation; in the second phase – bringing the technology to the market – tensions and conflicts emerged between these three parties around competition for profits and the large potential market.

Three Major Developers

Three institutions became core actors in developing the HJD-04 system: the Centre for Information Technology (CIT) in Zhengzhou Institute of Information Engineering of the People's Liberation Army, the military research team, which was the initiator; the Posts and Telecommunications Industrial Corporation (PTIC), the industrial procurement unit of the Ministry of Posts and Telecommunications (MPT) (see Figure 1.1); and the Luoyang Telephone Equipment Factory (LTEF) of MPT, originally a cross-bar switch producer and later the main manufacturer of HJD-04.

CIT's involvement could be traced back to the early 1980s. In the past, this institute worked on designing large capacity computers, but only for R&D projects on national defence. Once economic growth became a main target of the country, the state budget for national defence, including military R&D projects, decreased. At the same time, the Military Commission of the Central Committee of the

Communist Party issued an instruction calling for the army to make a contribution to the civil sectors. Under this pressure, the military research team of CIT started looking for some R&D projects in civil sectors.

Professor Wu Jiangxing played a key role in this episode. He was formerly a senior engineer and later the head of CIT. In the early 1980s, Professor Wu was working in Fuzhou,[55] as a research fellow doing computer design. This was the time and the place that the first foreign PDSS, the Japanese F-150 system,[56] was imported and installed. The Chinese encountered many problems with this system: from the day the contract was signed, it took two years to get the system into operation. This frustrating experience highlighted the dangers for China of lacking its own technology, and deeply impressed Professor Wu. Thereafter, he established a research team in CIT, which started working in the field of telecommunications.

The Luoyang Telephone Equipment Factory (LTEF) was one of four HJD-04 manufacturing firms under the MPT. It was also the earliest party to co-operate with the military CIT research team. LTEF was established in the 1970s to produce cross-bar telephone exchanges. One of 28 MPT firms, LTEF is a relatively newly equipped company. It initially benefited from being state-owned. Soon after economic reform began, however, its products became less favoured by users as foreign advanced PDSSs began to pour into the Chinese market. Following the 'foreign technology fever' (section 1.3), LTEF first bid, unsuccessfully, to be the Chinese side of the joint venture with the Belgium Bell Telephone Manufacturing Company (which eventually became Shanghai Bell) and, later, was involved in another bid organised by MPT, for one of ten joint ventures to produce private digital switches. Having failed twice, in 1986 LTEF decided to co-operate with the military CIT's research team to seek new technological opportunities.

PTIC was the industrial unit of MPT set up at the start of the economic reforms to co-ordinate the activities of the MPT's 28 firms. It had previously undertaken equipment provision for MPT's public network. As noted already in Chapter 1, MPT was one of a few ministries that were historically quasi-militarised. As a result, it had a very firm monopoly position in the country. However, economic reform had not left MPT untouched. PTIC, and MPT's R&D institutions, were allowed to become increasingly independent of MPT control. Under MPT, there were 31 R&D institutes. In the past, any technologies developed from these institutes were given freely to manufacturing firms. The reforms changed this relationship, because technologies were now perceived as profitable goods, valuable in the market. Without an R&D base of its own, PTIC feared the loss of its technological resources. The pressure to save its loss-making state-owned firms also concerned PTIC. As a result, PTIC took a risk, and joined in CIT's technology projects.

The Initiation and Creation of Chinese PDSS

In the early 1980s, under pressure to turn to civil projects, Professor Wu studied available written materials on foreign PDSS technologies being imported to China – System-12, F-150 and E-10b.[57] PDSS is based on a range of computer technologies, completely different from the old generation of electromagnetic switching systems. For people steeped in the telecommunications field, PDSS was not easy to master. But having experience in the field of computer technology, Professor Wu could readily understand it as simply another kind of computer system. This made him decide to attempt some work on digital programme-controlled switching systems.

The major task for the CIT research team was to find a partner with expertise in telecommunications, especially in telephone exchanges. LTEF as a telephone-exchange producer was immediately under consideration. It was also a good choice both geographically and politically, since LTEF was near – just over a hundred kilometres away from CIT – and the two cities in which LTEF and CIT were located are in the same province. However, at that time, LTEF was concentrating on bidding for joint ventures, and had no interest in the joint development project. So CIT enlisted another telephone equipment manufacturer in the city of Changchun, in Northeast China.

In September 1984, CIT and its partner embarked on the project of a digital programme-controlled private automatic branch exchange (PABX). CIT chose this as a way of getting into switching technology, but one that was smaller scale and simpler than a public telephone exchange (for example, it only needed to interface with a narrow range of equipment, and regulatory requirements were less demanding). The technology was thus not a big problem for Professor Wu and his team. However, a setback occurred as the work was near completion. CIT's partner was informed that the Directorate-General of Telecommunications (the top telecommunications administration unit of the country – see Figure 1.1) suspected that the proposed PABX was inadequate. It thus withdrew from the project, and the military research team was left to carry on alone. In June 1986, laboratory work was completed. The technical design of this PABX passed an examination organised by the provincial science and technology committee which concluded that the CIT research team had produced some 'novel ideas' in design. This result exceeded CIT's expectations and encouraged the research team to continue their R&D in this area.

In October 1986, after LTEF's attempts to establish a joint venture had failed, it expressed an interest in CIT's project and received a positive response. In November the two new partners signed a contract to improve the design, and convert the laboratory prototype for production. Engineers in LTEF had expertise in telephone-exchange technology, the requirements of telephone networks and the regulation of the telecommunication administration. The researchers in the military team were skilled in computer design. So the co-operation was quite successful. An improved PABX was delivered from the laboratory in August 1987 and, in May 1988, it entered into production.

At that time, as already noted, PTIC was also under pressure. After LTEF joined the R&D project, PTIC kept an eye on it, from time to time sending specialists to examine the product on the spot and to check the progress. Expectations arose in PTIC about the possibility of using CIT to develop a domestic digital programme-controlled switching system. Soon after, PTIC decided to invest three million Chinese yuan to develop a PABX with 2000 lines. This project was only the start of a bigger plan, of which the second step was to develop a terminal (local) PDSS with 6000 lines; the final target was a full-size PDSS.[58] Its investment in the military research team was, however, still risky for PTIC for both political and technological reasons: first, being outside the telecommunications sector, CIT was out of PTIC's control; and second, the stakes were large while CIT's technological capability was unsure. Nevertheless, PTIC saw CIT as a potential R&D base that could provide it with the opportunity to fulfil its ambition. After the research team had gained enough practice on PDSS technology, PTIC planned to send the team to Singapore to develop a Chinese PDSS, with more advanced equipment and assistance of some experts from Taiwan and Singapore.[59]

In 1987, a contract to develop a PABX with 2000 lines was signed between CIT and PTIC. Since then PTIC had played the role of general project manager and financial sponsor; CIT was the main technological force, with LTEF as a technical assistant as well as a test workshop.

PTIC's support was crucial to the CIT research team. The earliest result, a PABX of 1000-line capacity named HJD-03, was registered officially with the MPT. This was the largest capacity of digital programme-controlled exchange developed domestically at that time. The very success of HJD-03 and financial backing from PTIC greatly encouraged the CIT team. However, as a research organisation, largely driven by the motivation of technological novelty, it no longer had enthusiasm for developing another PABX (as PTIC planned). Instead, CIT aimed directly at a terminal (local) PDSS, which it saw as a necessary step to gain a full range of knowledge of PDSS technology.

PTIC's response to CIT's proposal was lukewarm, for two reasons: first, it was not confident of the capability of the military research team; and second, it feared that the project would offend MPT which, as mentioned above, had been investing for some time in the development of another PDSS, the DS series.[60] Duplicated R&D effort was always considered a waste of money; in addition, PTIC might be suspected of being unfaithful to MPT by attempting to build up its own technological strength. PTIC did not oppose the programme; it just took a watching stance, thus *de facto* allowing the CIT research team to carry on anyway.

Eventually, as the military research team had hoped, a workable terminal (local) PDSS, HJD-15, was developed. From the viewpoint of CIT computer specialists, their major technical obstacle – the lack of expertise in telephone switching systems – had been removed. In November 1989, PTIC agreed to the CIT's proposal to develop a full-size PDSS. It organised a conference to examine the development plan and the feasibility of the Chinese PDSS, to which it invited almost all authoritative experts in Beijing. The result was ambiguous. Although the telephone switching experts were not able to understand the detailed design (because of having less experience in computer technology), most of them found the architecture of the system distinctive. Nobody could be sure that the project would be successful in the end, but the conference concluded that 'if the design can be proved in practice then it will be a big success'. Consequently, the development project was initiated. This involved registration of the project with MPT. The system was registered by the PTIC with the name HJD-04, although officially, HJD was the name for a range of PABX technologies. By using this name, PTIC could avoid being accused of duplicating research or offending MPT. In fact, the development still irritated MPT, but so long as PTIC did not submit its application for approval, MPT could not respond to it.

The HJD-04 development project went smoothly, until test-system debugging was initiated in October 1990. Hardware debugging was completed, but serious problems arose on the software side. According to the original, rather optimistic plan, this test-system was to be put into test operation by the end of 1990, and simultaneously MPT would conduct a general examination. When the time came, MPT insisted on carrying out the examination on schedule, while the project was facing serious problems on the software side. This put the joint R&D group under enormous pressure to show that the product could succeed.

At that stage, MPT was not happy to accept the project, probably because the work was done by a military research team from outside the sector and, to their even greater irritation, because PTIC had become involved in the project without its approval. Besides, the system had been declared by its developers to be better than the system DS series which was developed by MPT's own research institutes.

Eventually, PTIC managed to get the examination postponed, but MPT set some other obstacles. It did not carry out the examination, but instead demanded documentary evidence that the initiation of the project was approved by the authorities in MPT. Because the HJD-04 had not got MPT's approval as a *bona fide* PDSS project, in December 1991 a presentation of the project proposal was held in Beijing, before the formal examination of the system. Eventually, MPT sent a 20-person inspection party (a daunting prospect since the HJD-04 research team was only 18 people) to carry out an initial examination of the machine. Among the examiners were some who had been involved in the development of DS-2000 and DS-30, and experienced engineers from Shanghai Bell. The final inspection party was even larger. Indeed, it was the most authoritative examining party ever sent by MPT, and included examiners from many relevant ministries and organisations. The final result was favourable, and the HJD-04 was, at last, officially acknowledged.

Further Development – Bringing the Technology to the Market

From then on, HJD-04 development entered another phase related to production and to markets. No longer a 'bastard child', the technology was sought after by many companies who saw its potential market to be immense. The three parties co-operating in the HJD-04 project began to face problems, such as product quality, further technology improvement, and resource allocation. New conflicts emerged among them with respect to each party's right to exploit the technology and each party's responsibility for the group's co-operative actions.

According to the contract, PTIC possessed the right to produce HJD-04, while CIT held intellectual property rights for the core technology – for which it received a certain percentage of the profit from the producers, and took responsibility for training engineers and technicians from factories to master the technology. PTIC allowed four of its manufacturing firms (including LTEF) to produce the HJD-04 system. LTEF had no special role or relationship once the other three firms had joined in as producers.

In China, economic legislation was new – for legislators, implementors and undertakers alike. The relevant legal system and provisions had not been completed and elaborated. In the past, if conflicts occurred between people or organisations, they went to the Party for justice. Now, with only a hazy understanding of the law, people were having to use legislation to protect their rights. At the same time, many businesses and organisations ignored the laws; some even took advantage of imperfections in the legal system, and people's immature understanding of it, to avoid the constraints of the laws upon their efforts to pursue profits.

In the HJD-04 case, the technological co-operation surrounding its development was not actually based on the contract between the CIT and the PTIC. Instead, it was largely based on mutual understanding of the importance of the roles of each party. This facilitated co-operation in the initial development of HJD-04. However as it moved towards commercial exploitation, efforts to maintain or enhance each party's strength in this co-operation led to a series of conflicts.

One conflict arose because CIT sold its technology to other manufacturing companies without PTIC's permission. The telephone switching market was so attractive that many companies wanted to obtain the HJD-04 technology – for instance, professional telephone equipment producers or newly-established electronic joint production ventures belonging to the Ministry of Machine Building and Electronics Industry (MMEI),[61] as well as some military factories. CIT's action increased the number of HJD-04 manufacturers to seven or eight. This greatly offended PTIC, which considered CIT's move an illegal action and a breach of the written contract. But PTIC dared not risk damaging its relationship with CIT, as their co-operation was obviously crucial for any further innovation of the technology.

So PTIC fought back, but without a head-on battle with CIT. MPT's monopoly in the management of the telecommunications sector was still unshaken, up to this point. Its administrative unit in telecommunications, the Directorate-General of Telecommunications, was in charge of the whole public telecommunication network and all telecommunications services. Each new type of switching system had to be approved by the Directorate-General of Telecommunications before being used in the public telecommunication network. However, at that stage the HJD-04 system had not obtained the necessary licence for installation on the network. In this situation, PTIC's strategy was to stop HJD-04 units produced by non-MPT companies from gaining access to the public network. Instead of applying for a full licence for the HJD-04 system to enter the public network, it managed to get Directorate-General of Telecommunications' permission with the proviso that the system was allowed to be installed in the network for the purpose of 'test operations'. This permission was exclusive for PTIC's companies. With this, *de facto*, PTIC's companies could produce and sell their products as much as PTIC wanted, whereas the other HJD-04 producers could not!

The attitudes of the ministries and top state leaders involved were interesting. The above dispute inflamed the already sore relationships between MPT and MMEI. Each stood by its own companies. MPT took the HJD-04 technology as its own and tried to protect the right of PTIC, while the MMEI accused MPT of exploiting its unfair monopoly over the PDSS market. PTIC was worried that MMEI could take revenge, through its control of the tariff rate on imported components needed for the production of HJD-04. The case was passed on to some senior leaders. One state councillor, who had once supported the HJD-04 project when it was in difficulties, expressed his personal opinion that 'as long as the HJD-04 is an indigenous Chinese technology, why not stand for the whole nation to develop the technology all together first and leave conflicts to later on'.[62] So, the dispute on the surface was calmed down. But, a major initiative aimed at establishing an alternative telecommunications network had been brewing within MMEI and several other ministries, in order to break MPT's monopoly in telecommunications services.[63]

The relationship between PTIC and LTEF was also complicated. On the one hand, PTIC had been doing its best to help LTEF in finance and marketing; on the other, it had been trying to tighten its control over LTEF in order to make more profit from it. In turn, the firm enjoyed PTIC's support, while trying to avoid its tight control.

PTIC pursued its interests in several ways. First, it successfully lobbied the government, with the result that the HJD-04 technological development project was put under a state scheme in 1992. A $4.98 million long-term loan with low interest[64] was offered by the state for the modernisation of the production assembly line in LTEF's workshop. With this sum of money, plus $300 000 which it generated itself, LTEF could purchase advanced machines and facilities needed both from abroad and within the country.

Second, PTIC persuaded the government to waive import tariffs specifically for the HJD-04 components with effect from late 1993.[65] This was critical, since the system used many imported components, the tariff on which might be as high as 140 per cent. Third, PTIC established a new company, Beijing Long Term Technology Corporation, to deal with all business and matters concerning HJD-04 technology – purchasing equipment, importing components, capital investment, technology control, and so on. As an independent company (which in fact had a very close relation with PTIC, as shown by the fact that its director was the head of PTIC's Directorial Office), Beijing Long Term Technology Corporation could freely partake in commercial activities. Since LTEF was not allowed to gain access to foreign business partners directly, the purchase of components and machinery must be carried out through other commercial companies. This was a highly profitable business. Soon after its establishment, Beijing Long Term Technology Corporation replaced the trade companies who had been undertaking LTEF's business, importing components and purchasing machinery from abroad. However, because of Beijing Long Term Technology Corporation's lack of business experience, problems in supply arose which proved expensive for LTEF.

Finally, as part of the reforms to bring in a market system, marketing became an undertaking of firms, rather than of the PTIC. This weakened PTIC's total control over the production volume of its firms, and threatened its ability to monitor effectively their production and commercial situation, and thus to draw profits from its daughter firms.[66] However, PTIC found an alternative way of exerting control over its firms. It kept secret from the firms the password necessary to process all the software for producing HJD-04 systems. Thus, when LTEF (and other HJD-04 producers) got orders from users, it must apply for decoded software from PTIC's new company, Beijing Long Term Technology Corporation, and pay a fee for production of each line of the system. In addition, to gain more technical control over its partners and daughter companies, PTIC established an HJD-04 software centre.

LTEF was unhappy with this PTIC control but, as a daughter company, it would not fight back. In any case, it relied on PTIC for finance, as well as for obtaining government support. LTEF had learnt the danger of lacking technology of its own, and was determined to strengthen its technological position. In February 1993, the firm established a research institute in which it assembled its best manpower. Ambitiously, the firm hoped that one day it would be able to master the entire technology of HJD-04 and to extricate itself from external technological dependence.[67]

LTEF had worked closely with CIT's research team during the technology creation stage. However, after the technology was developed for the market and became profitable, technological capability became an important card to play in the power balance among the three parties. Information flow between users, manufacturers and the R&D institution was crucial in this technological improvement stage. But LTEF and CIT were no longer exchanging their expertise freely, because both parties were trying to protect their technological position. For example, a problem had been occurring in the firm since the beginning of production, because of a component with two pins which had a larger diameter than the holes they were to fit in on the printed circuit board. Before soldering, the two pins had to be filed smaller to fit the holes.[68] It only needed a very minor change in the design specifications of the board to overcome this problem, but this had not been done by the time of the study (April 1993). The LTEF said that the change should been made by CIT, since the firm was not allowed to change any documented specifications. However, CIT argued that LTEF should be responsible for this matter. On another occasion, CIT asked LTEF to get regular feedback from users, with whom LTEF had close links, but LTEF did not respond. So, CIT had to send its own team members to the field to collect feedback.

The same type of technology protection activities occurred among HJD-04 producers under the MPT. They were competing with each other in almost all aspects, including resource allocation, marketing and technological capability. The desire to prevent technology leakage between these four firms ruled out information exchange and co-operation which could have promoted overall technological development.

Confrontation (both overt and covert) had been a recurring theme in this stage of the improvement of HJD-04 technology. In spite of these conflicts, however, all parties involved in the project knew that they were bound up with each other through the HJD-04 system. They all knew that they had to put these conflicts behind them. According to current plans, CIT was to complete a new version, HJD-04AD (advanced version) in 1994, with new functions (for example, using a No. 7 signalling system and remote modules). In a few years, ISDN and Intelligent Network functionalities would be available. The question was how to conduct a co-operative relationship at an appropriate level of competition. In order to achieve this, in 1993 PTIC established a new co-ordination organisation named 'Production Co-ordination Committee', with the aim of finding the best solution to conflicts between institutions, and of encouraging co-operation to accelerate improvement of the technology. LTEF (and other HJD-04 producers) knew very well how important PTIC and CIT were for it – with respect to financial, political and technological support – in the past, currently and in future.

4.2 BUILDING UP TECHNOLOGICAL CAPABILITIES AT FIRM LEVEL

Technological capabilities at firm level are ultimately critical. The blueprint HJD-04 technology had to be turned into products and thereafter to be tested in the market. This section explores how LTEF developed its production capabilities in the struggle to survive during the transition, and spells out the organisational reform of the firm to root out the inefficiencies and lack of incentives stemming from the old system. It also examines how technological learning took place under intense pressures to overcome obstacles arising from both the traditional economic system and the transition.

Pressures and Opportunities in the Transition

Luoyang Telephone Equipment Factory is a fairly typical state-owned enterprise, in terms of the institutional structure, incentives and operating mechanism. The project to build the new factory from scratch started in 1972 under the 'self-reliance' policy of the government, prior to economic reform, that the country must build up the telecommunications industry on its own. The factory came into operation in 1980, producing cross-bar public telephone switches with a maximum capacity of 200 000 lines per year. This domestically designed switch was an advanced technology at that time in China and the technology was freely transferred from an R&D institute under the state scheme.

Like many state-owned factories that were located away from the coastal area during the 'cold war' in order to avoid the perceived threat of imperialist attack, LTEF was situated in the middle of China. The factory lies in the remote outskirts of the city of Luoyang, in Henan province. This created inconvenience in transport between the city and the factory. Because of this, when the factory was set up it decided to establish its own social welfare facilities for its employees working in the factory: providing houses near by; kindergarten and schools for their children; a hospital, a post office, telecommunications service; buses to and from the city to the factory seven or eight times per day; restaurants and canteens, guest houses, bathhouse, travel agent and all kind of services. As staff described vividly: 'Here we have everything except for a crematorium.'

The factory employed a large number of staff, which was due partly to labour-intensive production and partly to the socialist ideology that was supposed to provide everyone with a job. By 1992, the number of employees was over 2700. The whole community including the families of its staff was estimated as around 7000. People's jobs were permanent. The director of the firm played a role as head of a community, and accordingly managers of each department and section took care of their staff to a large extent. For instance, if someone was ill, the company would be obliged to send him or her to hospital and pay the expenses. If someone's family experienced disaster, his or her boss should, on behalf of the group, offer help and express their sympathy. Similarly, if a member of staff could not find a partner, the trade union of the factory would possibly play the role of matchmaker.

As noted earlier, the LTEF was a newly equipped cross-bar switch producer. It used to produce almost every component for the cross-bar switch, and the process was conducted completely within the factory from the input of raw materials to the output of the finished switch. All raw materials were supplied, and products were sold, at fixed prices by arrangement of the state. All the chief officials regarded as important to the firm, such as the director, major department managers, chief engineer and accountant, etc., were appointed by the MPT. The recruitment of graduates the factory received every year from universities and technical schools (most of which were run by the MPT) was organised according to the state plan. Without the economic reform, a factory like the LTEF would be a plan-taker immune to any problems from the imbalance between input and output.

Soon after LTEF had established its production and social facilities, its social and economic environment and the underlying socialist doctrine began to change. In the first five years of the economic reform, it remained untouched within MPT's protection. But it sensed the insecurity of its position due to one event. In the beginning of the 1980s, MPT offered the newly equipped LTEF factory to its foreign partner BTM[69] to establish a joint production venture. The offer was turned down and the foreign partner chose another cross-bar manufacturer in Shanghai as its base. This made the LTEF feel sour. However, at that time, the economic reform was merely a gentle breeze for the firm, and it did not exert much pressure.

In 1984, the central focus of economic reform had gradually shifted to the reorganisation of the industrial sector, involving provision of greater autonomy to firms and reduction of government protection. In other words, firms had to organise fully or partly their resources and sell their products in markets.

This made LTEF face both internal and the external pressures. Financial constraints became stringent – how to sustain the unduly large workforce and more urgently to feed about 3000 staff. The existing institutional establishment – once well suited for the central planning system – did not provide the structure and incentives for high productivity. Instead, previous socialist advantages – the significant community function of the firm – became a heavy burden. The emergence of the PDSS market favoured foreign advanced systems rather than Chinese cross-bar technology even though international prices and import tariffs made them more expensive. At that time, some authorities suggested that cross-bar could remain for quite a while in China. As noted in section 1.3, however, orders for cross-bar products decreased sharply.

The LTEF was faced with two alternatives: either to co-operate with CIT in pursuing a new technological opportunity or to bid for joint venture projects. It turned down the earlier offer of CIT because it lacked enough momentum at that stage. After it failed twice in its bids for joint ventures, it could not afford not to join CIT. For LTEF, it was a chance to renew its technology and ultimately to maintain its position in the market.

In collaboration with CIT, LTEF provided expertise in exchanges and networks in the telecommunications field; it offered its workshop as a test ground and undertook the designing of a variety of racks for holding switches. In turn, it benefited from producing new technologies: the PABX HJD-03 which at that time was the digital switching system with the largest capacity developed in the country; and the terminal public digital switching system, HJD-15, which was also new for the country as a locally developed system. By producing these two systems, the firm turned around its loss-making position. Later, the firm obtained HJD-04 technology which had a great potential in the domestic PDSS market, although it had to compete with other HJD-04 producers inside and outside MPT's territory.

Reform to Survive

Efficient production capability was the key to turning the new technology from a blueprint to a product which could succeed in the market. The situation had reached a point where the firm could not move on without restructuring its entire organisation, to address productivity and the requirements for producing the new technology. However, this was the most thorny problem for a state-owned firm like LTEF. Restructuring would touch every member of staff and their individual vested interests. The stakes were so high that the firm would have avoided getting involved in these issues if this had been at all possible.

Instructions for reform eventually came from above. These were applied all over the country, although the speed and incidence of their application varied from place to place. At this stage, the major target was an administrative innovation in firms to shake off the rigid system; popularly known as 'smash the big rice bowl', it was based on a belief that employees of enterprises, from shop-floor workers to the director of the firm, lacked motivation to work hard. A new system was to be built, described as the 'responsibility system', based on contractual arrangements,[70] which also defined the respective roles of the enterprise director, Party secretary and the other chief managers. However, because the rules of the new arrangement, and the dogma of the 'socialist market mechanism' underlying it, were not explicit, people's understanding of the responsibility system varied considerably.

At LTEF, the most urgent problem was not the rigid administration system, but the unduly large workforce, especially since the new technology required much less labour. As it was a relatively new firm, and staff were newly enrolled and young on average, people's performances were not that bad. However, the production of HJD-04 was capital-intensive, requiring only 800 to 900 people, whereas the total work force in the firm was 2700. It therefore faced a dilemma: to follow 'socialist' principles the firm had to be concerned with the basic needs of the majority; to fit the 'market mechanism' it must cut off its community roles and be more efficient. How to solve this problem became critical for the firm, as well as a matter of concern for the director who was in charge. As he noted:

> The market economy is the market economy, no matter whether one calls it socialist or capitalist. What I care about is that I have been living with people here for so many years I can't see them jobless. If we just kick workers out after they have served this country for so many years, where is justice and humanity? We are trying to find a way for them to make a living. Otherwise we would rather wait for a solution from the central government.
>
> (Director of LTEF, 22 April 1993)

This was a common reaction in state-owned firms all over the country, especially from those who, like the director of LTEF, had lived to-gether with staff in the same living-quarters for many years. However, as the financial pressure on the firm intensified, some measures had to be taken.

LTEF eventually established an internal labour market. Surplus labour was allowed to stay at home on 70 per cent of their salary. A bureau was set up to organise the internal labour market and mean-while seek new jobs for them, e.g. to find some products which were in demand at the time for them to make; to arrange for them to work temporarily or long term in other companies which needed spare labour; to train them technically in order to return to workshops with different skills, etc. This had the positive result that each department of LTEF could choose better labour from the internal labour market. The internal labour market did not solve the fundamental problem of the unduly large workforce, but it created great scope for engineering a dynamic system. Its positive side was that it created a buffer that reduced the immediate pressures on LTEF. As it was accepted by the majority of its people, it did not produce any danger of instability which was a major concern of the administrative group of the firm.

Simultaneously, the firm reorganised its management institutions and operating systems, and introduced new incentives. In preparation for this reform, the firm sent a large group to visit Shanghai Bell, in order to adopt foreign managerial methods which were considered effective. In the last quarter of 1992 when the internal reform was unfolded, LTEF adapted the 'responsibility system' to introduce what it described as the 'optimum constituting system'. Under this new company constitution, posts became selective with appointments made on only a one-year contract; and the performance of an individual in his or her post was annually assessed. The role of each post was defined more clearly than ever before, especially that of the managers of each department. They had more scope to make decisions, and took on more responsibilities, compared to the previous tradition of collective decision-making. The biggest change was with the Department of Production. It became more autonomous and had its own internal accounting system which gave great scope for the department to fully use its income as a means to motivate workers to improve both quantity and quality of production.

A new salary structure was introduced, described as 'performance-oriented salary'. Under this system, the salary was broken down into two parts: basic pay and performance-related pay. The basic pay depended upon how long the employee had worked in the company or in other state-owned organisations; what qualifications he or she had, etc. The performance-related pay was based on performance, in so far as the employee's working hours and output met the standards set by the firm, and the output exceeded the quota. Alternatively, good group and departmental performance would lead to bonuses in the individual's salary. The sum of these two parts is then weighted by a measure of the quality of the individual's work.[71] In this way, control over workers was intensified through a set of detailed regulations and disciplines. In addition, because of the great size of the labour force, there were many to choose from for each post. Thus, for people with posts, the workers standing-by were a pressure on them – an 'internal' reserve army of labour!

All these changes focused upon improving the productivity of the system. Material incentives were seen as an important means of motivating every cell of the system to achieve the firm's aims. At the same time, efficient production organisation was put on the firm's agenda (see below). This reform, more or less, achieved its purposes. Workers on the shop-floor were working harder than before. When the firm needed, they worked in their lunch breaks and in the evenings. So did the engineers, especially young and unmarried engineers. Since they live alone in the dormitory of the firm (just 5-minutes' walk from the workshop), they often came back to work in the evenings.[72]

In spite of these achievements, the state-owned firm could not yet get rid of all its burdens. In comparison with private and joint venture companies, LTEF was still less productive. Because government tariff policy also favoured joint ventures,[73] the disparity between a state-owned firm and a private and/or joint venture firm was big. As one department manager said: 'We are competing with these companies on an unequal basis. As such, we will never catch them up' (Manager of the Planning Department, 23 April 1993).

Apart from these developments, the nature of the state-owned firm had not changed much to date. All of the social welfare facilities were still there; without them staff could not live. For instance, if the firm cancelled the bus, people living in town would have to walk for hours to get to the factory. The firm's role in taking care of staff well-being had not changed much either. According to the Director, recently, when a newly employed worker was seriously ill, the firm spent several tens of thousands of Chinese yuan on his medical expenses. As he explained:'Tell me, how could I just kick him out even though we are very tight in finance? We are a socialist country after all!' (Director of the LTEF, 22 April 1993).

When I was interviewing the manager of the Department of Production, somebody came in urging him to leave: he apologised to me that, as a head of the department, he must act on behalf of the whole department and go to visit a member of staff whose mother had just died. At that time (April 1993), the firm was laying pipes in its living-quarters to install a central heating system to improve their staff's living conditions. The former head of the Directorial Office of the PTIC viewed this situation in a broader sense. He said:

We state-owned enterprises were and are still undertaking the role as a backbone of this country. Now, the other companies can select people who are relatively young and healthy, and can escape from paying pensions, providing medical care or child care and the other expenditures. But it is us who are looking after possibly their parents, spouses and children. Everybody knows the ideal structure of a family is that father works for joint ventures and mother works for state companies, so their dependants can still be in the welfare scheme. Without us, this society would have already lost its balance.
(The former head of the Directorial Office of the PTIC, 6 April 1993)

4.3 TECHNOLOGICAL LEARNING

Pressures stemming from the new economic environment compelled state-owned companies like LTEF to seek newly emerging technological opportunities, and to strengthen their basic capabilities as an enterprise to survive in the more market-oriented system. The future facing them provided few options: either to become intensively involved in technological learning; or to drown slowly in the increasingly competitive environment.

In a state-owned company like LTEF, the environment for technological learning was not the best, compared with private and joint venture companies. Learning processes and adjustment were also not pleasant, as they had inherited substantial social burdens. However, LTEF was drawn into the learning process, and has gradually built up basic technological capabilities.

Resource Allocation in the Market-Oriented System

State control over raw materials had been gradually liberalised. A state-owned firm like the LTEF was ultimately bound to lose its privilege of getting low-price supplies. However, the firm remained dependent on the state, and in particular on MPT, until it found that the state price was much higher than that in the freely negotiated market. This discovery provoked an important change of attitude in LTEF. Its immediate reaction was that it sold its spare copper materials, bought in at a low state-regulated price on the negotiated market, at a much higher price without the state's permission. More important, through this the firm learned that it had to rely on itself.

To produce HJD-04 technology, a large number of components needed to be imported from overseas. But LTEF did not have direct access to overseas companies. Components had to be purchased through various means: usually through some domestic trading companies which then purchased the goods from trading companies in Hong Kong. And the companies in Hong Kong might have ordered the components through some other intermediaries. As a result, LTEF found it difficult to know who the real suppliers were; worse, the quality of components differed to a large extent, and the timing of the shipping-in of the goods was often off schedule. LTEF's frustrating experiences gradually taught its business team how to deal with these problems, e.g. to find alternative suppliers, to make more practical plans in provision, etc.

Despite its severe problem of surplus labour, LTEF was at the same time short of qualified technicians and engineers for the new technology production. The market economy had resulted in large disparities between state-owned companies and private and joint venture companies and with the latter having much higher ability to provide increased rewards for such skilled manpower. As a result, LTEF, which could not provide high wages and bonuses, lost its attractiveness as an employer.

In the past, once anyone was assigned to work in the firm they could only leave with the firm's permission, unless the transfer was ordered from a higher level. Now, because political control upon private and joint venture companies had been loosened, many firms accepted new employees without official leaving certificates as long as they had professional qualifications. Skilled workers and qualified engineers could quit and leave their firm for a better-paid job in a joint venture or private company locally, or even in the southern economic zones. LTEF had not experienced much of a problem with people leaving, because once people were settled – e.g. when their children were in school or kindergarten and their spouses were working in the same community – it was not easy for them to leave. However, there was an urgent need for the firm to recruit new manpower and then get them to stay.

One of the most reliable sources of new and skilled labour for LTEF had been the recruitment of new graduates, but even this became difficult. Under the centrally planned system, graduates from universities, and especially from those MPT universities, were annually assigned to MPT enterprises. The reforms which had made technology more important, for similar reasons increased demand for university graduates. Graduates, in particular those with a good degree or from a reputable university, could choose where they preferred to work. As a state-owned firm, the LTEF was clearly not a favoured choice, especially because of its geographical location. The manager of LTEF Personnel Department said of these difficulties:

> In the past, according to the state quota, graduates were assigned to our factory annually. They came but hadn't got enough to do. We often felt there were too many graduates and only a few suitable posts for them. Now, things have changed. My boss has been constantly pressing me to get some new graduates. It's not easy. We are not Shanghai Bell, which has got privileges. Well, as long as we are determined to do it and are not stingy with money, we will make it. I have been travelling around attending 'human resource exchanging meetings'.[74] We are not attractive, indeed. We can't get the best students, but it doesn't matter. I always tell them the truth: our living conditions are not that good, but our HJD-04 is good, it's a Chinese system; the mastery of this technology is like having personal

property [as the skills are in great demand]. We need those who are willing to work on the technology. We have got some contracts done this year [1993]. This year, our budget for this recruitment is about 100 000 yuan; with it we can get 40 graduates. You know, we have to pay for it. Well, it is understandable that universities need money too.

(Head of the Personnel Department, 23 April 1993)

On the one hand, the firm was actively recruiting manpower from external resources. On the other, it was running a retraining programme – by sending people to study in universities, notably, to CIT to be trained directly in its laboratory; and by inviting experienced and knowledgeable engineers within the firm, and experts from the CIT, to give lectures in the classroom or teach practically in the field. As the director of LTEF understood: 'Now, we see that competition means a race in technology rather than only in the market. After all, this is a competition for manpower' (Director of the LTEF, 22 April 1993). Also the firm had been trying its best to attract key staff to settle down in the community, by providing them with the best living and working conditions that the firm could afford. The new incentives were: higher salary, better housing and, moreover, job satisfaction.

Production Capability – to Achieve High Productivity

People in LTEF learned gradually that there is a profound difference between a centrally planned socialist system and a market mechanism. 'Efficiency' and 'high productivity' are essential for a market-oriented system, and are closely linked to the profitability of a firm. In the past, the socialist tradition was to a large extent designed to protect people from the competition that results in brutal class struggle. Under central planning, high productivity was hardly a major consideration. Now, two key factors affected the firm's manufacturing operation. The first was derived from the new technology. Cross-bar was based on electro-mechanical technologies, whereas digital switching like HJD-40 is based on electronics technology. Production of cross-bar switching technology was labour-intensive whereas the HJD-04 is technology-intensive. For the firm, it was a fundamental change not only in production technology, but also in production organisation. Hence, the second problem was how to effectively control production quality in this new situation.

In the previous production of cross-bar switches, LTEF used to produce almost every component by itself. However, the only part of this technology which could be used for the HJD-04 system is the technology of racks and rack units. LTEF believed that its capability in rack design and production exceeded the other HJD-04 producers. The very new and difficult undertaking for the firm had been the assembly of printed circuit boards. In the beginning, assembly was done manually. Later the firm was equipped with a wave soldering machine and a pin bending machine. After the machine bent the pins of circuit components, they were inserted into printed circuit boards by hand and delivered to the soldering machine. Some joints were still soldered by hand. The final procedure of the production was testing the products, for which the workshop lacked proper apparatus.

The first and biggest problem was product quality. In the past, the socialist economic phenomenon meant shortage of material supply. Because of this, products were allocated on a rationed basis. In practice, quantity therefore came to be more important than quality. As a result, there was little perception of the need for quality. However, the new HJD-04 production was put in a competitive environment in which advanced foreign systems had already set high-quality standards for any switching system. Since LTEF had lost the protection of the state and had been pushed into the market, it had to compete with foreign companies, joint ventures as well as the other HJD-04 producers. From the market it learned the vital importance of quality.

'No quality, no quantity' became an almost everyday phrase spoken by people in the firm from the director to shop-floor workers; it was discussed on programmes made by the in-house wired-broadcaster everyday; and mentioned by every manager I interviewed. It was not a phrase from propaganda; rather, it was a lesson learned from their experiences in markets. Without quality, there would be no market, and the firm would not survive. That was the reality they were facing. Hence gaining high product quality had become the major task of the firm. More importantly, people's perception of quality with regard to market standards had gradually been changing.

Changing people's perception of quality was not enough. In the past, people also paid attention to product quality, but because the production was not the only undertaking of the firm, quality control was often left behind while the other tasks took precedence. Quality control was addressed by a series of disconnected mass movements like other political tasks. After each campaign, quality would remain high for some time and then deteriorate until another movement was needed. From its recent experiences, the firm learned that quality control needed a set of well-designed methods and that these methods needed to be implemented over the whole production process. In the beginning of 1993, after the institutional reform of the firm, the Department of Quality was set up and a knowledgeable person[75] was made head of the department. Compared to the previous quality control organisation which involved several small teams working in individual departments, the new department had more power.

The first target of the new department was to improve the quality of imported components. As mentioned above, the firm had no direct access to international markets, with the result that these components' quality was unpredictable. For this, the firm increased its investment on testing equipment within the factory. At the same time, some components were sent out of the province to two electronic R&D institutes which had appropriate test apparatus, as the firm lacked qualified labour and necessary equipment at that time.

The implementation of quality control methods in the process of production was more difficult, given the shortage of expertise, manpower and the means of production needed. For instance, in the workshop many work procedures were done manually. Women workers sat in lines, soldering components on printed-circuit boards by hand. Under these conditions, the quality of production varied depending on individual workers, their experience, attitude towards their job and, possibly, upon the time of day and on how workers felt. In addition, uneven availability of components often made things worse. When one lot of imported components was rejected by LTEF due to poor quality and needed to be returned to the supplier, the time delay was severe. As a result, the workshop sometimes ran out of components while, at other times, too many piled up. As a consequence, workers had nothing to do on some days and on other days had to work over eight hours to catch up. The stress and fatigue of such long hours meant that quality became uneven on these occasions. Apart from that, even though some quality problems appeared, as long as they were not too serious, workers as well as their managers would not like to stop work, because their salary was also linked with the quantity of their work, according to the new salary system.

It was very hard to solve these problems within the firm, given the lack of development of production technology and production systems. This must be understood in the context of the 30-year history of Chinese socialism, in which people had got used to Mao's idea that 'Ants can move Mount Taishan' and 'The more people and the higher the inspiration, the better things will be'. Along with a system of non-market competition, this left the industries of the country with under-developed production organisation, including adequate production means, technical design of the production process and production management. In LTEF, when HJD-04 production was started the assembly procedure had to be completed manually. The practice taught the firm that (as described by the new manager of the Department of Quality):

> The HJD-04 production is technology-intensive. Its quality is not visible and tangible. You just can't expect such a technology to be made by hand and be of a good quality. This is in complete contrast to the traditional idea: 'The more people and the high inspiration' can't do any good to product quality. We've got to have an auto-mated production process. In assembling components, anti-electro-static measures are necessary. The fewer the people involved, the better the quality of production. Besides, while the degree of inte-gration of printed-circuit board gets higher, soldering on it by hand becomes more and more impossible. Automation is the only and best solution, whether we like it or not.
>
> (Head of the Department of Quality, 27 April 1993)

LTEF could not afford automation in the workshop. It was PTIC which successfully lobbied the government, and obtained financial support for the purchase of the facilities needed. All machines were to be shipped to the workshop in July 1993. The firm was looking forward to it, at the time of my visit.

The manager of the Department of Technology was still worrying about the management of the whole production process. He realised that the firm's capability of technical design for the production process was weak. The final documentation of technical design for the whole assembly procedure had not been completed by April 1993. Shop-floor workers were not used to strictly following documented instructions. Taylorism was never fully applied in socialist China; instead, workers were usually encouraged to work in their own way as long as they could complete their job. For example, ten different workers might drill a hole in a piece of work in ten different ways, rather than following a standardised procedure. Obviously, this could not meet the standards of mass production of the HJD-04 system. The manager pointed out:

> In the past, technical design of production used to be considered less important than the design of product itself. This was common all

over the country. As a consequence, innovations of production technology used to be considered less significant and, worse, technologists working on the production process were easily ignored. Because
of this, we now lack technologists and expertise on production
organisation. We have to learn gradually. It takes time; it's not easy.

(Head of the Department of Technology, 27 April 1993)

The internal institutional reform transformed the Department of
Technology. The department laid down new operating rules for
workers, and tightened the procedures in the workshop. In order to
speed up the improvement of production organisation, the firm raised
the salaries for all in this department, and allowed the department to
recruit technologists from different sources, as many as were needed.
'I have been working in the area since the 1960s; for me, the change is
remarkable', noted the head of the Department of Technology.

By contrast, the head of the Department of Quality, who was not
satisfied, could not help complaining:

Till now, many of our managers are still sticking on the old thought
that quality control is only the responsibility of our department.
Each department for different reasons tries to cover up quality
problems rather than put the problems on the table and track down
the sources so as to root them out. We lack co-operation between
departments and sections. Apart from this, pressures come from
PTIC which asked to produce 25 000 lines this year [1993]. When
production 'quantity' becomes critical, 'quality' can only be left
behind. You know, we have got too many problems, and new
machines have not arrived yet.

(Head of the Department of Quality, 27 April 1993)

'Product quality' can only be the result of a successful process made up
from the combination of every piece of qualified work done by each
worker. The experience of LTEF shows that this capability takes time
to build up with respect to expertise of quality control and know-how
of production organisation, as well as qualified workers, technicians
and engineers.

The firm had been strengthening its technological capability with
regard to production, installation and maintenance capabilities.
Between October 1992 when HJD-04 technology was put into production and April 1993, about 80 000 lines and ten systems had been
produced and installed.

Marketing

To sustain its financial situation and expand the domain of the HJD-04 system, the firm was doing its best to produce as many systems as it could.

Since the reform, LTEF had been enhancing its marketing department. There were over 20 sales persons in the department. They were sent away from home, travelling around the country for more than 200 days a year on average. The company encouraged them by offering a higher bonus which was related to the number of lines they sold. According to the manager of the marketing department, the average income in the department was 30 per cent higher than the whole company. The new approach was expressed strongly by the former head of the Directorial Office of the PTIC:

Now, firms are allowed to use material incentives. For instance, a good salesman, if he sold a 100 000-line system, why shouldn't we give him a certain commission fee? In the new commercial economic environment, we should not keep the idea of 'iron rice bowl'. Those who contribute more to the firm, must be paid more, more than expected.

(Director of Beijing Long-Term Data Technology Corporation, former head of the Directorial Office of the PTIC, 6 April 1993)

This would not have happened in the past, because people were taught by a socialist dogma that each job must be treated equally, as long as it was for the revolution. A gate-guard would not necessarily be paid less than an engineer. Income differences between different professions were never that big. In LTEF, since the reform, such differences have been gradually widened.

As mentioned above, because the PDSS market was so big, there was considerable scope for the HJD-04. However, one problem was that some foreign governments were providing soft loans that in most cases were for the purpose of supporting their own country's exports. Since many Chinese local Posts and Telecommunications Administrations had been operating at a loss and were not able to afford any PDSS, and the MPT was also short of finance, foreign soft loans had become an important source of finance. Having been offered this, recipients might be forced to buy foreign products as a precondition. Local administrations preferred using these loans to buy an expensive foreign system to buying a cheaper Chinese one. This involved two considerations. First, if it was a 20-year deferred loan, the official who took out the loan would not be in that post when the time came to repay it. Second, purchasing a foreign system might well mean a free tour abroad for some officials!

However, there were opportunities for HJD-04, considering that, first, applying for a soft loan takes time and the result was not always positive; and, second, even if it is successful, buying in a foreign system may be slow. Since profits in the telecommunications service were very high, the investment could be returned in a short time. In this circumstance, buying HJD-04 was also a reasonable option.

In order to compete with foreign products, LTEF introduced some new policies. As some users were too poor to afford this product, LTEF made its payment policies more flexible, and even allowed some to pay less. LTEF had been holding information exchange meetings with current and potential users about one to three times a year to introduce HJD-04 technology to them, to collect feedback from users and, in the meantime, sell its products. For this, it made a substantial expenditure, including arranging banquets and tours for all participants around the historical spots of the city of Luoyang in order to build and maintain good relations with users. This was impossible in the past, because of state regulations over accounting at firm level. Even corruption was used as a means of selling its system. It had arranged long-distance tours for local Posts and Telecommunications Administration officials in charge of purchasing the switching system, to different places around the country, and even further – to Hong Kong, Thailand and so on. These expenditures were then added on to the cost of the system sold. The director of the firm commented about this with sorrow: 'It's not the way we would like to go deep in our hearts, but it is "a way" against "no way". We have so many mouths to feed' (Director of the LTEF, 22 April 1993). In the recent period, marketing in China had involved many complicated factors. LTEF's behaviour had been led by the reality of and the requirements from the market.

With the effort made in marketing, LTEF's exchanges were currently operating in seven provinces, including Jilin province and Inner Mongolia in a far north, Yunnan and Sichuan provinces in the west, and the neighbouring Shandong province and the home province Henan. The firm was very proud that two systems with 20 000 lines had been installed in Shenzhen, the most advanced economic zone next to Hong Kong.

Co-operation with Others

Technological innovation in the production process also demands co-operation between R&D institutes and industry. In the past, under central planning firms could get full technical support from R&D institutions in accordance with state plans without any condition. Therefore, firms like LTEF were not familiar with the new type of co-operation in a context of production for profits. The co-operation with the CIT and PTIC was such a new experience for LTEF that they were sometimes confused, as described earlier. When the three were working together on the HJD-04 and to gain official approval, the things important to maintain co-operation, such as a written document with detailed items to clarify and guarantee responsibilities and profits of each side, were overlooked. But after the technology had demonstrated its enormous potential in the market, they had to face the problems arising from the conflicts of interest emerging between them.

It made LTEF really uneasy that the core technology was held in other people's hands: for some things LTEF had to ask for CIT's instructions, and for others it had to ask PTIC. Notwithstanding this, the firm had to work together with CIT, as the system was still new and there were many adjustments to be done. Problems, small and large, arose frequently, especially in the installation field. Similarly, LTEF needed the help of PTIC in many aspects. This did not rule out LTEF's intention to reduce its dependence upon CIT and PTIC. In order to strengthen its technological capabilities, LTEF decided to establish a research institute. However, it was not that simple. It brought its best manpower into the research institute and gave them privileges in terms of better working conditions and higher rewards as well as living conditions. Although the firm's provision, in a material sense, was far from the best, the firm intended to make these people feel their future would be promising.

However, to master entirely a technology like HJD-04 is not a matter of short-term endeavour, and may not be possible under certain conditions. As the firm was engaged every day in dealing with urgent problems arising in workshops or switching offices elsewhere, these engineers could not help functioning like a fire-brigade. They worked 14 hours a day on average and even often worked overtime through the night. This situation did not allow them to engage seriously in any research work. Despite the firm's ambitions to, one day, master the entire technology of HJD-04 and be able to extricate itself from the external technological control, it remained under immediate pressure to improve production. Although LTEF was the most successful producer in general amongst all HJD-04 producers (both MPT and non-MPT), the quality of its products was still poor according to CIT. From the CIT's point of view, LTEF should concentrate on production organisation and product quality, and leave technological innovation to CIT.

As mentioned in section 4.2, LTEF was also very worried that the other HJD-04 producers would become strong rivals. The desire to prevent technology leakage to these firms made its relationship with them very sour. One producer, who once ordered some racks from LTEF, complained that LTEF was so nervous that this company might steal its technology of rack design and production that it was reluctant to supply the company with racks of good quality. As a result, that supply of racks was not usable.

4.4   THE LOCAL SHAPING OF THE ARTEFACT: THE HJD-04 SYSTEM

HJD-04 technology was shaped by the particular social, economic and technological context in which it was developed and used, as well as by global developments in information and computer technology and PDSS technologies. The development of the Chinese HJD-04 system reaped benefits because its developers adapted existing technology without going through some of the developmental stages which preceded them in advanced industrialised countries. The HJD-04 was not a new technology in the strictest sense. When the development project started in 1989, many foreign PDSSs had already been introduced in China. R&D for most of the major PDSS technologies in the world started in the 1970s. By the end of 1989, these systems had been updated and were more sophisticated. The R&D for the Chinese system HJD-04 was built upon studies on several different advanced foreign systems, so it could integrate their advantages while avoiding their disadvantages. Moreover, by then, many software design tools could be purchased on the world market and many advanced electronic components (such as microprocessors) were available cheaply. There was thus no comparison between the development of HJD-04 and the earlier PDSSs, which had to start from scratch.

As noted earlier, the R&D project for HJD-04 was carried out by computer technology experts without a background in telephone-switching technology. They came up with a system with a comparatively simple structure. The system utilised cheap imported microprocessors: for example, the MC68000 microprocessor cost only 70–80 Chinese yuan each at that time. CIT's computer specialists were able to make a full-scale HJD-04 system, incorporating 1900 microprocessors, at a reasonable cost. The whole system only took about 2.4 Mb memory, while its software was packed on to only two diskettes.

As a latecomer, the HJD-04 had several special features. Significantly, its switching network consisted of a single time (T) switch. This is a 'duplicated T switching network', which is non-blocking with respect to call processing. The switching network consisted of up to 32 identical, relatively independent modules. The number of modules depended on the size and traffic requirements of a particular switching office. Its architecture design allowed a big processing capacity. Each switch module was capable of handling a traffic load of up to 360 Erlang with a processing capability of 2 million BHCA (busy-hour call attempts), whereas the average of the other PDSS systems was 1.2 million BHCA. If a switching office was equipped with 30 modules, and the average traffic-per-line was 0.18 Erlang,[76] the switching office could handle 60 000 equivalent lines. This capacity was large enough to meet most switching office requirements in China; it was equivalent to that of a business environment in North America. Additionally, the structure of each module was identical, and interconnection between modules was via cables linking the buffer memories of each module. This design allowed for extensive office expansion, since the modules could be located anywhere within the pre-defined distance laid down in the design specification (Chen, Yan and Li, 1993).

The HJD-04 system was not as sophisticated as advanced foreign systems. However, its development had kept pace with major user demands. The process of technological development was shaped by the exigencies of the market. Because of the constraints of time and finance, the project could only concentrate on those features necessary for the basic functions of a switching system which were required by a majority of its users.

The Chinese telecommunications market was as disparate as the nation's economic development – that is to say, demand was increasing rapidly in the south and east coast areas and big cities, while remaining very low in the west and especially the countryside. In advanced areas, users demanded sophisticated services, while in less-advanced areas, users required only the simplest adequate telephone lines. The specifications laid down by MPT had not requested advanced functions such as ISDN (Integrated Services Digital Network) and IN (Intelligent

Networks). Although many advanced systems installed in China had such functions, they had not been used by then. The HJD-04 project was planned in accordance with this reality: the use of the No.7 signalling system would be realised by the end of 1994, whereas ISDN and IN capabilities would be completed within the following few years, in line with user requirements.

Apart from flexibility, another target of HJD-04 was to keep its price low, in order to compete with advanced foreign systems in the market. In spite of the inefficiency of production in state-owned companies, and unfavourable tariff status until the end of 1993, the price of the HJD-04 was still lower than foreign PDSSs. Of the many foreign PDSS systems, Japanese ones and System-12 produced by Shanghai Bell were slightly cheaper than the others. Still, System-12 cost over 1000 Chinese yuan per line, whereas the HJD-04 was currently about 850 yuan.[77] As had been planned, when the volume of production increased, the price would decrease, and when the import tariff was waived it would no doubt fall further still. In addition, when buying System-12, users had to pay part of the price in foreign currency; this did not apply with HJD-04. Foreign systems were simply too expensive for low-level users and in any case were not necessary in terms of local demands.

As a Chinese-developed system, the HJD-04 design had been targeted on local network conditions and requirements. As indicated in section 3.2, in China, transmission quality and transmission lines varied greatly in different areas. The lower the network level, the poorer the conditions were. Foreign systems were rarely able to work under these circumstances. In addition, because of the combination of low telephone penetration rate and high demand throughout the country, most telephone lines were located in public services and each telephone set was used very intensively. Many foreign systems were designed around presumptions of lower usage of lines and had run into problems in this situation, sometimes even leading to breakdowns in the local network. The HJD-04, with a processing capacity of 2 million BHCA, was designed to overcome this problem. Apart from that, the HJD-04 screen menu was in Chinese, whereas all foreign systems used English. (Outside the big cities, it might be difficult to find operators who could understand English – see section 3.2.) Moreover, the HJD-04 system had a simple interface between operator and machine which made the system easy to run.

While all foreign companies were aiming at large cities, the Chinese system was aimed at lower levels in China's hierarchical public telecommunications network. Apart from the three international gateways, there were five levels in the public network: levels one to four (known as C1, C2, C3, C4) were transit switches, and level five (known as C5) was comprised of terminal switches. There were eight level-one (C1) transit switching centres; 22 level-two (C2) transit switching centres were located in the capital cities of provinces or autonomous regions; level-three (C3) transit switching centres were located in each district and level-four switches (C4) at the county level; and level-five (C5) terminal switches were located in every major city and town. The HJD-04 system could be used at C4 level or lower (although technologically it was designed also to meet the require-ments at C3 level). It had a capacity of approximately 30 000 subscriber lines and could be used as local or tandem (toll) switches. Up till 1993, the C3 and higher levels were dominated by foreign systems. However, there was a large market for the HJD-04 at the lower levels, which foreign systems either had not yet focused on or had difficulties in entering, because of the poor network conditions.

The HJD-04 developers developed a market strategy targeted on the large market for smaller C4 and C5 switches – its modular design allowed exchanges to be supplied according to the local capacity requirements (and expanded as demand grew). Within this strategy, the further development of the HJD-04 was planned as a remote terminal module. This would be very suitable for telephone exchanges in the countryside, where telephone stations are widely dispersed and the density of the network is low. To aid diffusion into these areas, it was intended that the suppliers would take responsibility for training operators and maintenance technicians on behalf of users. Since most of these areas had poor transportation, which made it inefficient to send service engineers to solve problems in person, users were allowed to adjust some software data in their local office when necessary.

4.5 SUMMARY AND CONCLUSION

The HJD-04 system emerged as a particular product of the social and economic environment in China during the transitional period. Polit-ical and economic pressures led the CIT military research team to turn to civil technology, and Professor Wu's personal experiences drew his attention particularly to modern switching technologies. These stimulated the initiation of the project. However, to develop a Chinese PDSS required: (a) computer technology expertise; (b) first-hand knowledge of switching technology and the Chinese telecommunications system; and (c) finance and political resources. Later on, the broader social context was again important. It drove the Centre for Information Technology (CIT), the Posts and Telecommunications Industrial Corporation (PTIC) and Luoyang Telephone Equipment Factory (LTEF) into a three-party coalition. With their respective strengths in financial, political and technical fields, the three made an effective collaboration.

The process can be seen as involving two phases. In the stage of technology creation, the project was unstable and vulnerable in the face of uncertainties and difficulties (relating to both technological and administrative aspects). The three parties worked hard together to overcome technical and financial problems, and to appeal for regulatory approval, in particular from MPT. However, once the development project succeeded and its potential market was recognised, the search for profit came to the fore. In this context, tensions developed between the parties and new conflicts began to undermine the co-operation between them. Nevertheless, common interests still ultimately bound them together.

We can see that during this process the changing behaviour of individual parties was significantly shaped by the broader social, economic and political environment of China's transition. MPT's attitudes, state policies and technology users' interest, as well as the development of the market mechanism, all played roles in this process.

The contributions of economic reforms to this technological development have been at least twofold: bringing in advanced technologies from abroad, and introducing the market mechanism. The latter created an environment for integrating technological development with economic development, which brought in pressures as well as incentives for R&D institutes, firms and organisations like PTIC to seek new technological opportunities. This development project *per se,* and such co-operation among organisations in general, are newly emerging in the transition. The PDSS was a relatively complex technology, and its development project required many different kinds of technical expertise as well as large financial investment and regulatory approval; a development project like this, initiated outside of state arrangements, had rarely happened in the past. Similarly, the type of co-operation between CIT, LTEF and PTIC was certainly a new phenomenon in the country. So were the problems and difficulties they encountered, and the conflicts between them during the development process.

The way in which the socio-technical constituency of HJD-04 technology was built exemplifies the new institutional relations, offering greater technological dynamism, which are emerging in society with the introduction of market mechanisms. However, this provides evidence that market competition is a two-edged sword. On the one hand, it compelled firms and other agents relevant to technological activities to seek technological opportunities and co-operation, encouraging technological changes in line with local demands and strengthening indigenous technological capabilities. On the other hand, it put pressures on them to keep technology secret from each other and therefore damaged the inter-firm co-operation and co-operation between different technical and social agents which were necessary for further technological innovation.

A state-owned firm like LTEF was pushed into organisational reform and a continuing technological learning process. Even some corrupt measures were adopted by LTEF in reaction to the emerging competitive market economy to survive in the new system of China's transition. As the previous traditions had not been completely removed and the new mechanism was still in the process of developing, many confusing elements arose in the course of transition – for example, an incomplete legislative system for protecting intellectual property rights or poorly established markets – which presented obstacles to technological collaboration. As a result, the process of building up indigenous technological capabilities at firm level proved to be uneven and unstable, heavily dependent on the contingencies of its particular setting and broader social changes.

The state proved to have played an important role during the transition period in many aspects. This case study suggests that the Chinese government's policies were essential in promoting PDSS technology development. Buying in and transferring advanced foreign technologies, meant that domestic technology development could start from a higher base line, whilst it provided opportunities for the Chinese to accumulate knowledge of different public digital switching systems. The government policy of decentralising financial control in constructing the telecommunications infrastructure facilitated this process. In addition, more sophisticated foreign technologies set standards for local technology development, whilst the existence of local technologies on the market reined in the price of foreign products.

Because that, as noted above, the effects of market forces are contradictory, and the pursuit of self-interest by individual firms can produce negative consequences for wider co-operation. In such cases, government intervention in general can be crucial. For example, by introducing measures to enhance the linkages between R&D institutes and industries, and for completing the legislative system relevant to ownership of technology and regulating market competition, it can promote the best use of available material and human resources within the country. As the LTEF case shows, technological capabilities in the firm were still at a very basic level. Some of the key issues to be addressed related to labour development, changing people's perception of product quality, getting proper production equipment, developing routine quality control procedures, etc. Without its co-operation with CIT and PTIC, LTEF would not have been able to develop any advanced technology like HJD-04. State intervention in controlling the pace of economic reform was also necessary. As the LTEF case shows, the large scale of labour redundancy of state-owned firms in pursuing high productivity might have serious consequences.

From a technological point of view, HJD-04 had unique features, shaped by both social and technical elements involved in the development process. The most obvious 'socio-technical' features of HJD-04 includes the special composition of the R&D team, which consisted of CIT's computer designers and LTEF's switching technicians; their knowledge crossed computer techniques, switching applications in the Chinese telecommunication network and MPT's specifications of it. By obtaining advanced technological information, development tools and cheap standardised electronic products (components) available in the international market the local development of PDSS like HJD-04 was made possible. The complex and convoluted process of development in the context of China's economic and social transition, included diverse factors such as the financial, market, cultural and political context. Features from the local development context were imprinted in the main features of HJD-04 which were adapted to local needs. Thus, it was capable of handling a dense traffic load – a challenge which had caused breakdowns of many foreign systems used in China. It had a simple machine–operator interface, a Chinese-language screen menu and a flexible maintenance strategy. In addition, its development had been in line with users' requirements for low prices.

As described so far, the process of building up the socio-technical constituency of PDSS HJD-04 had been completed in a relatively short time – from November 1989, when three parties all agreed to develop a full-size PDSS, to October 1992, when the technology was put in production and its technical features were able to meet the needs of the majority of its users. The case suggests that it is possible for a developing country to speed up its technological development by reaping benefits from existing overseas technologies. Although the Chinese HJD-04 system was not as sophisticated as advanced foreign systems, it was, arguably, more appropriate for the unsophisticated condition of the Chinese network, and much cheaper. This raises questions, which we shall return to in Chapter 5, about the range of strategies available for utilising foreign advanced technological capabilities to build up indigenous technological capabilities through effective technology transfer, and their consequences.

Another closely related issue concerns the national system of innovation. We have concluded that the current success of HJD-04 development and the collaboration (and conflicts) between CIT, LTEF and PTIC were associated with the broader social context in China which has been transforming from a centrally planned to a more market oriented economy. The question remains as to whether the further development of the Chinese HJD-04 system will be able to keep pace with global technological development, and the rapidly changing market. The further innovation of the Chinese PDSS depends largely on co-operative effort of many agents relevant to the technological activities in the whole country, as well as on the improvement of production capabilities at the firm-level. The problems facing the three parties involved in HJD-04 shows that the future remains unpredictable, even though the market is large and growing; it is uncertain whether the social and economic transition in China will continue to improve the technological dynamism of the entire system. These issues will be further explored in Chapter 6.

A Postscript

At the time that my fieldwork for this study ended, HJD-04, despite its undoubted achievements, still faced uncertainties, regarding its further commercial and technological development. In February 1998, five years later, I revisited China and was able to obtain some additional information about the Chinese telecommunications industry. Two news stories in particular threw light on the subsequent development of the Chinese PDSS industry:

The production of HJD-04 Programme Controlled Switchboards by our country has changed the situation of the domination of imported switchboard in China. The national switchboard industry made a breakthrough and has realised the exportation of switch-boards made in China.

As a leader of national switchboard production, GDT [Great Dragon Telecommunication (Group) Co., Ltd.] has sold ten million lines of HJD-04 programme controlled switchboards.

(*China Daily*, 28 August 1997, p. 3)

Now, PDSS products developed by ourselves [Chinese] have achieved a market share of 14%. Last year, over 5 000 000 locally developed PDSS (lines) were installed, and amongst the total new exchanges installed in the local telecommunication networks 23.4% were locally developed ones.

(*People's Daily* (overseas edition), 8 September 1997, p. 2)

This news about HJD-04 compelled me to arrange further telephone interviews with Mr Zhang Fengzhou (the key figure previously handling the HJD-04 project in PTIC, MPT) and Professor Wu. The HJD-04's future seems brighter than ever.

These revealed that the Great Dragon Telecommunication (Group) Co., Ltd. was established in 1995 through a co-operative effort by the State Science and Technology Commission, the Ministry of Electronics (formerly MMEI) and the Ministry of Posts and Telecommunications. The company is a collaboration between CIT and nine HJD-04 producers, including LTEF and the other HJD-04 producers under MPT and MMEI. It is in the process of reorganisation in order to make the HJD-04 production management, sourcing, and marketing more effective and efficient. LTEF is now the leading firm among the nine members, while CIT was transformed to the R&D base for the Great Dragon Telecommunication (Group) Co., Ltd. Professor Wu was the leading figure for the establishment of the corporation, and has been board chairman ever since.

Although it was not possible to investigate the detailed processes involved in this development, it is clear that the hitherto fragmented HJD-04 production facilities have been reorganised with the support of once-rival ministries, MPT, MMEI and central government, united under the single banner of the Great Dragon Telecommunication (Group) Co., Ltd. This group seems to have been successful in overcoming the production and marketing difficulties that threatened to hinder the prospects of the HJD-04 system.

The Great Dragon Telecommunication Group has achieved production capacity of 8 000 000 lines annually and sales revenues

4 000 000–500 000 000 yuan (RMB).[78] The price of HJD-04 is kept at as low as 70–80 per cent of other PDSS products; HJD-04's market share is expected to be 15–20 per cent of the estimated 20 000 000 lines of total domestic demand for PDSS; HJD-04 has been exported to some Asian and South American countries including Russia and some other former Soviet countries, Brazil, India, Cuba, etc. Some joint production projects were in process. Technically, the IN-equipped HJD-04 has been successfully operating in the public telecommunication network for over two years, and further developments (e.g. new concepts related to GSM mobile telephony and the Distributed Mobile Switching Centre technology) have been patented in China. Indeed the Chinese-developed PDSS has made remarkable achievements in production, market and technology alike.

Part III
Comparison and Analysis

5 Acquisition of Advanced Technological Capabilities

This chapter begins the process of analysing the detailed case-study findings presented in Chapters 3 and 4. By comparing and contrasting the processes of technological innovation in these two cases it seeks to throw light on the central concern of this study – how developing countries can accumulate indigenous technological capabilities and the contribution to this of advanced technology transfer from abroad. The next chapter will then seek to explicate the influence of the broader social setting, which was changing as a result of China's economic reform and transition.

Chapter 2 argued that the key for success in accumulating endogenous technological capabilities rested with the effective utilisation of exogenous capabilities. This study has shown that there is a range of different strategies and choices in selecting both particular technologies for transfer and particular types of technology transactions. Which strategy is chosen may depend on the objectives and requirements of the developing country. For example, what level and type of competence is needed? Is innovation competence required as well as productive capacity? Is there a difference between long and short-term goals?

This chapter examines these questions in detail through a comparative analysis of how China has acquired PDSS technological capabilities in the cases of System-12 and HJD-04. The analysis focuses mainly on how the characteristics of the different technologies and the type of transfer processes affect the possibility for China to gain access to appropriate foreign advanced technologies. It also examines the scope for local shaping of these technologies, and finally explores how these two strategies worked in the changing circumstances during China's economic reforms.

5.1 SELECTIVELY UTILISING FOREIGN TECHNOLOGIES: CONTRASTING THE SYSTEM-12 AND HJD-04 CASES

Chapter 2 introduced the idea that the nature of imported technology and the type of technology transaction together set the parameters of both the availability and appropriability of exogenous technological competencies embodied in imported technologies and the scope for local shaping of these imported technologies. Recipient countries can use different strategies for utilising foreign advanced technology to meet domestic requirements. This includes selecting different ranges and types of technology, e.g. between comprehensive 'system technologies' versus an array of more discrete 'component technologies' and between different types of transaction, varying between wholesale technology transfer and the purchase of finished commodified products.

Different Approaches

The System-12 case looks like the archetypal example of technology transfer – acquiring indigenous capacity by utilising foreign advanced technologies. Paradoxically, on further consideration so is the HJD-04 case, which in other ways was an indigenously developed PDSS. However, these two cases are very different in many aspects. First, drawing on the theoretical framework developed in Chapter 2, we can see that the artefacts imported in these two cases have very different characteristics. System-12 can be characterised as a 'system technology' (although it has application layers which are configurable), and the foreign technologies that the Chinese system HJD-04 comprises are 'component technologies'. A 'system technology' involves complexes of elements which mutually condition and constrain one another and which has its own more-or-less unique proprietary architecture and elements. A 'system technology' like System-12 involves a wide range of foreign components, e.g. LSI chips, microprocessors and other components, which had already been configured into a particular architecture before being transferred into China. These artefacts embodied foreign developers' technological, social and economic knowledge and rationales, and reflected the technological competencies which they had accumulated over time. This is in sharp contrast to 'component technologies' which are generally designed to be used in conjunction with other technological elements, building on standard interfaces, and are often available as cheap commodities in international markets (section 2.4).

Second, these two cases adopted extremely different types of technology transfer transactions. System-12 is a wholesale technology transfer project, which included the provision of manufacturing, engineering, and installation technologies, as well as management skills. A highly formalised and carefully planned process of technology transfer was adopted to ensure the transfer of all the skills needed to create productive capability for System-12 in China. In contrast, the HJD-04 technology development project involved importing foreign standardised components as building blocks for the system, based on an architecture designed by the Chinese. In addition, software design tools and some production facilities which China did not possess were purchased from abroad. Exogenous technological expertise was thus acquired, embodied in artefacts – artefacts that were themselves designed to be appropriable. This was underpinned and supplemented by the informal acquisition by the Centre for Information Technology (CIT) of general knowledge of global developments with PDSS technologies.

A 'system technology' like System-12 is much more difficult to master than the 'component technologies' that the HJD-04 system is using. In the HJD-04 case, imported foreign standardised components could be used for building PDSS exchanges. China could buy them in and deploy these components without needing to acquire all the capabilities required to develop or produce them. It would seem to be impossible to master a technology like System-12 without a comprehensive package of technology transfer. Equally, wholesale technology transfer like System-12 almost inevitably requires a large capital input, whereas the standardised components for HJD-04 were widely and cheaply available on the world market. This contrast highlights the enormous scope for choice about the extent to which a country imports these component technologies, rather than investing money and effort to produce them locally.

The availability of foreign technology depends largely on the way in which it is purchased and the means of technological learning. Buying-in finished foreign products obviously provides the least access to the technological competencies which are embodied in the artefacts and black-boxed before the delivery. (On the other hand, these artefacts were typically designed to be usable in this way, without the need to acquire these competencies – and the fact that such components are readily and cheaply available reduced the financial and strategic importance of acquiring such competencies locally.) In comparison, wholesale technology transfer provides access to a wide range of technological capabilities spanning from knowledge about the production of the artefacts to management techniques. Contrasting the two different approaches, clearly, the System-12 case provides much more extensive means than HJD-04 for the Chinese to gain access to advanced foreign technologies. System-12 technology transfer was, moreover, carefully planned, negotiated and formalised in a written contract.

On the other hand, we can see that the wholesale transaction of System-12 production capacities allowed very limited access to technology creating and innovating capacities. Even the capacity to adapt System-12 that was needed to match the characteristics of the Chinese telecommunications system, was confined to the application layers. Moreover, the export capacity of the Shanghai Bell joint venture was also substantially constrained as this would cut across BTM's interests in the world market (section 3.3). The Chinese HJD-04 case represents a very different model. Standardised foreign components and tools were purchased and used straight away in the design and production of the exchanges, without the need to obtain mastery over their design or production. Compared to System-12, the HJD-04 development required more creative effort on the part of the Chinese participants or actors. This context provided better opportunities for integrating the technical features of the system with local technological, economic and political requirements.

When considering differences between the System-12 and HJD-04 cases we must not forget that they were initiated at different stages of China's economic reforms. The broad social and economic contexts surrounding these two cases were so different that the driving forces and strategies by which they built up their own sociotechnical constituencies were markedly different. Different approaches were required for establishing their own technological capabilities, and particularly in marketing, resource allocation and management. As the social and economic context is so crucial for technological learning, this will be discussed more thoroughly in Chapter 6.

The final difference concerns the scope to shape and adapt the technology to meet particular local requirements, which differed substantially between the two cases. A technology, even a completed PDSS exchange technology like System-12, has to be adapted to meet the circumstances in which it will be used, and as noted in earlier chapters, the Chinese telecommunications system was a particularly challenging technical and social context.

Different Scope for Local Shaping of Technology

Both the nature of technology itself and the type of technology transfer transaction constrain the scope for local shaping. Contrasting the

System-12 case and the HJD-04 case, System-12 as a system has much less scope for local adaptation than a Chinese PDSS like HJD-04 which is made up from an assemblage of imported discrete components. The extent to which novel technological elements were developed indigenously was clearly far greater in the design of HJD-04 than in the limited level of adaptation to local markets which took place in System-12.

Because of the complexity of public switching technology, its application package has to be customised to meet the requirements of the particular country. We have seen that Shanghai Bell had gradually overcome the incompatibility between System-12 and the poor conditions and un-standardised features in the Chinese telecommunications network – by, for instance, developing ancillary equipment to help System-12 identify signals from the telecommunications network and by customising the CDE packages.

However, in System-12, the space available for adaptation and reconfiguration is limited, largely within the domain of the application layers. The fact that the generic part of the system is shared by all System-12 producers and users across the world allows little chance for the Chinese to make innovative changes to the technological core. We have seen that hardly any further development of System-12 technology had taken place in Shanghai Bell – either in the system *per se* or in its production technologies including equipment, process design and operation techniques. Rather, such technological changes were carried out in the parent company, and then fed down to Shanghai Bell. The most significant local adaptation activities were limited to the area of customer application technologies and human-factor-related management, e.g. the local development of some application software and the development of a distinctive hybrid management style in the production facility.

Since the generic technical features of System-12 were deeply embedded in its design, some of them could not be changed without considerable expense. For example, System-12 used the English language for its operator–machine interface: in theory, this could be changed into the Chinese written language but, because of the complexity of this task, it is not currently economical. Another example is System-12's limited capacity to handle the dense traffic loads often encountered in China, which caused breakdowns (section 3.2). This problem highlights the presumptions underpinning the technical design, which were to meet the requirements in an industrialised environment rather than those typical of poor countries like China.

By contrast, building a PDSS from an assemblage of imported discrete components, as in the HJD-04 system, leaves great scope for local configuration. Professor Wu and his team were able to develop a Chinese switching system to meet the technological, economic and cultural requirements of the local context and conditions for local production and operation, as well as international standards of telecommunications. CIT's core competencies in computer design, and LTEF's competencies in rack design and production and its understanding of the Chinese telecommunications network, were configured together with an array of available discrete foreign technologies – electronic components and development tools plus some foreign design concepts. As a result, HJD-04 is arguably the most suitable for the Chinese telecommunications network. It is also the easiest of the two systems to operate and maintain as it does not require operators who speak English. Being purposefully designed for the Chinese context, there is no problem of handling dense traffic loads. In addition, because the core technology is held in the hand of Chinese developers, further updating and innovation is possible.

However, in the case of HJD-04, because of the type of 'technology transfer' transaction – purchasing finished component technologies – the technological competencies embodied in these products, e.g. component design and production technologies, are black-boxed. As there is no clearly defined access to them for recipients, there is virtually no scope for their local shaping. On the other hand, there was little need to get inside these technologies. The microprocessors in particular offered generic technical functions that were rather transparently presented (price, processing power). They combined presumptions about their *technical context* of use – though these were features (e.g. particular functions, languages, interfaces) that were largely standardised at an international level – but made few specific constraints and presumptions about the *application context*. They could therefore be deployed as 'black-boxed' solutions by the Chinese developers. In this sense, local shaping was restricted to the choice of processors available on the market. But that did not matter. These processors were readily available on the market as cheap and standardised commodities. As far as the Chinese developers were concerned, it was cheaper, simpler and less risky to buy-in these technologies than seek to acquire locally the design and production competencies for building the necessary complex integrated circuits.

Different Strategies to Meet Domestic Demands

At the very beginning of the economic reforms, China lacked PDSS technological capabilities (both overall PDSS production capacity and capacity to build constituent components) while domestic demand for adequate telecommunications infrastructure was pressing. The wholesale transfer of System-12 seemed to be the best solution under these circumstances. This project helped China to build up production capacity in PDSS from scratch, thus more or less satisfying the increasing domestic demands for modern telecommunications services.

The System-12 technology transfer provided formally defined means and a broad avenue for the Chinese to gain access to a wide range of advanced foreign technologies, ranging from component production to production management. The flow of technological information from industrialised countries to China (as a nation, above and beyond that to Shanghai Bell) through the System-12 transfer project was substantial. The later design of system HJD-04 had, to some extent, also benefited from this informal flow of technological information into China (section 4.1). Even in developing its production facilities and management approaches, LTEF sought help by sending delegations to Shanghai Bell to explore suitable solutions (section 4.2). Equally significant was that Shanghai Bell, through its programme of domesticating component production, enabled transfer of advanced foreign technologies to local industries, creating components-production facilities to meet world quality standards and technologies (section 3.2). In a sense, without the wholesale PDSS technology transfer through System-12 or a similar project, the indigenous technological development of HJD-04 might not have been possible.

However, a wholesale technology transfer requires enormous investment and resource inputs. The selection of the particular technology for transfer is very crucial. In the case of System-12, the aims of the PDSS technology transfer were very clear. China sought the most advanced technology and the latest version of its development and a technology which was suitable for the Chinese telecommunications environment. To ensure the transaction would provide China with adequate means to obtain advanced technologies in both the short and long term, and limit technological dependency, it was important for the Chinese to insist on an experienced and reputable technology supaplier and a comprehensive package of technology transfer including the specified LSI chip production at the heart of System-12. This was moreaover a technological field in which China nationally was rather weak.

As discussed above, System-12 technology is difficult for a developing country like China to master. To function properly, it also requires adaptation to the Chinese telecommunications environment. Because China's telecommunications condition was so poor, and because of substantial technological and cultural differences from Europe and North America (where System-12 development took place), this technological undertaking was very difficult for China. In such circumstances, the Chinese selection of the technology and the type of technology transaction involved a high risk of failure. The System-12 case confirms the enormous difficulties that Shanghai Bell faced particularly in the early stages of production and installation of the exchanges (for more details see section 3.2). Without substantial and sustained support by the Chinese government, the whole project of technology transfer would have failed.

The Chinese system HJD-04 might not be as sophisticated as System-12, but it provides the Chinese telecommunications network with a PDSS which is able to meet user requirements that most foreign systems could not provide, in particular handling a dense traffic load. Compared with foreign systems, HJD-04 had a simple machine–operator interface, with a Chinese-language screen menu, so as to be easy to operate. Because of its low development and production costs, the system offers low prices to Chinese users, which are particularly important to those in less-developed and rural areas.

Most important to China is the coexistence of a foreign PDSS like System-12 and a local one like HJD-04, which creates a dual-development environment. First, resorting to foreign PDSSs provides a source of advanced technologies – which are continually developing globally. Through both the international market and proprietary channels (e.g. BTM), Chinese companies (e.g. LTEF and Shanghai Bell) can keep in touch with the state of the art. Second, this provides a competitive environment, which, on the one hand, sets up high standards for Chinese products and, on the other, reins in the price of foreign PDSSs and motivates the further transfer of upgraded versions of these technologies.

5.2   TECHNOLOGICAL LEARNING

In the chapter on theory (Chapter 2), technological learning was defined as the means by which exogenous technological capabilities are transformed into indigenous technological capabilities. Substantial technological learning took place in both the System-12 and the HJD-04 cases. The range of learning activities includes formally organised learning (such as staff and customer training courses arranged by both Shanghai Bell and LTEF) and the domestication of component production. The System-12 technology transfer utilised at least four different means for the Chinese in Shanghai Bell to obtain technological competencies: technological training, technical assistance from BTM's experts, BTM management participation in the joint venture, and the transfer of technological documents (section 3.2). Through these formalised means, the Chinese in Shanghai Bell have systematically obtained skills for manufacturing, installation and maintenance, as well as engineering technologies for System-12. Western managerial methods and values were also introduced into Shanghai Bell. This helped Shanghai Bell to develop its own strategies and policies for marketing, resource allocation and management. It allowed Shanghai Bell to achieve high productivity. As production quality is one of the most common problems in China's industry, the help of BTM's quality control specialist, who at the outset set up the routines for Shanghai Bell to gradually bring production quality up to world level, was critical.

Technological learning has not been solely confined to Shanghai Bell. Rather it has been widely spread through both informal and formal channels to System-12 users, component producers, and other related agents. The movement of Shanghai Bell's engineers to other establishments (R&D institutes, universities, firms, etc.) provided one means for the transfer of technological information across China. Many of the engineers and researchers who were gathered by MPT from across the country to help the System-12 project, subsequently returned to their original institutes, and thereafter used their knowledge of System-12 to carry out some technological projects for Shanghai Bell (section 3.2). Some of these specialists even contributed to the development (or at least recognition) of HJD-04 technology – being enlisted by MPT for the examination of HJD-04 for technical approval (section 4.1).

Unlike Shanghai Bell, in the HJD-04 case, technological learning was to a considerable degree through informal channels. Professor Wu, the key designer for HJD-04, acquired information about System-12 and other foreign PDSS through publicly available documents (section 4.1). LTEF sought information about production equipment and management through Shanghai Bell (section 4.2). Interestingly, it learned the importance of production quality through its *customers* whose quality standards for the Chinese system were set by foreign advanced products that had become available in the Chinese PDSS market. Apparently, market competition drove LTEF into an intensive learning cycle in order to improve its technological capabilities (section 4.2).

Informal and formal learning activities like these have taken place in almost all the players, involving not only those involved directly in the System-12 technology transfer and HJD-04 development projects, but also PDSS users, installation engineering teams (section 3.3), MPT's R&D institutes and the universities which helped Shanghai Bell to achieve System-12 adaptation and market expansion. More widespread learning activities encompass local industries, in particular System-12 component producers (section 3.4). The achievement of System-12 production capabilities required the involvement of a wide range of players within Shanghai Bell to inculcate not only understanding of manufacturing processes but also wider recognition of the importance of quality as well as production volumes.

As noted in Chapter 2, a supportive social and economic environment is crucial in providing incentives for technological learning. Without it, even formalised technological learning may be inefficient and incomplete. This was demonstrated in the case of System-12. The government's attempts to organise domestication of System-12 component production was not very successful in the beginning, because Shanghai Bell and local producers lacked appropriate incentives. A very different situation emerged, at a later stage, when local production of System-12 components became in the interests of Shanghai Bell and local industries. Both Shanghai Bell and local industries were seeking co-operation opportunities, and local producers became active in technological learning to improve their technological capabilities.

5.3　CHINA'S PDSS TECHNOLOGICAL CAPABILITIES

The two cases of System-12 and HJD-04 show that, from the viewpoint of the entire country, China now possesses a wide range of PDSS technological capabilities, from creation and design to production, installation, operation and maintenance. The development of technological capabilities in PDSS production, operation and services in China as a whole was extremely successful, through advanced technology transfer from industrialised countries, and in particular wholesale technology transfer. In the case of System-12, production capacity had expanded rapidly, from 15 000 lines in 1987 to 2 700 000 lines in 1993, during seven years' production (section 3.2). Shanghai Bell's productivity even out-performed BTM (section 3.3). Production capabilities for System-12 components have also been gradually established and upgraded, e.g. the custom LSI chips, an advanced technology in international terms (although quality was still a problem at that time).

However, individual firms are still at the stage of accumulating basic technological capabilities. As we have seen in both cases, the state of production capabilities in China was extremely poor, especially in relation to production engineering, quality control, and production management. This backwardness stemmed from the old centrally planned system, and the weak links not only between technology designers and producers, but also with technology users. Most technology designers lacked a sense of commercial issues; producers were mainly 'plan-takers'; and technology users were accustomed to having no choice but to accept what producers produced. This situation has begun to change since the economic reforms and the progressive introduction of market mechanisms. We can see that the manufacturing firms involved in both cases have gradually established capabilities in marketing and resource allocation, and have also been compelled by market pressures to improve production quality and efficiency. However, improving these basic technological capabilities is obviously a long-term task – not least because it is associated with the whole economic system, and a wide range of people within it. For example, to ensure the quality of System-12, Shanghai Bell had first of all to improve the production quality and quality control of each component when their sourcing was domesticated. This required an effort by local producers (as we saw in relation to the production of LEDs, resistors and even the screws used on the switches (section 3.4)).

There are very few firms like Shanghai Bell that possess these basic technological capabilities at firm level. Both these cases remind us that most state-owned companies involved in either System-12 component production or the Chinese HJD-04 manufacture were still struggling to improve their production quality and productivity, and to build up from scratch their capabilities in marketing, resource allocation and management. Even LTEF, which can be considered the most successful and major producer of HJD-04 exchanges, still had a long way to go to catch up with Shanghai Bell. In April 1993, its production capacity was merely 80 000 lines, compared with Shanghai Bell's then annual capacity of 2 700 000 lines.

Given China's urgent need to modernise its telecommunications infrastructure and provide adequate telecommunications services to underpin rapid economic growth, the development of production capabilities was arguably the most important priority for the country at that stage and more immediately significant than developing the capabilities to innovate telecommunications technologies. The development of these basic production capabilities to overcome the poor state of the telecommunications and electronics sectors was necessary and could also provide the basis for higher-level technological competencies in future.

The development of production capabilities required a quantum jump in production technologies in these sectors. No less important was recognition of the need to bring production quality in line with world-wide standards in terms of reliability and accuracy (both are particularly crucial for switching technology, but have a more general relevance). And this depended upon development of 'non-technical' capabilities, such as marketing (including recognition of the importance of user-requirements), production management and quality control and, crucially, understanding of all these issues by the workforce as a whole. To the extent that these objectives were attained, there was considerable scope for domestication of production – as demonstrated in the case of System-12 component supply. The Chinese domestic market is huge. And low Chinese wage costs could offset the weaker base in production technology, keeping Chinese production competitive with foreign supply.

The Capability of Innovation and Creation

Whilst developing production capacity had the most obvious immediate economic importance for a country like China, the indigenous capabilities to create and innovate technologies have been seen as more strategic in the long term in allowing China to avoid technological dependence on foreign firms and foreign market supply, as well as enhancing opportunities to meet local needs. At the firm level, Chinese switch producers are very weak in terms of technology innovating capabilities. Even Shanghai Bell, the most successful PDSS producer, had limited activities in PDSS technology innovation. This is due partly to the model of System-12 technology transfer, and partly to China's existing technological capabilities. Moreover, as Shanghai Bell was at the stage of rapid expansion of its production facilities, and its products were in constant and high demand, it had little interest in pursuing major technological changes to System-12. Although LTEF was one of China's most modern exchange producers, and became one of the three key developers of the Chinese HJD-04 system (with a strong technical base), it never seemed to be able to acquire the capabilities to carry out any research, development or innovation in PDSS on its own.

However, China has developed its own PDSS systems through co-operation between R&D institutions and industry. The Chinese HJD-04 system is the best example (though there is also the case of the DS-series). Such technological co-operation brought China as a country to a high level with regard to technological capabilities in PDSS creation and innovation.

The HJD-04 case displays the technological capabilities and ingenuity of Chinese developers, especially CIT who were able to combine foreign and local technological elements to create their own PDSS. The Chinese PDSS development took advantage of being later than that of other major PDSS technologies in the world, bypassing the often long and difficult history in PDSS design which preceding developers had been forced to confront – which involved enormous investments of time and money (Molina, 1990) – and reaped benefits from the available technologies. Most significant is that the Chinese developers were able to translate the technical challenges of PDSS development into the areas that they were good at. They utilised fully their strengths in computer technology design while bypassing their (and China's) weakness in electronic components design and production. As a result, the HJD-04 has distinctive technical features. It is not a copy of any other PDSS technologies in the world through reverse engineering or the like. HJD-04 is an extremely effective system in many respects, and moreover appropriate for the Chinese setting. The HJD-04 can cope with processing high densities of calls (a challenge for most foreign PDSSs used in China) and is easy to operate and maintain. More essential, this system is simple and easy for the Chinese to produce, given that production capabilities were poor in Chinese industries particularly in microelectronics. The Chinese HJD-04 is perhaps the only PDSS to have been developed successfully in as little as three years, by a small R&D team with only 18 people as fixed staff and with the investment of only a modest amount of money (section 4.1). Since the Chinese HJD-04 has a modular architecture and is designed to be open for future development, it allows Chinese developers to develop new technical functions (such as the No.7 signalling system, ISDN, IN, etc.)

separately, in line with Chinese users' requirements (section 4.4). This meanwhile keeps the R&D costs, and thus its market prices, at a low level.

By all these criteria, HJD-04 is a distinctive success for the Chinese. On the other hand, HJD-04 was a latecomer, compared to foreign systems like System-12, and at the time of my fieldwork its position in the Chinese PDSS market was far from secure and its production capacity far too low. Its capacity to expand was held back by the competition between MPT HJD-04 producers sponsored by MPT and their competitors under MMEI. However, the subsequent formation of a holding company to link these firms – Great Dragon Telecommunications Co. Ltd. – has done much to resolve this. By combining and co-ordinating these efforts HJD-04 has made remarkable achievements in production and marketing, and resources have been made available for further technological development. These should be attributed not only to the efforts of those directly involved – the designer Professor Wu and his team; producers like LTEF and the other key player, PTIC – but also to those of other relevant actors, such as government bodies like MPT and MMEI (now the Ministry of Electronics), the State Science and Technology Commission, etc., whose willingness to open up and expand the HJD-04 socio-technical constituency is related to changes in the broader social and economic context, and in particular to the changing institutional structures and incentives of the innovation system. Without collaboration between relevant government bodies, between R&D institutes and producers, and between producers and users, it might well have been impossible to obtain sufficient funds for the research and development needed for further technological innovation (such as that needed to improve the sophistication of HJD-04 and allow it to provide new services such as ISDN and IN), and for other improvements (for example, in production equipment). Further changes in government policy, and more progress in China's social and economic transformation, would be needed before state-owned firms like LTEF, which had inherited social burdens and continued to suffer from these, would find it possible to compete in the markets on equal terms with others.

Although the System-12 technology transfer was not designed to deliver technology innovation capabilities – and indeed could be said to have been designed *not* to deliver these – it did lead to the dissemination of PDSS technological knowledge across a network of players in the telecommunications producer and user industries and research institutes. They provided the basis for further development work on System-12 (and, indirectly, could be argued to have provided a springboard for the later HJD-04 project).

Comparative analysis of these two attempts to develop PDSS technological competence, suggests that there is not necessarily a rigid division between importing production competence (the focus of System-12 technology transfer) and developing indigenous technology innovation capacity (the focus of HJD-04). The two cases remind us that there are different routes to achieving technological capabilities. The wholesale import of production technological competence for a complete PDSS system (System-12) gave less scope for acquiring and applying innovation capabilities than the HJD-04 case, particularly in relation to the core technologies which were proprietary. However this did not prevent an important local innovation effort around adapting System-12 to Chinese circumstances. The Chinese HJD-04 development has been extremely successful in the way that it made selective use of imported technological elements – allowing the local developers to concentrate on those areas in which it was feasible and most advantageous to have indigenous development. There is considerable scope for such a selective approach that can combine pragmatic and opportunistic considerations.

Standing back from these two cases, it may be necessary to rethink earlier discussion of the 'technological dependency' thesis with its implications that only indigenous technology innovation capacity across the full range of technologies involved could avoid leaving developing countries in a dependent state. As these cases show, there are different routes for achieving technological capacity. It is possible to combine local technological capabilities flexibly with foreign technological capacities bought-in through the market (in various forms – varying from component technologies to finished solutions and the facilities to make them). The proprietary core technologies (including a dedicated LSI chip) at the heart of System-12 did pose an important constraint. On the other hand, it was not clear to what extent it would ever be desirable to seek indigenous innovation capabilities for all the elements of a complex technology such as a telephone exchange. The growth of inter-operability standards and the marketing of cheap, commodified and readily applicable tools and components represents a challenge to presumptions that the provision of technologies (even complex large-scale technologies such as PDSS exchanges) will necessarily be as finished 'system' solutions. The configuration of complex solutions from assemblages of bought-in and

1 elements is likely to become increasingly common. In this
t, technology innovation capability across the board is likely to
be unnecessary. It may also be undesirable. It potentially increases the
cost and time investment in a new technology. It may also encourage a
segregation of indigenous from global development – which in the
long term could result in local stagnation and loss of economic and

technological competitiveness. The development of new technologies
is becoming an increasingly global activity – particularly in the case
of information and communication technologies with their potenti-

ally enormous development costs. Only the strongest and most
advanced economies, if at all, could afford to 'go it alone'. Most
countries (and all developing countries, surely) will be faced with
resorting to global markets in addition to domestic development and
production – thereby reducing the costs and risks of wholesale
development.

Also at the firm level, the continued involvement of overseas
suppliers was seen as beneficial in that it kept Chinese firms in contact
with global developments – not only in the HJD-04 case but also in
the supply of components for Shanghai Bell. Technology production
in a dynamic and global sector like ICT (Information and Communication Technology) is likely to revolve around combinations of local
production and resort to the global market.

The other way in which the dependency thesis may need revision is
in its privileging of innovation over production capabilities. Despite
the undoubtedly amazing achievements of the HJD-04 constituency, it
still faced enormous problems in increasing production capabilities.
And the limitations in technology innovation capabilities in the
System-12 case does not seem to have been overwhelming and has not
threatened the ability of Shanghai Bell from becoming the major
PDSS supplier in China. More important here was the competitive
supply of PDSS technologies (shared between overseas supply, various
joint ventures and indigenous producers) which kept product prices at
a reasonable level. The presumptions which seemed compelling at the
start of this enquiry – which prioritised the acquisition of innovation capabilities over production capabilities – do not seem to be justified by these cases. Acquisition of production capacity and domestication of component supply led to the widespread uptake of PDSS
technological competencies in the Chinese telecommunications production sector and public sector research institutes. It also made
an immediate and vital contribution to Chinese telecommunications infrastructure.

During the last fifteen years of economic reforms (1978–93), China had succeeded in both modernising switching technologies and increasing telecommunications network capacity dramatically. At the end of 1993, China's telephone lines numbered 25 million, and the penetration ratio was 20 phones per 1000 people, compared with about 4 million lines and 4 phones per 1000 people in 1978. In terms of switching technology, China leapfrogged older vintages of technology, for example, analogue automatic switches. About 98 per cent of the cross-bar switches in provincial capital cities had been replaced by digital computer programme-controlled switching systems. Many rural manual exchanges had been replaced by digital programme-controlled exchanges, and in some areas the first telephone exchanges installed directly entered the digital age! These achievements in China's telecommunications infrastructure are remarkable, considering both the rate of expansion and its poor starting position in terms of technology.

We can see it would not have been possible to achieve such a quantum jump without introducing advanced foreign PDSS technologies. Alongside directly imported finished PDSS products, locally produced foreign PDSSs, such as System-12 by Shanghai Bell, EWSD by BISC and Neax-61 by a Sino-NEC joint production venture (section 1.3), contributed greatly to the rapid development of the Chinese telecommunications infrastructure, and helped to meet China's urgent domestic demands for adequate telecommunications services. In 1993, Shanghai Bell's share in the PDSS market was as high as 50 per cent (section 3.3), let alone the other two joint PDSS production ventures.

Chinese PDSSs also played a part in the improvement of the Chinese telecommunications network services. Though small, this contribution was important. As the economic development as well as existing telecommunications network conditions in different areas of China varies to a considerable extent, many inland districts and rural areas lag far behind the coastal urban areas and large cities. Thus demands for telecommunications services from inland districts or rural areas are often different from those of large cities. They are often not able to afford expensive foreign PDSS exchanges. Apart from this, because their local telecommunications network and other relevant conditions are usually poor, foreign exchanges are less suitable for them. In these circumstances, Chinese PDSSs, such as HJD-04, which were designed to meet these local requirements, being low cost and easy to operate, etc., are able to cover these areas very well.

5.4 CONCLUDING POINTS

The empirical case studies show that transferring foreign advanced technologies made a crucially important contribution to PDSS technology development in China. In the situation where indigenous PDSS technological capability is lacking, a wholesale technology transfer may be recommended; arguably, the weaker the existing technological capabilities the recipient possesses, the more a comprehensive package of technology transaction is needed.

The key requirement is *selective utilisation* of foreign technology. Here two elements are essential: the type of technology and the type of technology transaction. These two elements determine the availability and appropriability of the exogenous technological competencies which are embodied in the imported technologies. They also have an impact on the scope for local shaping of the imported technologies. The strategy used in the System-12 case can be seen as involving acquisition of a 'system technology' which embodied a wide range of advanced technologies from the industrialised world, plus foreign developers' technological, social and economic knowledge and rationales. It established the wholesale technology transfer through various formalised channels to allow the Chinese to gain access to these technologies. In contrast, the strategy adopted in the Chinese HJD-04 development involved using foreign standardised components as building blocks to create a Chinese PDSS technology to fulfil local requirements. It also used foreign production equipment and software design tools which China was lacking at that time.

Selecting a 'system technology' like System-12 seemed to be a correct choice at that time, given the circumstance that China badly needed PDSS technology. Because a 'system technology' is difficult to master, the selection of wholesale technology transfer was also necessary. As noted above, the transfer of a comprehensive package provided the Chinese in Shanghai Bell with access to virtually every technology of System-12. The weaknesses are that this strategy requires huge investments and brings technical difficulties. As it requires tackling a wide range of challenges, particularly in the production of proprietary LSI chips, there is a high risk of failure, and thus, potentially, of huge losses. Apart from this, because System-12 is a foreign-developed proprietary system, some core technologies of the system are not appropriable by the Chinese (due partly to the low existing technological capabilities and partly to the high expenses and effort that Shanghai Bell could not then afford). Because of the nature of the technology transfer transaction, the scope for social shaping of System-12 technology is confined to customising its application layers, and its export capacity is also very limited.

In contrast, by selective purchase of standardised and cheap 'component technologies', the HJD-04 developers bypassed the weakness of China's existing technological capability in electronic component design and production. At the same time, this allowed the Chinese developers to concentrate on parts of the system design in which they had strengths, and provided a space to focus on meeting local requirements, while leaving the technologies in component design and production to be black-boxed for the time being. As this is a Chinese-designed system, it can in principle always be improved and innovated in line with the needs of Chinese users. Of course, to pursue this strategy requires indigenous PDSS technology creating capabilities, i.e. Chinese developers must possess adequate knowledge about digital switching technologies. Apart from that, the shift of the main technology of switching systems from electro-mechanical to computer technology also provided a chance for CIT to get involved in PDSS technology design, enabling it to use fully its computer design expertise and apply rapidly upgraded technologies in electronics and computing to the Chinese PDSS.

It seems that the System-12 project and HJD-04 project are in many aspects complementary in their contribution to the modernisation of the Chinese telecommunications technologies and provide adequate telecommunications services to meet domestic demands in the rapid economic growth. It is the coexistence of foreign advanced PDSS systems like System-12 and Chinese PDSS technologies like HJD-04 which is most important for China. This has created a dual development environment, which allows two technologies to compete with each other. On the one hand, the existence of the foreign PDSSs forces Chinese PDSSs to meet international standards, and on the other, the existence of Chinese indigenous PDSS technologies means that many features not available in foreign PDSSs can be developed to better serve Chinese users who have particular needs, e.g. low price, a simple system that is easy to operate and maintain and is able to work in poor local telecommunications conditions, etc.

In the light of both the System-12 and HJD-04 cases, we can see that there are notable differences between firm level and national level in terms of technological capabilities. The alarming point is the considerably weak technological capabilities of individual firms in general. Serious attention needs to be paid to the improvement of their technological capabilities in production, marketing and management which are operational and basic for a firm to survive. To some extent, acquisition of these technological capabilities needed to produce and implement PDSS technologies is more essential than capabilities in creation and innovation, certainly at this stage in Chinese development. These capabilities are not just associated with a few extremely highly skilled and creative engineers and technologists, but rather involve a wide range of players including not only producers and technological specialists, but also users – and not only those within the same industry but also in other industries which are suppliers of materials or components or product consumers. In China, production capabilities at firm level were so poor that improvement almost has to start from scratch. Problems in production quality and efficiency are still major obstacles for almost all Chinese companies. Firms like Shanghai Bell, which have achieved high productivity and quality levels, are few and far between across the country. Firms like LTEF are more typical among those in the state-owned sector. There is still a long way to go before Chinese firms possess technological capabilities in creating and innovating technologies like the system HJD-04.

The System-12 and HJD-04 cases show the importance of technological learning – enabling the Chinese to master foreign advanced technologies, to adapt foreign technologies like System-12 to the Chinese telecommunications network, and moreover to create Chinese indigenous systems like HJD-04. Four elements are essential in the process of technological learning. First, formalised means are needed, e.g. technological training, operating with technical assistance, etc. Second, these are complemented by wider informal avenues for technological learning. Even making advanced technology products available through the market has given opportunities for users to compare different products and therefore learn what quality a user can expect. Third, mass involvement in technological learning is crucial particularly for improving firms' technological capabilities in production. Fourth, it is necessary to have an environment which creates incentives for technological learning. A supportive macro environment is so crucial for technological development that it is the other main analytic concern of this study, and we will discuss this in the next chapter.

6 China's Changing Socio-Economic Context

The key remaining issue to be discussed, which was not explored in Chapter 5, is the influence of the wider social and economic context of the country in which technology development takes place. This is also one of the two major concerns of this study, and is essential to the effectiveness of utilising foreign advanced technologies and building up indigenous technological capabilities. This chapter focuses on the link between technological development and the restructuring of the national system of innovation during China's social and economic transition from a centrally controlled socialist state to a more market oriented system. Two key elements have been crucial to the above issues: state intervention and market forces. As there has been long-standing debate about the issue of state versus market, this chapter will focus specifically on their roles in relation to the PDSS technology development in China.

6.1 THE INTRODUCTION OF MARKET MECHANISMS

As was discussed in Chapter 2, from the viewpoint of national systems of innovation, the conventional system of socialist states had two fatal weaknesses in relation to technological dynamism:

(a) the central planning mechanism could not effectively link technology developers, producers, financiers and users;
(b) it could not generate incentives on a regular basis for technological changes.

The empirical case studies have thrown light on the rapid changes occurring because of the introduction of market mechanisms. First, it brought about new types of collaboration between R&D institutes and manufacturing firms. As shown in the System-12 case, Shanghai Bell initiated technological co-operations with some local universities and R&D institutes on quite a few occasions. Equally HJD-04 was itself a successful product of technological collaboration between a military R&D institute (CIT), a state-owned switching producer (LTEF), and an industrial procurement organisation (PTIC), the financial sponsor and the manager of this project. The HJD-04 case, in particular, clearly demonstrates the emergence of a new type of collaboration that has brought in close links between technology creators (and designers), producers and users. It demonstrated the benefits of such co-operation for product design: it enabled the design of technology to match the existing production capabilities, and its technological modification and innovation to be carried out on the basis of a better mutual understanding between designers, producers and users.

Second, the introduction of market forces has changed attitudes of organisations and people toward technological activities. As the HJD-04 case shows, none of the three key developers would have become involved in a project like HJD-04 without the socio-economic transition from the centrally planned to a more market oriented system. CIT as a military R&D institute would not have turned its attention to a civil telephone switching development project, as its research projects were formerly decided by higher military authorities. With the transition it was not only given greater freedom to modify its activities to exploit financial opportunities, it was also under pressure to achieve commercial development to safeguard its own economic future. Opportunity and necessity were combined to force many People's Liberation Army units to embark on commercial ventures. Similarly, as LTEF under the old system did not need to worry about its production output, it could produce its cross-bar switches for a long time without any changes. To a large extent, it was forced to explore technological opportunities under increasing financial pressure given the rapidly falling demand for its existing product: cross-bar switches (section 4.2). The fact that PTIC as a newly established industrial unit of MPT became interested in this project was also because of the new phenomenon of market forces. Because technologies began to be commercialised, there was no longer any free technology transfer even within the sector (section 4.1).

Third, and perhaps the most important, is the creation of incentives in the system for technological learning, therefore leading to the accumulation of technological capabilities. As shown in both empirical case studies, firms like Shanghai Bell, LTEF and other local component producers have been compelled by market forces to master new technologies, to improve production management, to establish marketing skills and to allocate resources by themselves.

Although it was set up in the first place by the Chinese government and afterwards enjoyed privileges provided by the government, the new environment that Shanghai Bell found itself in stimulated the firm to learn to segregate its own business interests from that of the government. On the one hand, it resorted to technical, financial and political support from the central government, MPT and the Shanghai municipal government. On the other hand, it rejected interference from them which would cut across its best interests. It co-operated with government to expand its market share more rapidly. Shanghai Bell refused outright when MMEI (the machinery and electronics ministry) wanted it to take as its supplier of transistors and TTL circuits for System-12 the firm which produced electronic components (at high production costs) for the national defence sector. Managers in Shanghai Bell might all have been accustomed to state intervention in the old socialist tradition before they worked in Shanghai Bell, but they learned quickly in a more market oriented context what the company had to pursue. This was clearly shown by their interview responses (see in particular quotations in section 3.3 and 3.4). Their technological development activities, such as technology adaptation, domestication of component production, were selected in order to pursue Shanghai Bell's interests. Their resort to Western managerial methods was not a simple copying of their BTM parent company. Rather it developed a hybrid style of management between Western and Chinese methods through which it achieved high productivity. In marketing and resource allocation, local managers articulated Shanghai Bell's natural connections both domestic and overseas, and established specific measures and policies in customer training, staff recruitment, technical collaboration, etc. to maximise Shanghai Bell's profits (section 3.3 and 3.4). Without market pressures, Shanghai Bell might have become another 'state-owned' firm and would not have developed its capabilities in marketing, resource allocation and management.

Similarly, under high pressure from the new and changing environment, LTEF had to learn to build up its basic technological capabilities from scratch. The process was painstaking, as it could not shake off all of these social burdens inherited from the past. Management learned to motivate staff to work harder in the new environment by reforming the administrative system, by setting up an internal labour market, etc.; they learnt to manage production and quality more efficiently and effectively; to have greater autonomy in allocating human, financial and material resources; and to 'marketise' their products by providing better-quality products and services (and even adopt arguably corrupt measures) to win customers. It was signals through the market mechanisms which motivated under-standing of customers' requirements of 'quality', and established criteria for producers like LTEF to achieve. In addition, in such a more market-oriented environment, management and staff in LTEF were compelled to recognise the ownership of technology and the potential power and profit attached to technology. In addition to learning how to improve its basic capabilities, LTEF even decided to try to attain technology innovating capability by setting up its own R&D institute (section 4.2), although this aim seemed a long way from being achieved. Compared to Shanghai Bell, this learning process taking place in state-owned firms like LTEF was far more difficult. However, it was market forces which mobilised stark economic necessities which made them want to learn (it could be said forced them to learn), and this even involved a risk that state-owned firms might become bankrupt before having accumulated the basic capabilities needed to survive.

State versus Market

The contribution of market mechanisms to national systems of innovation, went hand in hand with the important role played by the state as a generator of incentives for technological development. The state's role has to be seen in the light of the potential negative effects of market forces and areas where markets fail to allocate resources optimally. In addition to the positive effects of market forces on the innovation system and the economic system more generally that were noted above, the case studies showed that market forces can produce negative consequences not only for social and economic development but also for the technological development of the society.

Profit is an essential element of the market mechanism. In the case of HJD-04, the incentives generated by market mechanisms also created barriers to technological collaboration: they induced techno-logical secrecy and protection amongst the three original developers and with the HJD-04 producers in different sectors and parts of the country. These tensions were most acute when HJD-04 technology development reached the stage of marketing, and immediate expec-tations of profit came to the fore. Friction emerged between the three players involved in the original development, as each party had its own vested interests and sought to maximise its own income and prospects. Their behaviour in pursuit of their immediate and sectional interests from the technology seriously threatened the technological collaboration between them. It inhibited the flow of technological information needed between designers, producers and users for further technology improvement and innovation. Subsequent conflicts about which producers should be able to exploit the HJD-04 market also slowed the expansion of HJD-04 production, at the level of individual firms and nation-wide. This had strategic importance for the Chinese PDSS development as a whole. HJD-04 was still embryonic and the technology was needed to compete in the Chinese market with foreign PDSSs, like System-12, which already had over half the market share. If HJD-04 could not expand its production capacity quickly enough, its small market niche might not be able to sustain the necessary technology improvement and lay the base for future innovation.

Market forces drive individuals to pursue and maximise their own interests. Highly competitive markets might also induce firms to pursue short-term profits, which could divert investment needed for longer-term technological development. We have seen in the empirical cases the clear difference between firms' interests and the interest of sectors and the state in technological development. For example, firms like Shanghai Bell had no interest in domestication of component production until importing large quantities of components became inconvenient for its production. It was also not keen to establish an R&D facility able to get involved in the core of the System-12 technology, because this would not bring the company any immediate benefit. It was the state which was interested in using System-12 as an advanced technological resource in order to bring the country to a higher technological level. Similarly, firms like LTEF had no interest in getting more switch producers involved in HJD-04 production. PTIC was only concerned to take care of firms in its own sector and tried to fend off all non-MPT producers. It was, in principle, in the state's interest to promote wider technological co-operation across the country (for example, between MPT and MMEI), to help expand production and promote the further technological development of HJD-04. In particular, MMEI was responsible for the electronics industry, which might, for example, be important for the future supply of components for HJD-04 or its successors, if one day it is decided to shift toward domestic manufacture, e.g. of microprocessors.

We can see that market forces are something of a two-edged sword which can produce both positive and negative outcomes for social, economic and technological development. However, as this study shows, market mechanisms do not constitute a uniform, unchanging or 'asocial' set of pressures, but can operate in quite different ways, with very different consequences, in different societal and historical settings. The key question is the broader social and political frameworks in which market mechanisms are embedded. For example, the HJD-04 case demonstrated that the incentives could lead to adoption of corrupt measures by firms (section 4.3). Given the newly established yet incompletely developed legislative system in China, coupled with the lack of a legal tradition under the socialist system, and weaknesses in the internal administration and culture of firms, companies tended to make deals in a 'simple' way, by providing rewards to the person who was in charge of the business. In these circumstances, economic incentives could damage the social order rather than bear a positive result for technology development.

The most common negative social consequences of market competition, including mass unemployment, a widening gap between the rich and the poor, etc., could lead to social instability and unrest, and perhaps ultimately threaten the survival of the whole system. As we have seen in the Chinese case, after the economic reforms, the immense labour surplus became one of the major burdens facing state-owned firms, seeking to be competitive in a more market-oriented system. Under increasing pressure, lay-offs of surplus labour by state-owned firms seemed to be inevitable. Under the old Chinese socialist system, work units took full responsibility for social welfare, so losing one's job would be equal to losing everything – being left with no social security and no health care, as well as no means of living. The market mechanism itself clearly has no facilities to look after its victims. If the market mechanism had been allowed to operate without limits in China, millions of people would have been immediately redundant, and social stability would have been at stake.

The empirical evidence presented above confirms the point noted in Chapter 2 that market mechanisms can fail and must be complemented by public controls. In practice, there is no unregulated market in the world. Market mechanisms always work within a broader social and political framework, e.g. the legislative system, cultural system, etc. of a nation. State intervention is therefore necessary to offset the inadequacies of the market mechanism and reduce some of the negative consequences produced by it.

Apart from these general considerations, in the case of China the introduction of the market mechanism began within the framework of the Chinese socialist culture and a centrally controlled system. As a result, the state's role was particularly crucial in *designing* the whole process of the social and economic transition, in *initiating* and *directing* the process, and gradually reducing the state's direct administrative control over economic affairs, while concentrating on the roles necessary and complementary to the market for national development as a whole. The state had to find more effective forms of intervention!

Both the case studies show that government intervention brought about a range of positive outcomes. First, the government policies set up the framework for Chinese PDSS technological development through technology transfer from abroad. This was particularly marked in the case of Shanghai Bell. The state directly intervened in selecting Western technology partners and negotiating the System-12 technology transfer agreement to provide China with independent productive competencies in both PDSS and component technologies and to pursue the ultimate mastery of foreign advanced technologies. The attention given by the state in this case of PDSS is rooted in the fact, as already noted, that this technology lies at the heart of the telecommunications network, which has particular economic and social significance. Telecommunications is a public good and a strategically important technology: the backbone supporting the social and economic development of a country. Government therefore pays considerable attention to strategies for the telecommunications sector, which is subject to planning and regulation in pursuit of a variety of goals, to protect and balance economic and public interests across the country, and between different regions. This included questions of core telecommunications. For example, using too many different PDSS systems could result in unnecessary large costs and complexity of maintenance, because of their interfacing and different maintenance skills.

Second, the state's involvement in dealing with foreign companies and governments lifted the PDSS technology transfer from the level of a business deal between firms to the level of relationships between states. This helped ensure the reliability of the agreement, and offset the weaknesses that would have beset individual Chinese companies with little experience in foreign trade. The fact that the deal was sponsored by the Chinese government placed the Chinese side in a powerful bargaining position (particularly given the enormous size of China's telecommunications market which made it an extremely tempting prospect for all large PDSS producers world-wide) and helped them obtain a very advantageous deal. Chinese government pressure on the Belgian government sponsors was also critical to getting lifted the COCOM sanctions against high technology transfer to China.

Third, state intervention successfully gathered adequate financial, material and human resources across the country in the support of the wholesale System-12 technology transfer project. Like most developing countries, China's technological competencies in general are weak. However, technological competencies at the national-level are stronger than at the firm-level. This is also the case in relation to the firm's financial, material and human resources. Only the state was able to overcome these weaknesses. Such direct state intervention provided a powerful momentum for initiating modernisation of the Chinese telecommunications infrastructure. Direct intervention was definitely necessary in dealing with a technology as complex as PDSS – and at the outset of economic reforms. In the case of System-12, the state's role was so crucial that without it the whole project would not have been possible or successful, in the circumstances that China lacked PDSS technological capabilities and the national system lacked dynamism for technological development.

Fourth, the economic reforms led by the government transformed China's national system of innovation. This had broader significance, and is fundamental for the country's technological development in the longer term. We have seen that during the course of the System-12 project, there was a progressive shift in state policy towards a more market-oriented economic system through a gradual introduction of market elements, accompanied by loosening and decentralising state administrative control over economic affairs, that transformed the entire system towards technological dynamism.

Even though the creation and development of HJD-04 technology did not directly involve government intervention, unlike the System-12 case, the new environment created by the government also contributed greatly to the building up of the Chinese HJD-04 socio-technical constituency, and to the subsequent achievements of HJD-04 in production, marketing and further technological improvement.

Finally, the state made considerable efforts in facilitating and promoting technological development at national level. For example, it pursued the domestication of System-12 component production; the rapid expansion of System-12 production; the integration of System-12 technical upgrading with the new regulations and demands for the Chinese telecommunications infrastructure; the spin-off of foreign advanced technologies from Shanghai Bell to local industries; etc. All these confirm that the state can play a crucially important role, especially for the longer-term development of the country.

However, not all of these efforts were successful, as state intervention proved to have potentially negative consequences too. The System-12 case showed that state intervention could result in inefficient resource allocation. The government policy of pursuing import substitution was not very successful at first in the case of the domestication of System-12 component production, and the investment of government finance and effort on this project did not bear expected results. The main question is not whether or not the state has a role, but may well be more properly concerned with how best to implement state intervention. We discuss this in the next section.

6.2 POLICY IMPLICATIONS

The previous sections have already made a number of observations about the role of state intervention in PDSS technology development in China. It is important at this point to discuss further two related questions, which the case studies throw light upon: first to note the changing patterns of state intervention over time during the social and economic transition, and second to identify the different forms of intervention adopted and their different consequences, positive or negative. In this way, this section seeks to spell out the lessons from the Chinese empirical cases for the policies of the Chinese government for technology development and for transforming the national system of innovation in relation to future PDSS technological development.

Changing Forms of State Intervention

The form of state intervention has changed since the beginning of the transition. When the System-12 project was initiated, state intervention was still so direct that the state was the sole project designer, organiser, conductor and manager. Through an array of policies – including the wholesale System-12 technology transfer; component import licences (and the quota allocated for low tariff imports) and compulsory objectives for domestication of component production; measures to restrict the number of kinds of foreign PDSSs in the Chinese telecommunications networks; and initiatives for technology spin-off to local industries – we can see that the System-12 project embodied almost every element of government strategy for technology development of the country, relating to its three-step technology development policy.

With the deepening of the economic reforms, government control over firms like Shanghai Bell and LTEF became more indirect. Apart from the particular link with MPT and the Shanghai municipal government, Shanghai Bell benefited from being a joint venture and the 'source of foreign advanced technologies' in particular. It enjoyed general support from government policies: low taxation rates, more autonomy in business management, direct trading with foreign companies, more flexibility in currency exchange, etc. In the domestication of System-12 component production, apart from the fact that the government still kept the control of component import tariffs, direct intervention was largely reduced. It would seem that, as firms became more independent from the state and tended to pursue their own objectives to survive in the market, direct government intervention became more difficult and less appropriate.

In the HJD-04 technology development, the government did not give any direct support until the technology design had been proved successful. This project was indirectly catalysed and stimulated by a series of government economic measures and the general policies of the government for national technology development. HJD-04 represented a very different model to the conventional top-down approach, exemplified by System-12 in which the government directly decided the objective of technology development, laid out a large investment, and appointed technology developers. Instead, the idea of developing a Chinese PDSS was conceived by a technologist. His personal attributes, which were crucial for HJD-04's success – his creative personality, entrepreneurial gifts and required technology expertise – would have mattered little had it not also been that the Communist Party had called for the shift of the central focus of military R&D while the market began to give out strong signals indicating the enormous and increasing demand for PDSS technologies. Moreover, the government dual development policy made foreign PDSSs available in the Chinese market (including the System-12 technology transfer), which allowed PDSS technological information to diffuse within the country, through both formal and informal channels. Similarly, the eventual construction of the HJD-04 sociotechnical constituency can be more or less directly linked to government policies to introduce market mechanisms and increase the dynamism in the whole national system. The state budget and schemes for supporting new technology production were not attributed according to prior centralised plans, but rather they were granted to projects like HJD-04 after the technology proved to be successful.

We discussed the negative consequences of the centrally controlled system in Chapter 2. Briefly, the system itself was so rigid that it could not handle effectively the information flow between the R&D sector, industries and users and the complex processes of interaction between them. Take the project of the domestication of System-12 component production as an illustration. For each sub-project, many factors had to be considered by the organiser, the Shanghai municipal government. These included not only technological problems but also the finance for each sub-project, the attitudes of Shanghai Bell and local producers, and the changing trends of technological development. Moreover, while the major players were not fully committed to the domestication programme, much important information could simply be withheld by them. These problems might in principle be overcome through more careful planning and closer monitoring of the process of projects by the government. However, it would simply have been too demanding for the government to deal with every single project in this detailed way. The state's ability to become directly involved in such economic planning, particularly in a context of technological dynamism, is constrained both by its lack of access to the requisite technological information and its limited decision-making capacity.

In addition, as already noted, state intervention is not homogenous. The state itself is fragmented, and its different parts tend to have more-or-less diverging sectional perspectives depending on their responsibilities, traditions, external constituencies and knowledge base. For example, MPT was the main state body involved in conducting the System-12 project. However, it was primarily concerned with the development of the telecommunications systems. It gave as much support as it could to Shanghai Bell to make the project work. When conflicts arose between PTIC and MMEI (the machinery and electronics ministry), MPT took the side of PTIC, trying to keep the HJD-04 exchanges that were being produced by MMEI's firms out of the public telecommunications network. On the other hand, MPT was not really involved in the domestication of System-12 component production, although this could be seen as also being in the interests of the state and the nation as a whole. In contrast, MMEI and the Shanghai municipal government both actively pursued the domestication project. Differences emerged between them. MMEI wanted Shanghai Bell to take its own firms as component suppliers, while the Shanghai government preferred Shanghai Bell to resort to local Shanghai industries and bring them up to the required level of technological capabilities.

The above analysis may suggest three points in relation to technology development in China. First, the government role in technological development, and in particular a complex technology like PDSS, seems to be evolving from direct intervention towards more indirect actions, seeking for example not to direct facilitating technological change, but to facilitate change and promote technological activities in a direction that would seek most benefit for the entire country in the long term. This represented a gradual transition from the previously top-down process.

Second, some direct intervention may still be needed, as the state is the body responsible for taking a general longer-term view – for example, the requirements for national technological development. Since developing countries like China are constrained by a lack of resources, especially in relation to technology, human resources and finance, nationwide co-operation through government intervention could be effective in creating and pulling together scarce resources.

This is not to suggest a particular model for state intervention. The form of government intervention can be extremely diverse – ranging from direct control over individual projects, as the state undertook in the case of System-12, to facilitating and promoting technological changes, as exemplified by the role the state played in creating economic incentives for technological dynamics, which indirectly helped the emergence of the HJD-04 project. These deliberations suggest that direct intervention may be most liable to give rise to negative side-effects or inefficiencies given the complex social elements involved in technological development processes. If direct state intervention is adopted, it needs to be carefully planned and implemented.

This brings us to a third and final conclusion – that state intervention is not homogenous, and that different ways of implementing state policies may well bear different results. The forms of state interventions and the ways of implementing the state policy need to be carefully considered. We are now in a position to assess the effectiveness of the policies adopted by the Chinese government and draw some lessons for further policy advance.

Policy Implications for China's Future PDSS Technology Development

Government policies in two areas need to be reviewed here: first, policies having an impact on PDSS technological development; second, policies which create new national systems of innovation. The former encompasses the dual-technology development policy and three-step development strategy, the import substitution policy in accompaniment with import licensing and tariff control, etc. The latter consisted of a broader series of policies being introduced in the course of socio-economic transition over time.

The government's dual technology development policy – of so-called 'walking on two legs' – combining foreign and national aspects in the technology development seems to have been extremely effective in PDSS technology development during China's socio-economic transition. Within this policy, the specific three-step technology development strategy identified by the Chinese government – involving, respectively, bringing in foreign products; technology transfer; and then indigenous development – has been successfully pursued in the PDSS technology field, and has yielded fruit. The import of foreign-finished PDSSs at the start of the economic reforms in particular, helped solve the urgent problem of meeting acute domestic demands for PDSS technology, in the face of the lack of indigenous technology capability, and contributed to rapid renewal of the Chinese telecommunications infrastructure. This also had the consequence of providing information about advanced technologies and in particular allowed the society to develop new requirements and criteria for PDSS technologies. At the same time, government policies to deepen the economic reform, such as progressively introducing market mechanisms, loosening state control over economic activities, facilitated this process.

Wholesale technology transfer into China of telecommunications switching technology, the second step, began early, around the same time as the first purchase of foreign advanced PDSS exchanges, with the clear intention of building up Chinese PDSS production capacities and to meet the foreseeable increasing domestic PDSS demand. Local PDSS production capacities has contributed greatly to the modernisation of the Chinese telecommunications infrastructure and curbed the increasing import of finished PDSS exchanges. More important, the first two steps effectively enabled a wide range of people – designers, producers, users – to get involved in technological learning and to accumulate technological capabilities – as indicated in Chapter 5.

Indigenous technological development as the third step, including adapting foreign advanced technologies, spinning off advanced technologies to other local industries, and even developing Chinese PDSS technology, has benefited very clearly from the previous technological activities. Without them, the Chinese HJD-04 technology development might not have been possible, as this involved a strategy of developing Chinese digital programme-controlled switching technology by selectively utilising the international technology market rather than seeking to repeat the protracted development stages which were involved in PDSS development in the industrialised world.

The coexistence of Chinese and foreign PDSS technology in the Chinese telecommunications market not only helped to meet diverse requirements of domestic customers for PDSS technologies, it also propelled both technologies towards further technology improvement and innovation and towards high-quality products and service as well as low prices.

Ironically, the development of HJD-04 did not get much attention and support from the government, especially in the initial stage of technology creation. MPT even tried to stop the process, regarding this project as an unnecessary 'duplication' and potentially in competition with its own candidate for an indigenous PDSS. This attitude did not change until the HJD-04 technology proved to be successful. At a later stage, the dispute between MPT and MMEI did not help to unite HJD-04 production capacities across their respective industrial sectors. Rather it ruled out the cross-sector technological co-operation which could have enabled the rapid expansion of HJD-04 production.

HJD-04 technology was still embryonic when I finished my field-work. The state-owned companies that produced it faced constant problems and pressures from the broad economic transition. Compared to privileged joint ventures like Shanghai Bell, state-owned firms like LTEF clearly needed more government support. For example, HJD-04 producers might have expected to look to the government to grant them direct access to the international electronics market and autonomy in arranging adequate foreign currency for purchasing HJD-04 components, as was given to Shanghai Bell. As we have noted, state-owned firms like LTEF faced problems not only of resource shortages, but also the inherited social and economic burdens. In addition, market forces do not automatically ensure the success of indigenous technologies like HJD-04. A major challenge facing the HJD-04 constituency was the need to expand production capabilities. Here a key potential obstacle was the conflict of interest between MPT and MMEI, each of whom oversaw firms that were seeking to produce HJD-04 exchanges on licence. When my fieldwork ended, MMEI-producers were still unable to get their products accepted on the public telecommunications system. It would seem clear that intervention by central government is needed to encourage the further development of indigenous technological capabilities (both productive and innovation capabilities). The validity of this last argument is confirmed by a number of very recent developments that have taken place. In particular, the various MMEI and MPT HJD-04 producers have been united into a co-operative venture – Great Dragon Telecommunications Corporation Ltd. – which has enabled massive expansion of production capabilities. The broader terrain for this development is the government decision to introduce competition in telecommunications services, with the launch of the Unicom[79] network sponsored by a consortium including MMEI and other industrial Ministries.

Contrasting MPT's attitudes toward HJD-04 and System-12, up to the point I left China, it seemed that MPT had been more concerned with the rapid expansion of local production of foreign PDSSs like System-12 to modernise the public telecommunications network and meet urgent domestic demands for new lines, than to promote the development and market diffusion of the Chinese HJD-04 PDSS technology even though this might bring about considerable benefit to China in the longer term. Indeed, it proved rather difficult for MPT to balance short- and longer-term objectives surrounding PDSS technological development for the country, given the acute need for PDSSs in a rapidly growing domestic telecommunications market.

The government's early attempt to restrict the number of different types of foreign PDSSs was not continued in the face of the pressure from Western governments and the USA in particular to open the Chinese telecommunications market to the world even wider (section 1.3). This does not mean that the government's earlier effort was wrong. Rather, it demonstrates the complex array of factors that surround the central government – in carrying out this important role of dealing with foreign trade – and the need to balance divergent pressures and interests across the country.

The difficulties encountered by the government's efforts at import substitution do not necessarily suggest that the policy was wrong. The policy at least helped local industries to understand the essential requirements for their production to meet world standards and compelled individual firms to accumulate the basic technological capabilities needed to survive in a more market-oriented environment.

The goals and challenges of Chinese government policy for PDSS were changing over the course of this study. Achieving PDSS innovation capabilities was less of a priority for MPT in the early stages, compared with meeting domestic demand for telecommunications through first importing foreign PDSSs and later acquiring foreign PDSS production capability. The emergence of the Chinese indigenous HJD-04 technology was not anticipated (or even initially welcomed) by the main players in Chinese telecommunications – but could be clearly traced back to the process of broader economic reform aimed at promoting dynamism in China's economy and innovation system, coupled with earlier PDSS technology transfer. The broad thrust of China's dual, three-step, technology development strategy seems to have been validated in this case. Chinese policy developments in such a strategic technological field are carefully considered and debated. Although there were, inevitably, some areas where policy proved less effective or appropriate than hoped, and some players were slow to respond to new developments (e.g. the emergence of the HJD-04 constituency), there is an important element of pragmatism in Chinese policy formation, which enabled lessons to be learnt from the new developments (e.g. about HJD-04).

6.3   CONCLUDING POINTS

Technological development is a complex social process which involves a much wider range of groups and organisations than was presumed in traditional models of socialist planning. In Chapter 5, it was already noted that mass involvement in technological learning is crucial for improving technological capabilities of a firm and a nation. Technological learning is not only associated with those directly involved in the processes of technology creation and design, but also with wider networks of producers and users. Indirectly, the circle of relevant actors may well be much larger, involving perhaps financiers, educators, students, local and central policy-makers, etc. To enable the effective exchange of technological information between institutions and individuals in the society requires a supportive institutional framework and incentives for technological changes. In this respect the old centrally planned system in China certainly could not provide such a national system of innovation.

China's social and economic transition has introduced market elements into the system. State administrative control over economic affairs has been gradually replaced by market forces. With regard to the Chinese PDSS cases, we have seen that the transition brought about at least three major important changes:

(a) new types of technological collaboration have emerged between R&D institutes and manufacturing firms;
(b) the attitudes of people and organisations, including R&D institutes, manufacturing firms and others, towards technology have changed, and these bodies become more involved in technological activities;
(c) technological learning has been encouraged and has involved more people and a wider range of organisations in society, which has helped the accumulation of technological capabilities at both firm and national levels.

As noted in Chapter 5, firms have been motivated to seek technological opportunities and to build up technological capabilities. In particular, there has been rapid improvement in basic technological capabilities at firm level, e.g. production, marketing, resource allocation and management.

As the transition started from a highly centrally controlled system, the newly introduced market mechanisms started working alongside the existing but gradually reducing state powers. This study has shown that government intervention relating to PDSS technological development has, so far, brought about a range of broadly positive outcomes. Without these state actions, neither the System-12 nor the HJD-04 project would have been possible and successful. In relation to the national systems of innovation, the state played a major role in transforming the old rigid system into one with more technological dynamism. Apart from that, state intervention in PDSS technological development provided a powerful impetus to the modernisation of the Chinese telecommunications infrastructure. The Chinese PDSS cases show that the state and market forces can combine to generate incentives for technological development. Moreover, because China's transition has been a more or less top-down process directed by the government, the role of the state as its designer, conductor, monitor and executive, is therefore particularly crucial.

The Chinese PDSS case study shows that market forces can produce negative consequences not only for social development but also for technological development. Some of these have been particularly marked in the course of China's transition, in which old structures and traditions inherited from the centrally planned system exist alongside the newly established systems. Moreover, some important features of a market-based system, such as an appropriate legislative system and government regulations relevant to market operation, are still incomplete, or have not been fully established within the whole society. The newly introduced market mechanisms are still far from mature.

The implication is that both during and after the transition, state intervention is necessary to compensate the inadequacy of the market mechanism, to confront negative consequences and to balance the interests of individuals, institutions and the nation as a whole. Moreover, the state needs to continually adjust its role in accordance with the increasing role of market forces during the period of transition. Some functions carried out by the state can be effectively replaced by the market, whereas others are always needed and may need to be strengthened.

State intervention was particularly necessary in the case of PDSS technology development for several reasons. First, is the critical role of the state in setting up the longer-term development strategies and frameworks, e.g. through wholesale technology transfer from abroad to build up indigenous technological competencies. There were some particular features of PDSS technology that underpinned its importance to the state (stemming from the previously mentioned points: that PDSS is the technology at the heart of the telecommunications network which is very crucial for the social and economic development of a country). Second, as PDSS is such an advanced complex technology, its development and technology transfer from abroad needed large investments of financial, material and human resources. Thus, government effort may well be needed to gather sufficiently strong resources nationwide and effectively utilise them to ensure the success of technological development. This was particularly important at the beginning of economic reforms when China had been isolated from the international business community for thirty years, and individual companies lacked capabilities and experience in foreign trade and certainly were not able to handle a technology transfer project like System-12. Even if they had been allowed to, foreign companies like BTM (and indeed the Belgian government) would not have been sufficiently confident to commit such a large investment in China without Chinese government involvement.

On the other hand, state intervention can produce negative consequences. As these case studies show, technological development involves many elements – social, economic and political as well as technical. Many of these elements may be more or less in tension with each other. In addition, there is enormous uncertainty inherent in the development process. Because it is always difficult for the state to manage such complicated and often contradictory technological development processes, state direct involvement often results in some negative side-effects. One aspect is that much of the information needed to manage this process may be in the hands of private actors who may withhold it for their own particular interests.

This study has shown that major problems surround the form of intervention, that is, the manner in which state intervention is carried out. State intervention is not homogenous, and different bodies of the state, while developing and implementing state policy, might well conflate their local interests with the interests of the whole state or indeed nation.

The study also shows that the forms of state intervention have changed over time during the transition period. With respect to PDSS technology development, extensive government direct control, instruction, management and financial and material support in the beginning of the economic reforms has been reduced over the period of time. State intervention has become more indirect, through establishing a legislative system and issuing regulations, through restructuring institutional frameworks, and by setting up supportive schemes. Many of these are generalised in their approach, procedures and effects rather than being concerned with specific matters.

On the basis of the above points, we may suggest that: (i) there is a need to explore diverse forms of state intervention, which can range from direct control over individual project to an indirect role of facilitating and promoting measures and regulations; (ii) direct state intervention to achieve particular social and economic goals may bring about unintended negative side-effects, because of the difficulties inherent in managing a complex technological, social, economic and political situation; (iii) there is a need to identify different forms of intervention and to select appropriate ways of implementing policy and suitable state bodies to carry this out; (iv) indirect measures – e.g. through using markets to motivate technological dynamism as well as regulations and fiscal measures – are also needed.

We may also conclude that, in general, the broad framework of government policies for technological development and restructuring a national system of innovation, relevant to the Chinese PDSS technological development, are correct and necessary. In particular, the government's dual technology development policy of 'walking on two legs' and its three-stage technological development strategy have greatly contributed to Chinese PDSS technological development. In the first stage, China imported foreign-finished PDSS technologies which helped meet the urgent domestic demands for tele-communications and started the reconstruction of the Chinese telecom-munications infrastructure and, moreover, provided a window for the Chinese to learn about advanced PDSS technologies. This paved the way for the second stage – transferring complete PDSS technologies like System-12 into China. This step has successfully built up China's PDSS production capacities and has also greatly contributed to a quantum leap in the Chinese telecommunications system – rapidly restructuring and expanding its telecommunications infrastructure in a short period, leapfrogging earlier generations of switching-technology, as noted in Chapter 5. The first two stages provided technological resources for indigenous technological development and both direct and indirect means for technological learning. In a very real sense, without these, the Chinese HJD-04 technological development might not have been possible. Moreover, the coexistence of Chinese and foreign PDSS technologies, as promoted by the government's dual technological development policy, helped to meet the requirements of domestic customers and in particular compelled indigenous technol-ogy producers to improve the quality of production and services and further innovate, as already noted in Chapter 5.

However, at the time of this study the Chinese PDSS technology was still embryonic, and the problems facing HJD-04 were enormous. I concluded that, to compete with foreign PDSS products (including those locally produced like System-12), rapid expansion of HJD-04 production capacity would be needed, as well as further technological innovation. Expanding production capacity alone called for nation-wide technological co-operation (e.g. between MPT and MMEI, and its affiliated HJD-04 producers). Such a collaborative effort could also be needed to provide the resources for marketing and for further innovation of HJD-04 products. With increasing production, domes-tication of components production for HJD-04 might also need to be considered. In this case there was an obvious and key role for the government in co-ordinating these developments. Subsequently the state has made some important moves in this direction (with the creation of a consortium of HJD-04 producers, Great Dragon Telecommunications Co., and the establishment of competition in China's telecommunications services). The Chinese PDSS case shows that there is a gap to be filled by the state, including regulating the operation of the market.

The Chinese case proved that import substitution policies (through licensing and tariff control as well as the domestication project directly organised by the government) more or less helped to propel local industries into technological learning processes. However, it is equally clear that these policies made little headway in the early stages. They lacked support from local firms. Only later, when there was a broad coincidence between the self-interest of firms and the goals of the state, did these policies prove fully effective. Clearly, the form of state intervention needs to take into account the circumstances – in this case of domestic component producers.

The restructuring of the national system of innovation is clearly crucial for technological development. However, it still has a long way to go. Although some kinds of state intervention are always required to complement the market mechanism, the form of intervention needs to evolve continuously to match changing circumstance, e.g. the maturing of market mechanisms. In the meantime, an appropriate social framework needs to be set up to work together with market forces in order to reduce the negative consequences on technological development as well as on broader society.

7 Conclusions and Wider Implications for Developing Countries

The last two chapters, 5 and 6, compared the two empirical studies in considerable detail to yield a detailed analysis, respectively, of the process of acquisition of technological competencies and the influence of China's centrally planned economic system and its transition. This final chapter seeks to present the overarching conclusions of this study, linking the empirical research findings to the theoretical framework and concerns of the research. It further examines how relevant these findings are to the main policy issues and concerns of developing countries, especially for developing countries which have been socialist states. It revisits discussions about whether the resort to exogenous technologies will involve *development or dependency* (and considers the extent to which the optimistic findings about the prospects for developing countries may be specific to China and/or the particular PDSS technology). It explores the processes by which indigenous technological capabilities were acquired through *technology transfer*, emphasising the scope for technological learning and for *local shaping of technology*. It then reflects upon the changes in China's social and economic system, and in particular its *innovation system*, during the transition, emphasising the complementary roles of *state intervention* and *market forces*.

Development or Dependency

This study has shown how in PDSS technological development China has successfully utilised advanced foreign technological competencies through technology transfer to fulfil its national objectives in both technology and economic development. In less than fifteen years, China managed to expand its telecommunications network capacity by 21 million telephone lines. It also modernised its switching technologies and leapfrogged older vintages of technology by replacing

187

other lower-technology switches with digital programme-controlled switching systems. At the same time, China as a whole has built up PDSS technological capabilities not only in production, operation and maintenance, but also in innovation and creation of new technological knowledge.

This study shows that, given the right conditions, it is feasible for developing countries to catch up and overcome existing 'gaps' in technological capabilities between the developed and developing countries. Developing countries can indeed benefit from advanced technologies developed in the West. Technology transfer provides a means for developing countries to reap benefits from these technologies without the need to recapitulate the processes of technological development that led to their creation. Developing countries while transferring advanced foreign technologies may also be able to avoid some of the mistakes that the West (and more recently NICs) may have made in the course of earlier technological development and/or technology transfer.

The study thus calls into question the modernisationist view that technology transfer needs to resemble the Western model of development in its structures and patterns. Nor does it support the critical view, articulated by dependency theorists, of technology transfer as a simple linear process of geographically transporting a technology (with all its embedded social values) from one place to another. Instead, this study confirms the view of technology transfer, proposed in Chapter 2, as a complex process of unpacking, mastering and assimilating imported technologies. Strictly speaking, in the process of technology transfer, the original technologies are altered. The success of technology transfer is bound up with the behaviours of both suppliers and recipients, which involves substantial uncertainties and variability in outcomes. Whether the results of technology transfer favour recipients – the developing countries – depends greatly on how the processes are carried out. This raises important questions about how technology transfer projects are strategically planned and implemented.

The Chinese PDSS case highlights the need (and scope) for effective strategies to use available domestic resources, as well as to identify and exploit opportunities emerging in the dynamic global economy. This is particularly an issue for developing countries given their limited financial and technological resources. The latter places developing countries in a rather weak bargaining position in the international technology markets. In this respect, this study provides some support for the cautionary view articulated by dependency theorists and structural underdevelopment approaches (see Chapter 2). It is useful for developing countries to understand the potential pitfalls in resorting to exogenous technologies. However, these pessimistic analyses provide DCs with little practical advice about how to avoid these hazards and make best use of emerging technological opportunities.

The challenge is for DCs to find ways to escape economic and technological dependencies, given that some of the problems which were pointed out by dependency theories still exist. However, this study takes issue with the monolithic view of technology articulated by their analyses, which presents DCs with stark and limited choices. Instead this study shows that technology is both diverse and heterogeneous, and suggests that problems of dependency might be reduced, for example, by the selective use of foreign technological competencies and their combination with local competencies, through the local shaping of imported technologies. The empirical cases presented in this study provide clear (albeit radically different) examples of this. These underpin the conclusion in section 5.4 that the key questions for developing countries seeking to reduce dependencies concerns whether they can successfully build up technological capabilities through technological learning during the course of technology transfer.

This study suggests that the problems of dependency should not be reified or overstated. In some ways there is always a mutual dependency between technology suppliers and recipients. For instance, in the Chinese case, China needed to gain access to foreign PDSS technologies, while foreign switch-producers were extremely keen to gain access to the Chinese market. The question thus concerns the balance between them, and the extent to which China can maintain the advantage or gain an even stronger position. These considerations underpinned a number of important choices in the technology transfer of System-12 technology. If China could not produce the specialised components required – in particular, custom LSI chips – for System-12, China would have to rely on foreign producers. If their production was monopolised, then the situation would have been less favourable for China. In this situation, China could have lost the balance of power and might have suffered from unfair treatment, such as excessively priced components, outdated technologies, etc. What actually transpired in this case was the opposite. China has gained a stronger position through technology transfer. More important, this contributed to the development of indigenous Chinese PDSS technologies like HJD-04 which may have the potential, one day, to compete on equal terms with foreign products in the market. In these circumstances, China's dependence on foreign technology suppliers does not necessarily mean that China is in an unfavourable bargaining position.

This also bears upon the controversies in development studies about whether the NICs' experiences are relevant to other developing countries. The Chinese case confirms that although their circumstances may be rather different, some of the lessons drawn from the NICs' experiences have wider applicability – for example, the fact that NICs not only acquired the capacity to produce Western technologies, but also developed innovation competencies. The key question for developing countries thus becomes how to achieve technological dynamism. The Chinese case also shows that the state can play a complementary role to the market mechanisms in providing a supportive environment for technological development. We return to these points below.

However, there may also be limits in the extent to which one can generalise from the Chinese experiences in PDSS technology development for developing countries. First, China is an extremely large country. Its size and population alone give it a special position in the world economy and politics. Its huge market makes it an extremely attractive arena for many businesses across the world. For the same reason, it is feasible for China to develop its own PDSS technology which can best suit the Chinese conditions and compete with foreign products for a share of the huge domestic market. For small countries, it may not be economical to do so, since the development costs for PDSS technology are so huge, and a small domestic market might not be able to sustain a domestic production capacity, let alone the capacity to innovate the technology further. Second, PDSS technology, as the technology at the heart of modern telecommunications, has particular social, economical and political significance, and is thus frequently subject to state intervention. This may give rise to particular opportunities and incentives for state intervention that may well not apply in relation to other technologies with rather different features.

Technology Transfer and Indigenous Technological Capabilities

To a large extent, we can conclude that China's technology transfer from abroad has been effective in respect of the acquisition of technological capabilities. The wholesale transfer of System-12 technology provided avenues for the inflow of technological information and a wide range of avenues for technological learning. Technology transfer also indirectly provided the basis for the Chinese HJD-04 technology to emerge. However, HJD-04 involved a very different means of resorting to exogenous technologies. It was made possible by the selective purchase of foreign components (cheap, standardised microprocessors and design tools) and their combination with locally available expertise in computer design, and knowledge of the Chinese telecommunications system.

Technological learning – by using, operating, producing, adapting, designing, creating, innovating, etc. System-12 and component technologies – involved a wide range of people who greatly contributed to the accumulation of indigenous technological capabilities. The study highlights the importance of informal as well as formal links and knowledge flows for this.

Chapter 5, drawing on the empirical cases, discussed the close relationships between technology transfer, accumulation and development of indigenous technological capabilities and technological learning (section 5.4). These findings verify the presumption noted in section 2.4 that technology transfer provides valuable, and I would say necessary, opportunities for developing countries to build up technological capabilities. The key processes in effective acquisition of exogenous technological competencies embodied in imported technologies are the selection, unpacking and adaptation of imported technology. This involves strategic choices that require careful consideration. Rather than counterpose technology transfer with the acquisition of indigenous technological capabilities, a close and well-chosen relationship is needed between technology transfer and indigenous technological capabilities, especially in technologies like telecommunications which is a globalised and highly complex network technology with huge development costs. Indeed the empirical findings confirm the argument in section 2.4, based upon the literature review, about the close relationship between technology transfer, indigenous technological capabilities and technological learning.

At the outset of the study I noted the distinction that has been drawn in relation to technological capabilities between the 'basic' capabilities of production, operation, maintenance, resource allocation, marketing, management, etc. and the 'advanced' capabilities of indigenous innovation and creation (section 2.4). My initial presumptions prioritised the (advanced) technological capabilities of innovation and creation, in line with much research in the field which has regarded these as particularly important if developing countries are to overcome dependency. Having completed the analysis of the two Chinese PDSS cases (section 5.4), it seems to me that this presumption was perhaps misplaced. Instead, the cases demonstrate the enormous importance for DCs of developing and strengthening basic (operational) technological capabilities. There are two main reasons for this view. First, the basic (operational) technological capabilities create the basis for wider advances in economic growth and provide a foundation for the development of more advanced technological capabilities, for example by enabling the effective use of foreign advanced technological competencies. It must be remembered that in most developing countries, like China, even these basic capabilities are in general weak. This is particularly true for former socialist states in which the central planning system gave individual firms little incentive to develop many of these basic capabilities (for example, in production and marketing) and which were, as a result, poorly developed.

Second, I would argue that the emphasis on developing advanced capabilities in technology creation unhelpfully focuses attention rather narrowly on the activities of a handful of (maybe highly trained and capable) engineers and technologists. In contrast, the development of basic (operational) technological capabilities requires *mass involvement* in technological learning by a wide range of players including manufacturers, suppliers and customers, and also requires a supportive social and economic system.

This study further confirms that it is useful to distinguish the technological capabilities at the national level from those at the level of the firm (section 2.4). It shows that in a developing country like China, technological capability at the national level can be much stronger than that at the level of the firm, although its mobilisation depends on effective technological collaboration between organisations. For example, virtually no individual Chinese firms have PDSS R&D capacity. However, in co-operation with R&D institutes, they can develop and produce PDSSs like HJD-04. This highlights one of the major issues of this study, the important role of institutional linkages and government policies in supporting technological co-operation and in fully utilising existing technological competencies across the country.

Local Shaping of Technology

This study challenges classical intermediate/appropriate technology theories, which suggested that advanced Western technologies incorporated social and economic presumptions from their development context that would be reproduced when transferred to DCs and thus would prove inappropriate for developing countries. The implication was that DCs should avoid such alien technologies, also thereby forgoing the benefits that these powerful and efficient technologies might offer (section 2.4). Instead this study applies insights from the social shaping of technology approach to explore how developing countries can effectively and beneficially acquire advanced foreign technological competencies. It highlights the scope for developing countries to utilise foreign technologies selectively, and adapt them to local circumstances. This opens up a range of government policies and technology strategies that may be pursued.

The social shaping of technology approach draws attention to the *process* of innovation, and specifically:

- to the choices inherent at every stage of technological change and the way these are affected by their socio-economic context as well as narrowly technical considerations;
- to the negotiability of technology and the way that artifacts, once developed, are not fixed after they leave the R&D laboratory, but may evolve and be further innovated as they enter commercial production and use.

Applying this perspective to technology transfer highlights the various possibilities for the selective acquisition of exogenous technologies as well as the variety of choices about which elements of technology should be unpacked, adapted to local conditions or developed and produced locally. Therefore, there is in principle a range of strategies available for developing countries to adopt, according to their domestic requirements and their existing technological capabilities as well as external opportunities. The empirical cases demonstrate how widely differing strategies have been successfully applied in Chinese PDSS technology. Chapter 5 has already analysed and compared in detail the two strategies presented by the case of System-12 and HJD-04, and discussed the advantages and shortcomings of using them in different circumstances.

The SST approach is very useful here in distinguishing different types of technologies in terms of the form of the physical artefact which may be developed in different ways and offer different scope for local shaping. In particular following Fleck (1988a) (section 2.4) this study suggests that complex modern technologies are increasingly 'configurational' (they may be acquired as complex assemblages of more or less standardised component technologies configured together with customised elements) rather than internally homogenous, monolithic 'systems technologies'. Such configurational technologies can more readily be reconfigured in their implementation and use. This study shows that even large-scale proprietary technologies such as System-12 PDSS can be unpacked and further innovated. This study also suggests that Fleck's ideal type of 'system technologies', against which concepts of configurational technology have been counterposed, may not in fact exist.

Finally, as concluded in section 5.4, the study proposes that the type of technology, and the type of technology transaction, together determine the availability and appropriability of exogenous technological competencies which are embodied in the imported technologies, and provide different means for technological learning. This confirms the presumption that underpinned this study that an effective account of technology transfer and acquisition of technological competencies needs to address the content of technology, and the detailed processes of innovation, as well as the 'social' setting.

National System of Innovation

The concept of national systems of innovation helped frame this study, and may be helpful for a country considering how to assess its current situation and future strategies – and especially a developing country seeking to catch up with technologically advanced and dynamic economies. It usefully draws attention to the socio-economic institutional framework for innovation and to the influence of government policies. It highlights the importance of linkages between actors involved in technological activities and of incentives for technological innovation rooted in the broader context.

From this perspective, we can see that China's social and economic transition, involving the introduction of market elements into the system to replace some state roles, has contributed to the increasing technological dynamism of China's national innovation system. This has gradually overcome problems that had beset the socialist central planning system, and which arose in particular from the poor links between R&D institutes, producers and their customers. The study showed how, in the transition, market forces and government policies combined to provide powerful incentives for these players to seek opportunities from new technologies, to get involved in technological learning, and to engage in collaboration to pursue these ends.

However, to some extent, the concept of a national system conveys an image of a process that is systematic, ordered and stable. The findings of this study point to the fragmented and chaotic nature of the social and economic system. The rapid changes in the social and economic context during China's transition suggests that it is unhelpful to search for a single best model for a particular nation's system for innovation. National systems need to evolve in order to be best suited to promote innovation in a changing commercial and technological world. Just as important, there may be no single 'best' national system for a country as a whole, not just because of regional differences, but also because the circumstances and requirements for innovation systems in different industries and different technologies may be rather different. Thus, although the concept of a national system of innovation has usefully drawn attention to the crucial role of the broad social and economic context of technological development in a country, the concept may prove deeply unhelpful if it stimulates attempts to characterise and pursue a single monolithic and fixed model of 'best practice'.

State Intervention versus Market Forces

One of the main areas of debate among the different schools of thought within development studies and studies of socialist economies and their transition (reviewed in Chapter 2) concerns the role of state intervention. On the one hand there has been the recent emphasis on the role of market forces. On the other are suggestions that the state played a positive role in economic development in NICs, and by extension needs to be active in DCs. The empirical findings from this study show that state intervention can indeed play a positive role; however, it can also fail. Chapter 6 analysed certain failures in state intervention in the two PDSS cases.

Two key aspects have significant impacts on the outcomes of state intervention: the form of intervention and the state body which carries out the tasks (see section 6.4). This study in particular stresses the need to explore diverse forms of state intervention which may need to be adopted to meet continually changing domestic and international environments. Also, it points out that state intervention is not homogenous; the state itself is fragmented, and different parts of the state have their own vested interests and commitments which shape the ways they intervene.

In relation to the debate about whether state intervention is necessary (sections 2.2 and 2.3), this study rejects firmly the schools of thoughts which pursue exclusively *laissez-faire* approaches. The empirical findings from this study show that although many state roles can be more effectively replaced by market forces (particularly in promoting technological dynamism in the system, primarily by generating incentives for individuals and organisations), state intervention continues to be needed to fulfil other traditional roles, for example, to represent national interests, and carry out some new functions. This study confirms the findings from studies of the NICs' experiences which emphasise the importance of their governments' roles in providing appropriate macro-economic policies and infrastructure; in maintaining restrictions on imports and other kinds of industrial promotion, etc.; in formulating the long-term national plans for investment and industrial development needed to guide the market; and in controlling the content and pace of industrialisation (section 2.2). In its roles in guiding capital investment and technological development, the state is able to provide strategic direction which could not be guaranteed by the market-oriented behaviour of individual firms. An important aspect of this intervention is that it complements rather than displaces competition and the market system.

Chapter 6 also analysed some of the negative consequences of introducing market mechanisms in the course of China's economic transition and the diverse (including unintended) reactions of agents involved in technological activities to market forces which arose in the differing circumstances of the two PDSS cases (section 6.2). This shows that market forces represent a two-edged sword. The analysis further reminds us that market mechanisms always work within a broader social and political framework. For example, markets are always subject to some form of regulation (section 2.3). Markets in the real world are far-removed from idealised descriptions of the free market. This study argues further that state intervention is needed to compensate for some of the failures of the market mechanism, in particular to take responsibility for reducing some of the negative social consequences that may be produced by market forces. Relating this to the debates about socialist economics, it suggests that the 'simple dichotomy' between socialist and capitalist systems has little relevance for developing countries. In practice, governments always face a challenge to counteract potential areas of 'market failure', to balance public interests and economic efficiency, and to combat, or at least ameliorate, negative social consequences which could lead to social instability and could well jeopardise the development process of a country altogether.

Summary

This study of the development of PDSS technological capabilities in China supports an optimistic view – that it is possible for developing countries to acquire advanced technological capabilities through technology transfer from industrialised countries. It highlights the range of different strategies that may be used by developing countries in *selectively* transferring foreign advanced technologies in the light of available indigenous technological capabilities and opportunities in the international market.

This study demonstrates that developing countries can master advanced technologies by combining internal and external technological competencies, and suggests that this is likely to become an increasingly common feature. In the face of increasing globalisation, particularly in areas of advanced technologies, the goal of self-sufficiency of a country is becoming less relevant – even if it were feasible. Most developed countries may not be able to maintain the full range of capabilities in a technology (as is already the case in relation to micro-electronics and computing, for all but a handful of the most developed countries). On the other hand, developing countries and small industrialised economies may be able to acquire partial competencies in advanced technological fields.

This study sees technology transfer as not a narrowly technical issue, but as a broad social, economic and political one, linked not only to the domestic situation, but also its global context. The study suggests a shift away from the static model of technological dependency that has underpinned structuralist and dependency theories in development studies, towards a dynamic one, that presents developing countries with a number of options (including threats and opportunities). It flags the *balance* that exists between suppliers and recipients (at firm and at national levels) and sees technology development as a strategic issue for developing countries in choosing how to deal with a changing world, as well as an issue of how recipients can strengthen their position by building up technological capabilities alongside the attempts of overseas suppliers to maximise and sustain their position in the global market.

Much research has tended, more or less explicitly, to prioritise the development of indigenous technology creation capabilities (i.e. the capacity to create novel technologies), seeing them as more advanced, and more important than technology production capabilities to overcome dependency. (This was also a personal presumption at the outset of the study.) However, one of the key findings is that the firm's acquisition of basic (operational) capabilities is perhaps the most pressing task. They are of most immediate importance in allowing a developing country to benefit from advanced technologies; they strengthen the local economy, and also provide the basis for further technological development, including technological innovation not only in the firms which have received technology transfer but also in their local suppliers and industrial customers. The development of basic (operational) capabilities requires not just capital equipment and engineering knowledge, but also broader changes in the social and economic system. For example, a key feature was recognition of the importance of quality and of meeting customer requirements. Such developments were not restricted to technical and managerial specialists, but called for mass involvement in technological learning. Given that innovation is not a linear process, limited to initial R&D, the boundaries between technology production and creation capabilities may not be clear-cut – given the need to adapt technologies to local socio-economic and technical contexts. Moreover, technology production capabilities may provide the basis, through technological learning, for developing more advanced indigenous technological capabilities, including, as the HJD-04 case shows, technology creation capabilities.

Drawing on diverse theoretical roots the study highlights some of the features underpinning the lack of technological dynamism in China's former socialist system. It broadly confirms findings from studies of other socialist economies that the major obstacles for technological development in China have been the weaknesses associated with the socialist central planning system: the weak operational technological capabilities of individual firms, and the poor linkages (and lack of incentives for such links) between R&D and manufacturing organisations and with their customers. This study shows how the increasing influence of market forces in the course of the transition contributed to technological dynamism in China. However, it does not favour a *laissez-faire* approach. Instead it supports the view that the role of market and state are complementary rather than being counterposed, and in particular provides evidence that state intervention plays an important role in technological development –

in supporting the development of technological capabilities as well as in pursuing broader and longer-term interests. These issues pertain to a number of societies, as well as just the case of China, suggesting that the traditional dichotomy between 'socialist' and 'capitalist' countries may no longer be helpful.

Apart from these substantive points, this research confirms the value of case studies combining the detailed focus of actor-related studies with approaches that address the influence of broader structural and historical factors (section 1.3). It also highlights the importance of detailed analysis encompassing the content of technology artefacts and processes of technological innovation. Such an approach has allowed a better understanding of the changing behaviours of the actors involved in technology development in response to changes in the broad social and economic context in China's economic transition, and of the complex interplay between the content of technology and its societal context. Opening the black box of technology enables a reassessment of traditional views of technology transfer. In contrast to the pessimistic presumptions of dependency theorists, the study shows that developing countries are able to benefit by carefully chosen strategies for technology transfer, despite possessing limited capabilities compared with industrialised economies. What is at issue here is how to acquire *partial competencies* in advanced technological fields that are increasingly extensive and globalised. In this case, China's dual-track technology development strategy has proved remarkably successful, both in relation to its planned goals and in the indirect and unanticipated consequences (e.g. HJD-04) arising from the growing dynamism mobilised in the transition.

The study is completed. Globally, processes of technological development are accelerating and becoming more demanding. It is hoped that this study will help to improve understanding of how China and other developing countries can best march forward on the road to advanced technology.

Notes

1. Figures from internal materials circulated by MPT.
2. Figures from my interview with the Chief Consultant of the Economic and Technological Development Research Centre of MPT and confirmed by several other officials in MPT.
3. There were on average 60.95 telephone sets per 100 inhabitants in OECD countries in 1985 (Ypsilanti, 1988).
4. Each province, autonomous region, and municipality has its own Posts and Telecommunications Administration to administer the MPT's policies locally.
5. According to my interviews with officials in the MPT and the MMEI (in Beijing, April 1993).
6. This state-supported scheme for technological innovation selects various technological projects considered to be of national importance. This is a continuation of earlier state initiatives. In China, the state has been running 'Five-Year Plans' since 1953, which, in respect of Science and Technology development, have included a series of national R&D programmes. The R&D project for PDSS technology was under 'the key project plan during the sixth five-year plan'.
7. According to my interview with Prof. Liu Ximin, a specialist in telephone-exchange technology and leader of the R&D project of Chinese system DS-2000 development (interview in Shanghai, March 1993).
8. Interview with China's leading switching experts, Xie Xiaoan and Liu Ximin, who were themselves involved in such overall search of the opportunity of technology transfer from outside China.
9. Zhou was the director of the Shanghai Telecommunication Construction Bureau in overall charge of the System-12 project, and the Chairman of the board of the Sino-Belgian joint venture, Shanghai Bell, at that time.
10. Kerkhofs was the programme manager for the BTM-China contracts in 1985, and the general manager of Shanghai Bell in 1986.
11. The city where LTEF is located.
12. Interview with Xie Xiaoan (see note 8), and other interviews in Shanghai Bell.
13. In 1949 the USA, Japan, and the NATO countries created COCOM to restrict the flow of strategic goods and know-how, concerned that technology transfer might strengthen the strategic and military potential of socialist countries. Industrial sectors such as electronics and telecommunications were of particular concern in this context.
14. Information provided by the first Chinese general manager and the present general manager of Shanghai Bell on my interviews in February 1993.
15. Interview with the deputy manager of the Operations Department, 6 November 1992.

16. Interview with the deputy director of the Engineering Department, 30 January 1993.

17. The development of switching system technology is characterised according to the circuit technology. The earliest is 'analogue line circuit' with a microprocessor controlling 60 lines; the next was 'evolution line circuit' with a microprocessor controlling 128 lines, and the newest one is 'new generation line circuit' with a microprocessor controlling the same number of lines as the previous one but with the number of modems reduced.

18. Interview with a deputy director of the Engineering Department, 30 January 1993.

19. Interview with Mr De Graeve, who was the fourth Belgian general manager. His predecessors were: Mr J. Loontiens, Mr M. Kerkhofs and Mr S. Abbeloos.

20. Figures were provided by a deputy manager of the Engineering Department, 30 January 1993.

21. According to the director of Productivity and Quality Management, 'He is a very experienced manager. Apart from building up a quality control system in Shanghai Bell, he also introduced his knowledge to other local companies and had a very good relationship with the Shanghai Quality Management Association' (Director of Productivity and Quality Management, 9 November 1992).

22. Most detailed material about production quality control was provided by the manager of the Department of Productivity and Quality Management in an interview, on 9 November 1992.

23. The first System-12 exchange in use anywhere in the world was in June 1986 in the Netherlands. It was only six months before the first Shanghai Bell-made System-12 was put into operation in China.

24. Those with such a degree of education could have better jobs than being a phone operator in these places.

25. According to my discussion with shop-floor engineers and workers in Shanghai Bell's workshop, 1 March 1993.

26. Ibid.

27. Interview with the vice-chief engineer in the Shanghai Telephone Administration, 10 February 1993.

28. Interview with a deputy manager of the Personnel Department, 3 November 1992.

29. Figures provided by a deputy manager of the Department of Operational Finance at PTIC.

30. According to *The Law of the People's Republic of China on Joint Ventures Using Chinese and Foreign Investment*, Article 7, 'a joint venture equipped with up-to-date technology by world standards may apply for a reduction of or exemption from income tax for the first two to three profit-making years'. This law was adopted on 1 July 1979 at the Second Session of the Fifth National People's Congress; promulgated on 8 July 1979 (Shanghai Municipal Foreign Trade and Economic Committee, 1985c).

31. Interview with the deputy manager of the Department of Operational Finance at PTIC.

32. Domestic enterprises did not have such rights (see more detailed description in Chapter 4).
33. Interview with the vice-chief engineer in the Shanghai Local Telecommunications Administration and confirmed in other interviews in Shanghai Bell. I did not see the internal circular. However, there is the State Council No. 56 dispatch in 1989 which indicated clearly, 'it is requested for all purchasing of foreign switching systems to use the ones which have already been selected by the government' (Telecommunications Administration Bureau at Zhejiang Provincial Posts and Telecommunications Administration, 1992, p. 93).
34. Many of the young managers I interviewed in Shanghai Bell belonged to this batch of recruits, which was arranged by MPT.
35. About the CCG group, the deputy director of the Engineering Department provided most details at the interview, 30 January 1993.
36. Details of RASM from an interview with the deputy director of the Engineering Department, 30 January 1993.
37. This material was provided by the deputy manager in the Engineering Department at the interview on 30 January 1993.
38. Interview with the Belgian general manager of Shanghai Bell, 10 February 1993 and the Chinese general manager, 1 February 1993.
39. Which is technically more complicated than the exchanges used for telecommunications switching within the country.
40. Interview with the deputy manager of the Engineering Department.
41. Interview with the manager of Marketing Department, 28 February 1993.
42. According to the deputy manager of the Engineering Department, who was in charge of installation.
43. Interview with the manager of Personnel Planning and Education in the Personnel and Administration Department, 3 November 1992.
44. Interview, 31 January 1993.
45. Interview with the Chinese general manager, 1 February 1993.
46. Interview with the deputy manager of the Operation Department, 6 November 1992.
47. Housing in Shanghai was extremely scarce, as a popular saying vividly described: 'It is easier to find a wife than a flat.'
48. The manager of Personnel Planning and Education at the Personnel and Administration Department, Shanghai Bell, gave me the details about material incentives which Shanghai Bell provided to its staff.
49. The manager (associate professor) of the Training Centre provided the most detailed material.
50. The mayor Zhu Rongji is now the Premier of the state council.
51 Interview with the deputy director of the Shanghai Bell System-12 Project Conducting Group.
52. Interview with the head of the Domestication Division.
53. This was according to the deputy manager of the Engineering Department.
54. The head of the Domestication Division at Shanghai Bell provided detailed material in this section.
55. Fuzhou is the capital of Fujian province on the southeast coast of China.

56. In December 1980 the contract for importing the system F-150 between Fujitsu and the Post and Telecommunications Administration of Fujian province was formally signed. It was eventually put into operation in November 1982 (Gu, 1992).

57. A French switching system, also the first commercial digital local exchange system of Alcatel-Thomson.

58. By that time, digital computer programme-controlled exchanges developed by CIT were small-size PABX and terminal (local) exchanges. Full-size PDSS meant that the new system would have a capacity of approximately 30 000 subscriber lines and could be used as local or tandem (toll) switches.

59. This is according to my interview with Professor Wu, Director of CIT, in Zhengzhou, 26 April 1993.

60. The system DS series was a range of Chinese PDSS technologies. DS-2000 was the first successful PDSS developed by Chinese R&D teams and the latest version was DS-30 (see also section 1.3).

61. The MPT was originally established as a posts and telecommunications administration entity for the country. The MMEI was an industrial management ministry. However, under Mao's self-reliance philosophy, the MPT and MMEI both established their own industrial enterprises during the Cultural Revolution. As they both have their own telephone switch producers, this gave rise to confrontations between them.

62. This is according to my interview with a high-ranking official in the Ministry of Machine Building and Electronics Industry (now, Ministry of Electronics Industry).

63. Apart from the public telecommunications network, in China, there were several private networks run individually by the Ministry of Railways, the People's Liberation Army, the Ministry of Electronics Industry, etc. which have excess capacity. In early 1993, they planned to initiate a joint company, Lian Tong Corp. ('Unicom' in English), and to jointly establish a rival public telecommunications network, in order to challenge the MPT. This plan was still being debated when I was there in April 1993.

64. This is according to my interview with the official who was in charge of the HJD-04 technology. However, when people in the LTEF mentioned the sum of money, they simply called it 'the money given by the state'. For state-owned companies, a long-term loan is equivalent to a gift, because the firm does not belong to anybody, neither director nor the others in the firm. In the case of a 20-year term, these directors and managers will probably have left by the time of repayment. Whether this will make trouble with their successors is not their concern.

65. This is according to my interview with a key official in PTIC, 6 April 1993.

66. The PTIC as an entity which functioned as an administration organisation also lacked money, under China's economic transition, in a context in which everybody and every work unit was trying to make profits.

67. On one occasion, some people in the firm talked about breaking the security code of the software of the HJD-04, but the head of the firm immediately received an angry response from the PTIC, indicating that

it would definitely not be allowed. In contrast, Professor Wu did not take the idea very seriously. He laughed and said to me in the interview that it would probably have been impossible anyway.

68.   This impairs the quality of soldering, because the coating material of the pins is designed for making a good soldered joint.

69.   It was Bell Telephone Manufacturing Company of ITT; now it belongs to Alcatel.

70.   This kind of contract varied from firm to firm. Usually, workers signed contracts with the head of their department, heads of departments signed with the director of the firm and the director with his boss in higher-level organisations, respectively.

71.   The formula for counting is 'Total salary = (Basic salary + Performance-oriented salary) × Quality as weighted variable from 0–1'.

72.   This is according to my personal interview with three engineers and technicians. All of them had graduated from university and left their home town and come to work in this factory. One had got married and was living in the dormitory, the other two were single.

73.   To attract foreign investment in Chinese industry, the government issued several tariff bills: 'Regulations for the Implementation of the Law of the People's Republic of China on Joint Ventures Using Chinese and Foreign Investment', promulgated by the State Council on 20 September 1983, indicated that, ' . . . A joint venture can apply for reduction or exemption of industrial and commercial consolidated tax for a certain period of time . . . ' (Shanghai Municipal Foreign Trade and Economic Committee, 1985a, pp. 223–56); 'Some Provisions of the People's Republic of China Concerning the Reduction of or Exemption from Income Tax in the Absorption of Foreign Funds', 21 September 1982, indicated that, ' . . . A newly-established joint venture, jointly operated for a period of more than 10 years, with the approval of tax authorities upon an application filed by the enterprise, may be exempted from income tax in the first profit-making year, and allowed a 50 per cent reduction in the second and third years . . . ' (Shanghai Municipal Foreign Trade and Economic Committee, 1985b, pp. 386–91). Along with that, many coastal cities and districts added some more radical local policies to give joint ventures more privileges.

74.   These were organised for the purpose of letting companies and students get to know each other.

75.   According to my interview, he had been involved in quality control work since 1973 and was sent to study production management in some college during that time.

76.   Units of communications traffic. Defined as the average number of calls existing simultaneously.

77.   This is according to my interview with the manager of Sales Department in LTEF in April 1993.

78.   Figures provided by Professor Wu.

79.   Unicom (Lian Tong in Chinese, see section 4.1, and note 63) is referred to as the National United Communications Corporation. It was established in 1994 after the project was eventually approved by the central government. The establishment of Unicom introduced competition into

the Chinese public telecommunications network which had been under monopoly control by the state ever since the foundation of the People's Republic of China in 1994.

Bibliography

ADRIAANSEN, WILLEM L.M. and WASRDENBURG, J. GEORGE (eds) (1992), *A Dual World Economy: Forty Years of Development Experience*, New York: Oxford University Press.

AHMAD, AQUEIL (1988), 'Western Science and Technology in Non-Western Cultures', in Aqueil Ahmad and Hugh C. Russell (eds), *Science and Technology Policy for National Development – A Window on the Asian Experience*, Foundation for International Training and UNESCO, pp. 4–6.

ALCATEL BELL TELEPHONE (1992a), *Report on the Cooperation Between Belgium and the People's Republic of China in the Field of Telecommunications*, Antwerp: Bell Telephone Manufacturing Company S.A. Antwerpen.

ALCATEL BELL TELEPHONE (1992b), *Technical Cooperation and License Contracts*, Antwerp: Bell Telephone Manufacturing Company S.A. Antwerpen.

AMSDEN, A. (1989), *Asia's Next Giant: South Korea and Late Industrialisation*, New York: Oxford University Press.

ANDORS, STEPHEN (1987) *China's Industrial Revolution – Politics, Planning, and Management, 1949 to the Present,* New York: Pantheon Books; New York and London: M.E. Sharpe.

ASHTON, JOHN (1989), 'Science and Technology in China Today', *Technology, Industries and Society,* vol. 2, no. 1 (Sydney) pp. 5–8.

BAARK, ERIK (1978) 'Commercialised Technology Transfer in China 1981–1986: The Impact of Science and Technology Policy Reforms', *The China Quarterly*, pp. 390–406.

BAARK, ERIK (1980), 'Techno-Economics and Politics of Modernization in China: Basic Concepts of Technology Policy under the Readjustment of the Chinese Economy', *Discussion Paper no. 135*, November, Research Policy Institute, University of Lund, Sweden, pp. 390–406.

BAARK, ERIK (1988), 'Mainland China's Technology Exports', *Issues & Studies: A Journal of China Studies and International Affairs*, vol. 24, no. 9 (Institute of International Relations, Taipei, Taiwan) pp. 96–119.

BAARK, ERIK (1991) 'Fragmented Innovation: China's Science and Technology Policy Reforms in Retrospect', in *China's Economic Dilemmas in the 1990s: The Problems of Reforms, Modernisation, and Interdependence*, vol. 2, Study Papers, Submitted to the Joint Economic Committee Congress of the United States, April 1991, US Government Printing Office, Washington, pp. 531–45.

BAARK, ERIK (1991b), 'Computer Software and Biotechnology in the PRC: Analytical Perspective on High-Tech Politics', *Issues & Studies, a Journal of China Studies and International Affairs,* vol. 27, no. 9, (Institute of International Relations, Taipei, Taiwan) pp. 70–93.

BAARK, ERIK (1991c) 'The Accumulation of Technology: Capital Goods Production in Developing Countries Revisited', *World Development,* vol. 19, no. 7, pp. 903–14.

BAARK, ERIK and JAMISON, ANDREW (eds) (1986), *Technological Development in China, India and Japan – Cross-Cultural Perspectives*, London: Macmillan.

BALASUBRAMANYAM, V.N. (1973), *International Transfer of Technology to India*, New York: Praeger Publishers.

BALÁZS, K., FAULKNER, W. and SCHIMANK, U. (1995a), 'Transformation of the Research System of Post-Communist Central and Eastern Europe: An Introduction', *Social Studies of Science*, vol. 25, pp. 1–25.

BALÁZS, K., FAULKNER, W. and SCHIMANK, U. (1995b), 'Science and Technology Studies and Policy in Central and Eastern Europe: What Next?', *Social Studies of Science*, vol. 25.

BALLS, EDWARD (1983), 'Survey of China (4): The Cage Opens and the Bird Learns to Fly – but China's Economic Flight Path Will Remain Erratic for Some Years/Economic Reform', *Financial Times*, 18 November, p. 3.

BARDHAN, P.K. (1988), 'Alternative Approaches to Development Economics', in Chenery and Srinivasan (eds) (1988) *Handbook of Development Economics, 1*, Amsterdam: North Holland.

BARRATT BROWN, M. (1974), *The Economics of Imperialism*, Harmondsworth: Penguin.

BECKERMAN, WILFRED (1995), *Small is Stupid: Blowing the Whistle on the Greens*, London: Duckworth.

BELL, MARTIN (1984), ' "Learning" and the Accumulation of Industrial Technological Capacity in Developing Countries', in M. Fransman and K. King (eds), *Technological Capability in the Third World*, London and Hong Kong: Macmillan, pp. 187–210.

BELL, MARTIN and PAVITT, KEITH (1992), 'National Capabilities for Technological Accumulation: Evidence and Implications for Developing Countries', Paper prepared for the World Bank's Annual Conference on Development Economics, Washington D.C., April 30 and May 1, 1992.

BETTELHEIM, CHARLES (1971), *Calcul économique et formes de propriété*, Paris: F. Maspero.

BHALLA, A.S. (1992), *Uneven Development in the Third World: A Study of China and India*, London: Macmillan.

BI DACHUAN (1988), 'China's Reform of S&T, the Management System and the Strategy of S&T for Development', in Aqueil Ahmad and Hugh C. Russell (eds), *Science and Technology Policy for National Development – a Window on the Asian Experience*, Foundation for International Training and UNESCO, pp. 201–11.

BORNSTERIN, MORRIS (1985), *East–West Technology Transfer: The Transfer of Western Technology to the USSR*, Paris: OECD.

BRADY, T., TIERNEY, M. and WILLIAMS, R. (1992), 'The Commodification of Industry Applications Software', *Industrial and Corporate Change*, vol. 1, no. 3, pp. 489–514.

BRUS, WLODZIMIERZ and LASKI, KAZIMIERZ (1989), *From Marx to the Market: Socialism in Search of an Economic System*, Oxford: Clarendon Press.

CAMPBELL, NIGEL and HENLEY, JOHN S. (1990), *Advances in Chinese Industrial Studies – a Research Annual Volume 1 (Part B), Joint Ventures and Industrial Change in China*, Greenwich, Connecticut: Jai Press Inc.

CARDOSO, FERNANDO H. and FALETTO, ENZO (1979), *Dependency and Development in Latin America*, Berkeley: University of California Press.
CHARSLEY, SIMON R. (1994), 'A Technology Too Appropriate? The Indian Silk-Reeling Charka', *Science, Technology & Development – Journal of the Third World Science, Technology & Development Forum*, vol. 12, no. 2 and 3 (August/December) pp. 25–36.
CHEN, EDWARD K.Y. (1993), 'Foreign Direct Investment in East Asia', *Asian Development Review – Studies of Asian and Pacific Economic Issues*, vol. 11, no. 1 (Asian Development Bank) pp. 24–59.
CHEN JINGXIE (1991), 'Changes in the Relations Between Technological Progress, Enterprises, Science and Technology', in W. Konig, H. Poser, W. Radtke and W.H. Schnell (eds), *Technological Development Society and State – Western and Chinese Civilizations in Comparison*, Singapore, New Jersey, London, Hong Kong: World Scientific, pp. 155–64.
CHEN JUNLIANG, YAN LIEMIN and LI YONGLIN (1993), 'Switching Systems and Switching Software Development in China', *IEEE Communications Magazine*, July, pp. 56–60.
CHEN YUNQIAN (1993), 'Driving Forces Behind China's Explosive Telecommunications Growth', *IEEE Communications Magazine*, July, pp. 20–3.
CHENERY, H.B. and SRINIVASAN T.N. (eds) (1988), *Handbook of Development Economics, 1*, Amsterdam: North Holland.
CHILD, J. and LOCKETT, M. (eds) (1990), *Advances in Chinese Industrial Studies – a Research Annual Volume 1 (Part A), Reform Policy and the Chinese Enterprise*, Greenwich, Connecticut: Jai Press Inc.
CHOOI, K.Y., WEBB, J.R. and BERNARD, K.N. (1994), 'Technology Transfer and International Organisations: The Question of Localisation', *Science, Technology & Development – Journal of the Third World Science, Technology & Development Forum*, vol. 12, no. 2 and 3 (August/December) pp. 198–214.
CLAPHAM, CHRISTOPHER (1992), 'The Collapse of Socialist Development in the Third World', *Third World Quarterly*, vol. 13, no. 1, pp. 13–25.
CLARK, NORMAN (1985), *The Political Economy of Science & Technology*, Oxford: Basil Blackwell.
COLBURN, FORREST D. and RAHMATO, D. (1992), 'Rethinking Socialism in the Third World', *Third World Quarterly*, vol. 13, no. 1, pp. 159–73.
COLMAN, DAVID and NIXSON, FREDERICK (1994), *Economics of Change in Less Developed Countries*, 3rd edn, New York and London: Harvester Wheatsheaf.
COOPER, CHARLES (1994), 'Technology Policy and Industrialisation Policy in the Global Economy', *Science, Technology & Development – Journal of the Third World Science, Technology and Development Forum*, vol. 12, no. 2 and 3 (August/December) pp. 159–171.
DAVIS, JOHN D. (1977/78), 'Appropriate Technology for a Crowded World', *New Universities Quarterly*, vol. 31, no. 1 (Winter) pp. 25–36.
DEAN, GENEVIEVE C. (1972), 'Science, Technology and Development: China as a Case Study', *The China Quarterly*, July–September, pp. 520–534.

DENG SHUZHENG (1991), 'China's Technology Policy and Technology Legislation', in W. Konig, H. Poser, W. Radtke and W.H. Schnell (eds), *Technological Development, Society and State – Western and Chinese Civilizations in Comparison*, Singapore, New Jersey, London and Hong Kong: World Scientific, pp. 216–225.

DIRLIK, ARIF (1989), 'Postsocialism? Reflections on "Socialism with Chinese Characteristics"', in Maurice Meisner and Arif Dirlik (eds), *Marxism and the Chinese Experience – Issues in Contemporary Chinese Socialism*, New York: M.E. Sharpe Inc., pp. 362–84.

DORE, RONALD (1984), 'Technological Self-Reliance: Sturdy Ideal or Self-Serving Rhetoric', in Martin Fransman and Kenneth King (eds), *Technological Capability in the Third World*, London and Hong Kong: Macmillan, pp. 65–80.

DOS SANTOS, T. (1973), 'The Crisis of Development Theory and the Problem of Dependence in Latin America', in H. Bernstein (eds), *Underdevelopment and Development*, Harmondsworth: Penguin.

DOSI, GIOVANNI, FREEMAN, CHRISTOPHER, NELSON, RICHARD, SILVERBERG, GERLD and SOETE, LUC (1988), *Technical Change and Economic Theory*, London and New York: Pinter.

DUTT, AMITAVA KRISHNA and JAMESON, KENNETH P. (eds) (1992), *New Directions in Development Economics*, Cheltenham: Edward Elgar.

DUTT, AMITAVA KRISHNA, KIM, KWAN S. and SINGH, AJIT (1994), 'The State, Markets and Development', in Dutt, Kim and Singh (eds), *The State, Markets and Development – Beyond the Neoclassical Dichotomy*, Cheltenham: Edward Elgar, pp. 3–21.

EAST CONSULTING LTD (1995), *Telecommunications in China: Entering the Market of the Decade,* London: Financial Times, Telecoms & Media Publishing.

EDQUIST, CHARLES (1985), *Capitalism, Socialism and Technology: A Comparative Study of Cuba and Jamaica,* London: Zed Books Ltd.

ERNST, DIETER and O'CONNOR, DAVID (1992), *Competing in the Electronics Industry – the Experience of Newly Industrialising Economies*, Paris: OECD.

FLECK, JAMES (1988a), 'Innofusion or Diffusation? The Nature of Technological Development in Robotics', *Edinburgh PICT Working Paper No. 4*, Edinburgh: Edinburgh University.

FLECK, JAMES (1988b), 'The Development of Information-Integration: Beyond CIM?', *Edinburgh PICT (Programme on Information and Communication Technologies) Working Paper No. 9*, Edinburgh: Edinburgh University.

FLECK, J., WEBSTER, J. and WILLIAMS, R. (1990), 'Dynamics of Information Technology Implementation', *Futures*, August, vol. 22, pp. 618–40.

FRANSMAN, MARTIN (1984), 'Technological Capability in the Third World: An Overview and Introduction to Some of the Issues Raised in this Book', in M. Fransman and K. King (eds), *Technological Capability in the Third World*, London and Hong Kong: Macmillan, pp. 3–30.

FRANSMAN, MARTIN (1991), *The Market and Beyond – Cooperation and Competition in Information Technology Development in the Japanese System*, Cambridge: Cambridge University Press.

FREEMAN, CHRISTOPHER and PEREZ, C. (1988), 'Structural Crises of Adjustment, Business Cycles and Investment Behaviour', in Dosi *et al.*, (1988), *Technological Change and Economic Theory*, pp. 38–61.

GAO QIUZHAO (1992), 'Introduction of the EWSD Switching System and Its Future Prospect', *China Telecommunications Construction*, vol. 4, no. 1 (January/February) pp. 27–31.

GERSCHENKRON, A. (1966), *Economic Backwardness in Historical Perspective*, Cambridge, Mass.: Harvard University Press.

GLAESER, BERNHARD (ed.) (1987) *Learning from China? Development and Environment in Third World Countries*, London: Allen & Unwin.

GOULET, DENIS (1983), 'Value Orientation in Technology Policy', *Bulletin of Science & Technology Society*, vol. 3, pp. 299–310.

GU BAOGUI (1991), 'The Mechanism of International Technology Transfer and the Related Policies of China', *Technological Development Society and State – Western and Chinese Civilizations in Comparison*, Singapore, New Jersey, London, Hong Kong: World Scientific, pp. 252–60.

GU MING (ed.) (1992) *China's Efficacious 14 Years of the Reform – the Volume of Posts and Telecommunication*, China Economic Law Society and China Economic Publishing House.

HAQUE, IRFANUL (1994), 'International Competitiveness: The State and the Market', in A.K. Dutt, K.S. Kim and A. Singh (eds), *The State, Markets and Development – Beyond the Neo-classical Dichotomy*, Cheltenham: Edward Elgar.

HIRSCHMAN, ALBERT O. (1981), *Essays in Trespassing: Economics to Politics and Beyond*, New York: Cambridge University Press.

HODDER, RUPERT (1992), *The West Pacific Rim*, London: Belhaven Press.

HODGSON, GEOFF (1984), *The Democratic Economy*, Harmondsworth: Penguin.

HU YAOXING (1991), 'Science and Technology in China: Transition and Dilemma', *Science, Technology & Development, Journal of the Third World Sciences, Technology & Development Forum*, vol. 9, no. 1 and 2 (April/ August) pp. 64–72.

HU YAOXING (1993), 'Market-Oriented Reforms in China', *Development Policy Review*, vol. 11, pp. 1–10.

HUGHES, THOMAS (1983), *Networks of Power*, Baltimore: John Hopkins University Press.

HUQ, M.M. (1991), 'Introduction: Science, Technology and Development: North–South Co-operation – An Overview', *Science, Technology & Development, Journal of the Third World Science, Technology & Development Forum*, vol. 9, no. 1–2 (April/August) pp. 1–7.

ITU (International Telecommunication Union) (1986), *Yearbook of Common Carrier Telecommunication Statistics*, Geneva: ITU.

JAMES, JEFFERY (ed.) (1989) *The Technological Behaviour of Public Enterprises in Developing Countries*, London: Routledge.

JI DUOZHI (1991), 'Cultural Conflict and Technology Transfer', in W. Konig, H. Poser, W. Radtke and W.H. Schnell (eds), *Technological Development Society and State – Western and Chinese Civilizations in Comparison*, Singapore, New Jersey, London and Hong Kong: World Scientific, pp. 83–91.

JONES, L.P. and SAKONG, I. (1980), 'Government, Business and Entrepreneurship in Economic Development: The Korean Case', in Harvard University Council on East Asian Studies, *Harvard East Asia Monographs*, No. 91, Cambridge, Mass.

KORNAI, JANOS (1986), 'Efficiency and the Principles of Socialist Ethics', in Janos Kornai *Contradictions and Dilemmas: Studies on the Socialist Economy and Society*, Cambridge, Mass. and London: MIT Press, pp. 124–38.

LALL, SANJAYA (1992), 'Technological Capabilities and Industrialisation', *World Development,* vol. 20 no. 2, pp. 165–186.

LALL, SANJAYA (1993), 'Policies for Building Technological Capabilities: Lessons from Asian Experience', *Asian Development Review,* vol. 11, no. 2, pp. 72–103.

LARDY, NICHOLAS R. (1992), *Foreign Trade and Economic Reform in China, 1978–1990,* Cambridge University Press.

LATOUR, B. (1988), 'How to Write "The Prince" for Machines as well as Machinations', in B. Elliot, *Technology and Social Process*, Edinburgh: Edinburgh University Press, pp. 20–43.

LEE, PAUL S.N. (1991), 'Dualism of Communications in China', *Telecommunications Policy,* December, pp. 536–544.

LEFTWICH, ADRIAN (1992), 'Is There a Socialist Path to Socialism?' *Third World Quarterly,* vol. 13, no. 1, pp. 27–42.

LEYS, C. (1975), *Underdevelopment in Kenya: The Political Economy of Neo-Colonialism*, London: Heinemann.

LEYS, C. (1977), 'Underdevelopment and Dependency: Critical Notes', *Journal of Contemporary Asia,* vol. 7, no. 1, p. 89–96.

LI PENG (1994), 'Government Year Report' [Zhen Fu Gong Zuo Bao Gao], *People's Daily* (overseas edition), 24 March 1994, p. 1.

LI TIEYING (1994), 'China's Reformation of Economic System and Its Establishment of a Socialist Market Economy' (Zhongguo jingji gaige he shehuizhuyi shichang jingji tizhi de jianli), *People's Daily* (overseas edition), 5 November, 1994, p. 3.

LI WAN (1991), 'China's Strategy of Technology Development and the Reform of Technology Policies', in W. Konig, H. Poser, W. Radtke and W.H. Schnell (eds), *Technological Development Society and State – Western and Chinese Civilizations in Comparison*, Singapore, New Jersey, London and Hong Kong: World Scientific, pp. 33–45.

LIANG SHIHE (1991), 'Technological Progress and Structural Changes in Industry', in W. Konig, H. Poser, W. Radtke and W.H. Schnell (eds), *Technological Development Society and State – Western and Chinese Civilizations in Comparison*, Singapore, New Jersey, London and Hong Kong: World Scientific, pp. 180–9.

LIPPIT, VICTOR D. (1987), *The Economic Development of China*, New York: M.E. Sharpe.

LONG, FRANKIN A. and OLESON ALEXANDRA (1980), *Appropriate Technology and Social Values – a Critical Appraisal,* Massachusetts: Ballinger.

LUCAS, BARBARA G. and FREEDMAN, STEPHEN (eds) (1983), *Technology Choice and Change in Developing Countries: Internal and External Constraints*, Dublin: Tycooly International Publishing Ltd.

LUEDDE-NEURATH, RICHARD (1988), 'State Intervention and Export-Orientated Development in South Korea', in G. White (ed.), *Developmental States in East Asia*, ODS, Basingstoke: Macmillan, pp. 68–112.

LUNDVALL, BENGT-AKE (ed.) (1992), *National Systems of Innovation*, London: Pinter Publishers.

LUNDVALL, BENGT-AKE (1993), 'User–Producer Relationships, National Systems of Innovation and Internationalisation', in Dominique Foray and Christopher Freeman (eds), *Technology and the Wealth of Nations – The Dynamics of Constructed Advantage,* London and New York: OECD, Pinter Publishers, pp. 277–300.

MACKENZIE, D. (1992), 'Economic and Sociological Explanations of Technological Change', in R. Commbs, Paul Saviotti and V. Walsh (eds), *Technological Changes and Company Strategies: Economic and Sociological Perspectives,* London: Academic Press, pp. 25–48.

MACKENZIE, D. and WAJCMAN, J. (eds) (1990), *The Social Shaping of Technology,* Milton, Philadelphia: Open University Press.

MALECKI, EDWARD J. (1991), *Technology and Economic Development: The Dynamics of Local, Regional, and National Change,* London: Longman.

McNALLY, DAVID (1993), *Against the Market: Political Economy, Market Socialism and the Marxist Critique,* London and New York: Verso.

MEISNER, MAURICE and DIRLIK, ARIF (1989), 'Politics, Scholarship, and Chinese Socialism', in their edited *Marxism and the Chinese Experience – Issues in Contemporary Chinese Socialism*, an East Gate Book, New York: M.E. Sharpe Inc., pp. 3–26.

MITRA, ASHOK (ed.) (1988), *China: Issues in Development*, New Delhi: Tulika Print Communication Services Pvt. Ltd.

MOLINA, ALFONSO H. (1987), 'The Socio-technical Basis of the Microelectronics Revolution: A Global Perspective', PhD thesis, 2 vols, Edinburgh University, Edinburgh.

MOLINA, ALFONSO H. (1990), 'The Development of Public Switching Systems in the UK and Sweden: The Weight of History', *Edinburgh PICT Working Paper No. 19*, Edinburgh: Edinburgh University.

MOLINA, ALFONSO H. (1995), 'Sociotechnical Constituencies as Processes of Alignment: The Rise of a Large-Scale European Information Technology Initiative', *Technology in Society*, vol. 17, no. 4, pp. 385–412.

MU GONGQIAN (1991), 'The Status and Role of Government in Technological Progress', in W. Konig, H. Poser, W. Radtke and W.H. Schnell (eds), *Technological Development Society and State – Western and Chinese Civilizations in Comparison*, Singapore, New Jersey, London and Hong Kong: World Scientific, pp. 64–72.

NELSON, R. (ed.) (1992), *National Systems Supporting Technical Advance in Industry*, Oxford: Oxford University Press.

NOVE, ALEC (1983) *The Economics of Feasible Socialism*, London: Allen & Unwin.

NOVE, ALEC and THATCHER, IAN D. (eds) (1994), *Markets and Socialism*, Cheltenham: Edward Elgar.

NUTI, DOMENICO MARRIO (1992), 'Market Socialism: The Model That Might Have Been But Never Was', in Anders Aslund (ed.), *Market*

Socialism or the Restoration of Capitalism?, Cambridge and New York: Cambridge University Press, pp. 17–31.

OECD (1987), *Science and Technology in the People's Republic of China*, Paris: Organisation for Economic Corporation and Development (OECD).

PACK, H. and WESTPHAL, L.E. (1986), 'Industrial Strategy and Technological Change: Theory versus Reality', *Journal of Development Economics*, vol. 22, no. 1, p. 87–128.

PALMA, G. (1978), 'Dependency: A Formal Theory of Underdevelopment or a Methodology for the Analysis of Concrete Situations of Underdevelopment?', *World Development*, vol. 6, nos 7/8, pp. 881–924.

PEREZ, CARLOTA (1985), 'Microelectronics, Long Waves and World Structural Change: New Perspectives for Developing Countries', *World Development*, vol. 13, no. 3, pp. 441–63.

PILLAI, K. VIJAYAN and SHANNON, LYLE W. (eds) (1995), *Developing Areas: A Book of Readings and Research*, Oxford: Berg Publishers Limited.

POMFRET, RICHARD (1992), *Diverse Paths of Economic Development*, New York and London: Harvester Wheatsheaf.

PRYBYLA, J.S. (1987), *Market and Plan under Socialism: The Bird in the Cage*, Stanford: Hoover Institution Press.

PUTTERMAN, LOUIS (1992), 'Dualism and Reform in China', *Economic Development and Cultural Change*, vol. 40, no. 3 (April) pp. 467–93.

QADIR, SHAHID and GILLS, BARRY (1992), 'Fracturing Socialism: A Fragile Future', *Third World Quarterly*, vol. 13, no. 1, pp. 8–12.

RIEDIJK, W. (eds) (1982), *Appropriate Technology for Developing Countries*, Delft University Press.

RISKIN, C. (1981), 'Markets, Maoism and Economic Reform in China', *Bulletin of Concerned Asian School*, vol. 13, no. 3, pp. 31–41.

ROSENBERG, N. and FRISCHTAK, C. (eds) (1985), *International Technology Transfer – Concepts, Measures, and Comparisons*, New York: Praeger Scientific.

SAHAL, DEVENDRA (1981), *Patterns of Technological Innovation*, London: Addison-Wesley.

SARUPRIA, SHANTILAL (1994), 'Paradigms of an Integrated Technology Policy for Development', *Science, Technology & Development*, vol. 12, no. 1 (April) pp. 12–24.

SCHUMACHER, E.F. (1973), *Small is Beautiful*, London: Abacus.

SECRETARY-GENERAL OF UNCTAD (1994), *Trade and Development Report, 1994 – Overview*, UN, New York and Geneva.

SELDEN, MARK (1989), 'Mao Zedong and the Political Economy of Chinese Development', in Maurice Meisner and Arif Dirlik (eds), *Marxism and the Chinese Experience – Issues in Contemporary Chinese Socialism*, an East Gate Book, New York: M.E. Sharpe, pp. 43–168.

SHANGHAI MUNICIPAL FOREIGN TRADE AND ECONOMIC COMMITTEE (1985a), 'Regulations for the Implementation of the Law of the People's Republic of China on Joint Ventures Using Chinese and Foreign Investment', *Shanghai Overseas Investment Utilisation Manual*, Shanghai Translation Publishing House, pp. 223–56.

SHANGHAI MUNICIPAL FOREIGN TRADE AND ECONOMIC COMMITTEE (1985b), 'Some Provisions of the People's Republic of China

Concerning the Reduction of or Exemption from Income Tax in the Absorption of Foreign Funds', *Shanghai Overseas Investment Utilisation Manual*, Shanghai Translation Publishing House, pp. 386–391.

SHANGHAI MUNICIPAL FOREIGN TRADE AND ECONOMIC COMMITTEE (1985c), 'The Law of the People's Republic of China on Joint Venture Using Chinese and Foreign Investment', *Overseas Investment Utilisation Manual*, Shanghai Translation Publishing House, pp. 217–22.

SINGH, AJIT (1992), 'The Actual Crisis of Economic Development in the 1980s: An Alternative Policy Perspective for the Future', in A.K. Dutt and K. Jameson (eds), *New Directions in Development Economics*, Aldershot: Edward Elgar, pp. 81–116.

SINGH, AJIT (1994), 'State Intervention and the 'Market-Friendly' Approach to Development: A Critical Analysis of the World Bank Theses', in A.K. Dutt, K.S. Kim and A. Singh (eds) *The State, Markets and Development – Beyond the Neo-classical Dichotomy*, Cheltenham: Edward Elgar, pp. 3–21.

SMITH, BEN and JORDAN, JAMES (1990), 'Trade Transformation and Technology Transfer', in Hadi Soesastro and Mari Pangestu (eds), *Technological Challenge in the Asia-Pacific Economy*, London: Allen & Unwin

SMITH, TONY (1995), 'Requiem or New Agenda for Third World Studies?', in K. Vijayan, Pillai and Lyle W. Shannon, (eds), *Developing Areas: A Book of Readings and Research*, Oxford: Berg Publishers Limited, pp. 14–30.

SOLINGER, DOROTHY J. (1991), *From Lathes to Looms: China's Industrial Policy in Comparative Perspective, 1979–1982*, Stanford, California: Stanford University Press.

SOUTH COMMISSION (1990), *The Challenge to the South*, Oxford: Oxford University Press

STATE SCIENCE AND TECHNOLOGY COMMISSION (1992), High Technology Research and Development Programme of China, Beijing.

STAUBER, LELAND G. (1987), 'Capitalism and Socialism: Some General Issues and the Relevance of the Austrian Experience' in Alec Nove and Ian D. Thatcher (eds), *Markets and Socialism*, Cheltenham: Edward Elgar (1994), pp. 320–348.

SUN WENGE (1992), 'Industrial Output Rises, But State Firms Do Badly', *China Daily – Business Week*, 15–21 November, pp. 2.

SWEEZY, PAUL M. *et al.* (eds) (1978), *The Transition from Feudalism to Capitalism*, London: Verso.

TAYLOR, LANCE (1992), 'Structuralist and Competing Approaches to Development Economics', in Amitava Krishna Dutt and Kenneth P. Jameson (eds), *New Directions in Development Economics*, Cheltenham: Edward Elgar, pp. 35–56.

TELECOMMUNICATIONS ADMINISTRATION BUREAU AT ZHEJIANG PROVINCIAL POSTS AND TELECOMMUNICATIONS ADMINISTRATION (1992), 'Dispatches of the Application Management of Digital Switching Systems Installation in the Public Telecommunications Network', *Selected Dispatches and Documents on Telecommunications*, (Internal Circular), pp. 93–4.

TICKTIN, HILLEL (1992), *Origins of the Crisis in the USSR: Essays on the Political Economy of a Disintegrating System*, New York and London: M.E. Sharpe.

TODARO, MICHAEL P. (1994), *Economic Development*, (5th edn), New York and London: Longman.

UNCTAD (1994a), 'The World Economy: Performance and Prospects', *Trade and Development Report, 1994*, UN Conference on Trade and Development, New York and Geneva.

UNCTAD (1994b), *The Outcome of the Uruguay Round: An Initial Assessment Supporting Papers to the Trade and Development Report, 1994*, UN Conference on Trade and Development, New York and Geneva.

UNCTAD (1994c), *The Visible Hand and the Industrialisation of East Asia*, UN, New York and Geneva.

VICKERS, JOHN and GEORGE YARROW (1986), 'Telecommunications: Liberalisation and the Privatisation of British Telecom', in John Kay, Colin Mayer and David Thompson (eds), *Privatisation and Regulation: The UK Experience,* Oxford: Clarendon Press, pp. 221–40.

WADE, R. (1985), 'The Role of Government in Overcoming Market Failure: Taiwan, South Korea and Japan', in H. Hughes (ed.), *Explaining the Success of East Asian Industrialisation*, Cambridge: Cambridge University Press, pp. 129–63.

WADE, R. (1990), *Governing the Market: Economic Theory and the Role of Government in East Asian Industrialisation*, Princeton: Princeton University Press.

WARREN, B. (1980), *Imperialism: Pioneer of Capitalism*, London: Verso.

WHITE, GORDON (1988), 'State and Market in China's Socialist Industrialisation', in White, G. (ed.), *Developmental States in East Asia,* Basingstoke: Macmillan, pp. 153–92.

WHITE, G. and WADE, R. (1988), 'Developmental States and Markets in East Asia: An Introduction', in White, G. (ed.), *Developmental Sates in East Asia*, Basingstoke: Macmillan, pp. 1–29.

WHYTE, MARTIN KING (1973), 'Bureaucracy and Modernization in China: The Maoist Critique', *American Sociological Review*, vol. 38, no. 2 (April) pp. 149–63.

WILLIAMS, ROBIN (1997), 'The Social Shaping of Information and Communications Technologies', in H. Kubicek, W. Dutton and R. Williams (eds), *The Social Shaping of Information Superhighways*, Frankfurt: Campus Verlag.

WILLIAMS, ROBIN A. and EDGE, DAVID (1996), 'The Social Shaping of Technology', *Research Policy*, vol. 25, pp. 865–99.

WINTER, SIDNEY G. (1987), 'Knowledge and Competence as Strategic Assets', in D.V. Teece (ed.), *The Competition Challenge: Shortages for Industrial Innovation and Renewal*, Cambridge, Mass: Ballinger, pp. 159–84.

WOLF, C. (1990), *Markets or Governments: Choosing Between Imperfect Alternatives*, Cambridge, Mass.: MIT Press.

WORLD BANK (1991), *World Development Report, 1991: The Challenge of Development*, World Bank, Washington DC.

YENAL, OKTAY (1990), 'Chinese Reforms, Inflation and the Allocation of Investment in a Socialist Economy', *World Development*, vol. 18, no. 5, pp. 707–21.

YPSILANTI, DIMITRI (1988), *The Telecommunications Industry – The Challenges of Structural Change*, Paris: OECD.

ZALESKI, E. and WIENERT, H. (1980), *Technology Transfer Between East and West*, Paris: OECD.

ZHANG XIAOBIN (1982), 'Multidisciplinary Approach to S & T Policy for Human Needs – Case of the People's Republic of China', IFIAS Paper, IFIAS Stockholm, Sweden, 1 September.

ZHANG ZHIZHENG (1992), 'The Development and Progress of Communications and the Designing Institute of the MPT in the time of Reform and Opening', *China Telecommunications Construction*, vol. 4 no. 1 (January/February) pp. 4–8.

ZHAO HONGXIN (1995), 'Technology Imports and Their Impacts on the Enhancement of China's Indigenous Technological Capability', *Science, Technology & Development – Journal of the Third World Science, Technology & Development Forum*, vol. 31. no. 4 (April) pp. 585–601.

ZHENG SIZONG (1992), 'An Unprecedented Advance by Leaps and Bounds', *People's Post and Telecommunications*, Beijing, 3 November, p. 2.

ZHOU HUASHEN and KERKHOFS, M. (1987), 'System 12 Technology Transfer to the People's Republic of China', *Electrical Communication*, vol. 61, no. 2, pp. 186–93.

ZHOU SHULIAN (1982), 'The Market Mechanism in a Planned Economy', in Lin Wei and Arnold Chao (eds), *China's Economic Systems: Essays in Honour of Ota Sik*, Basingstoke: Macmillan, pp. 186–92.

Index